MINNESOTA SUPPLEMENT FOR
Modern Real Estate Practice

EDWARD J. DRISCOLL
THOMAS A. MUSIL

Fourth Edition

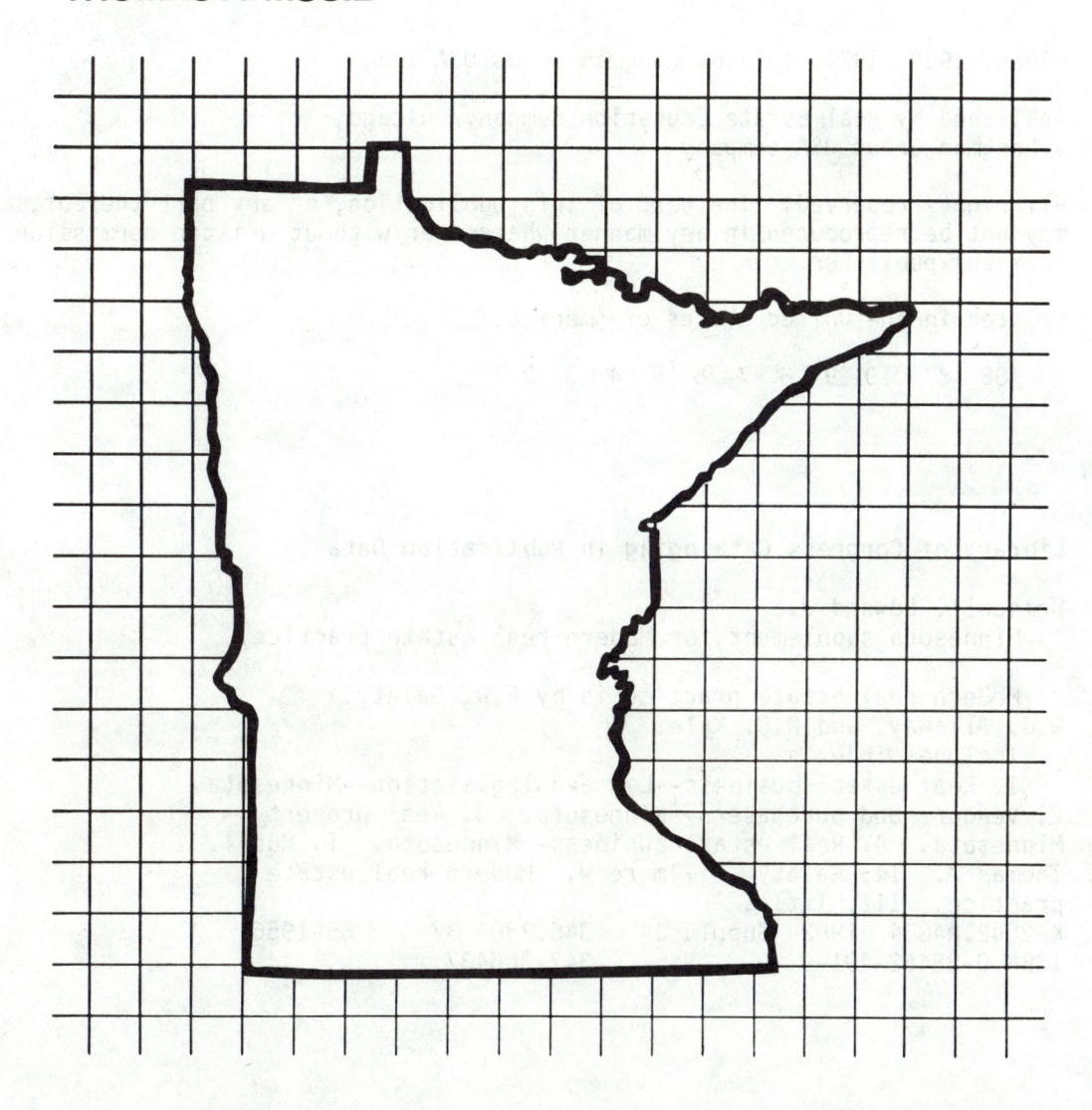

REAL ESTATE EDUCATION COMPANY/CHICAGO
a Longman Group USA company

While a great deal of care has been taken to provide accurate and current information, the ideas, suggestions, general principles, and conclusions presented in this book are subject to local, state, and federal laws and regulations, court cases, and any revisions of same. The reader is thus urged to consult legal counsel regarding any points of law--this publication should not be used as a substitute for competent legal advice.

©1985, 1980, 1979, 1977 by Longman Group USA Inc.

Published by Real Estate Education Company/Chicago,
a Longman Group USA company

All rights reserved. The text of this publication, or any part thereof, may not be reproduced in any manner whatsoever without written permission from the publisher.

Printed in the United States of America.

86 87 10 9 8 7 6 5 4 3 2

Library of Congress Cataloging in Publication Data

Driscoll, Edward J.
  Minnesota supplement for Modern real estate practice.

  Modern real estate practice is by F.W. Galaty,
W.J. Allaway, and R.C. Kyle.
    Includes index.
    1. Real estate business--Law and legislation--Minnesota.
2. Vendors and purchasers--Minnesota. 3. Real property--
Minnesota. 4. Real estate business--Minnesota. I. Musil,
Thomas A. II. Galaty, Fillmore W. Modern real estate
practice. III. Title.
KF2042.R4G34 1982 Suppl. 14   346.7304'37   85-1956
ISBN 0-88462-491-9   347.306437

Contents

PREFACE v

ABOUT THE AUTHORS vii

5 REAL ESTATE BROKERAGE 1

6 LISTING AGREEMENTS 5

7 INTERESTS IN REAL ESTATE 15

8 HOW OWNERSHIP IS HELD 19

9 LEGAL DESCRIPTIONS 29

10 REAL ESTATE TAXES AND OTHER LIENS 35

11 CONTRACTS 43

12 TRANSFER OF TITLE 57

13 TITLE RECORDS 65

14 REAL ESTATE LICENSE LAW 69

15 REAL ESTATE FINANCING 87

16 LEASES 103

18 REAL ESTATE APPRAISAL 107

19 CONTROL OF LAND USE 111

20 SUBDIVIDING AND PROPERTY DEVELOPMENT 117

21 FAIR HOUSING LAWS AND ETHICAL PRACTICES 129

23 CLOSING THE REAL ESTATE TRANSACTION 135

REAL ESTATE SECURITIES   147

REAL ESTATE LICENSING EXAMINATION   151

APPENDIX A: REAL ESTATE LICENSE LAW AND RULES AND REGULATIONS   163

APPENDIX B: SUBDIVIDED LAND SALES PRACTICES ACT   207

APPENDIX C: SAMPLE FINAL EXAM   227

ANSWER KEY   235

INDEX   237

Preface

Real estate practice in every state, in addition to being controlled by federal laws and regulations, is also based upon state laws and regulations. Each state has its own constitution, legislation, courts, and commissions that govern activities in that particular state.

The Minnesota legislature convenes each year on the first Monday in January. It may also be called into special session by order of the governor. In any of these sessions, new laws may be passed or changes made in existing laws that affect real estate practice.

The practice of real estate in any specific location may also be influenced by local agencies, bureaus and organizations, such as county and city governments or local Realtor® boards.

The purpose of this supplement is to discuss the laws and operating procedures that concern real estate and are specifically applicable to the state of Minnesota. This supplement builds on the basic information presented in the text, Modern Real Estate Practice, by Galaty, Allaway, and Kyle. Because every effort has been made not to duplicate information already presented in Modern Real Estate Practice, you should first study each subject area in the basic text and then refer to the same subject area in this book.

Following each chapter is a test. These tests can be both evaluative and teaching devices. As you finish each chapter, and before you go on to the next chapter, you should be certain that you understand and are able to answer each question in the test following the chapter. An answer key section for all the tests is included at the back of this supplement.

When used in conjunction with Modern Real Estate Practice, this fourth edition of the Minnesota Supplement can be used as a text for the first 60 hours of the 90 hours of real estate instruction required of all license applicants in Minnesota. In addition, the book is designed to help an applicant pass the state license examination. A special chapter devoted to the state exam is included at the end of the supplement.

Although the exact format of each course may vary depending on the school, the following is the approved state outline for both Course One and Course Two in real estate instruction. The outline indicates where specific information covered in each session may be found in both the Minnesota Supplement and Modern Real Estate Practice.

COURSE I (30 hours)

Time	Subject	MREP chapters	Minn. chapters
1 hour	Introduction to Real Estate	1, 3, 5, 21	5, 21
4 hours	Real Estate Licensing Law	14, 20	14, 20, Licensing Exam
4 hours	Law of Agency	5, 6	5, 6
5 hours	Law of Contracts	9, 11	9, 11
6 hours	Real Estate Financing	15	15
3 hours	Types and Classifications of Property	2, 7, 8, 12	7, 8
1 hour	Examination of Title	13	13
6 hours	Title Closing	23	23

COURSE II (30 hours)

Time	Subject	MREP chapters	Minn. chapters
3 hours	Deeds	12	12
1 hour	Search and Examination of Title	13	13
6 hours	Residential Appraisal	18	18
2 hours	Residential Construction	Appendix	6, 18
3 hours	Land Development and Use	19, 20	19, 20
3 hours	Condominiums, Cooperatives, Planned Unit Developments, and Manufactured Housing	4, 8	8
4 hours	Taxation	4, 10	10
4 hours	Investment and Appraisal	22	
2 hours	Real Property Management	17	
2 hours	Leases and Leasing	16	16

About the Authors

The Minnesota Supplement, Fourth Edition, was prepared by Edward J. Driscoll and Thomas A. Musil. Mr. Driscoll practices law as a partner in the firm of Larkin, Hoffman, Daly & Lindgren, Ltd., in Minneapolis. From April 1971 to March 1975, he served as Commissioner of Securities, Department of Commerce, for the state of Minnesota. He was thereafter named chairman of the Commerce Commission. Prior to his appointment, Mr. Driscoll was a practicing attorney for the firm of Torrison and Driscoll in the city of St. Paul.

Mr. Driscoll served as president of the Midwest Securities Administrators Association, and was a director of the National Association of Real Estate License Law Officials.

Mr. Driscoll earned a Bachelor of Arts degree from St. Mary's College in Winona, Minnesota. He subsequently attended De Paul University College of Law in Chicago, where he earned a Juris Doctor degree.

Thomas Musil is the Director of the Real Estate Program at the University of Minnesota. Through his teaching, advising and research activities, he is closely involved in the educational needs of students and in real estate as a field of study.

He has written several papers and articles, is a charter member and former Chair of the Papers Committee for the Real Estate Educators Association, Minnesota Membership Chair for the American Real Estate and Urban Economics Association, and is an active member of the Minneapolis Community Housing Resource Board, the American Association of Housing Educators, the Minneapolis Board of Realtors®, and the National Association of Corporate Real Estate Executives. In addition, Mr. Musil is owner and broker of American Real Estate and Financial Corporation.

Mr. Musil holds a BA degree from Macalester College, a Masters in Business Administration from the College of St. Thomas, and was a participant in the Higher Education Consortium for Urban Affairs at the University of Oslo, Norway.

The authors would like to thank the following persons for their kind help and assistance in technically reviewing the manuscript for the fourth edition of the Minnesota Supplement:

Gayle Nelson, Broker, The More Professionals, Minneapolis.

Sydney I. Weisberg, Broker, Sidney I. Weisberg and Associates. Real estate faculty member at the University of Minnesota and Anoka-Ramsey Community College.

Barry L. Wittenkeller, Esq., Tischleder, Tatone and Wittenkeller. Vice President, Careers Institute, Inc.

Robert J. Galush, S.R.A., Assistant Vice President and Manager of Corporate Real Estate, Twin City Federal Savings and Loan, Minneapolis. Instructor in Real Estate Appraising for the University of Minnesota and the Society of Real Estate Appraisers.

Peggy Karsten, Anoka-Ramsey Community College.

Danielle M. Gaines, Director of Fair Housing and Equal Opportunity Division, Minneapolis/St. Paul Office of the U.S. Department of Housing and Urban Development.

Thomas D. Cary, Lakeland Realty. Instructor at Wadena AVTI, Detroit Lakes, and Bimidji AVTI.

Special thanks are extended to the Greater Minneapolis Board of Realtors® and the Minnesota Association of Realtors®, whose gracious cooperation was essential in the publication of this text.

5

Real Estate Brokerage

In Minnesota, a person must be a licensed real estate broker in order to perform, negotiate, or attempt to perform or negotiate, for others and for a fee, any of the following activities involving real estate or a business opportunity among others: listing, selling, exchanging, buying, renting, managing property, dealing in options, or arranging for financing. In other words, <u>a person must have a broker's license in order to operate a real estate brokerage and collect commissions</u>.

REAL ESTATE LICENSE LAW

Minnesota real estate licenses are granted by the State Commissioner of Commerce, Commerce Department, under the provisions of the Real Estate License Law, Minnesota Statutes, Chapter 82. In addition to the law, a number of rules and regulations have been adopted. Commerce Department Real Estate Brokerage Licensing Rules elaborate on the basic law and provide additional guidelines for real estate licensees.

The specific provisions of the Minnesota Real Estate License Law will be discussed in Chapter 14 of this Supplement.

THE BROKERAGE BUSINESS

Agency and Commission

A listing agreement, as described in the text, creates an agency between a broker (the agent) and the seller of real estate (the principal). Minnesota law provides that listing agreements must be in writing before a broker is legally entitled to collect a commission for performing any service that he or she was hired to do.

A Minnesota broker earns a commission when he or she delivers to the seller a buyer who is "ready, willing, and able" to purchase the property on terms that are acceptable to the seller. It is not always necessary that the transaction be completed for the broker to earn a commission. For example, if the seller defaults on a valid contract prior to sale, the broker is still entitled to a commission. At the same time, the buyer must in fact be ready, willing, and able to perform. If, for example, Broker Smith finds a seemingly ready, willing, and able buyer for Jones's house, but the buyer cannot obtain adequate financing for the property, then Broker Smith would not be entitled to collect a commission from Jones. The buyer, although ready and willing, was by no means (financially) able.

Ethical Considerations

A broker is responsible for the truth of his or her statements (as well as the statements of his or her salespersons) to all parties to a real estate transaction. A broker who makes a material misrepresentation of anything likely to influence the consummation of a transaction, or who allows or permits another to make a material misrepresentation to a client, may have his or her real estate license suspended or revoked. Likewise, withholding pertinent information (such as the fact that the building's roof leaks when it rains) from a potential real estate buyer would make the broker guilty of misrepresentation by silence.

Minnesota law specifies several activities real estate licensees are prohibited from engaging in. These include: acting in the capacity of both licensee and undisclosed principal to a transaction; violating state or federal fair housing laws; violating laws pertaining to trust accounts; making material misstatements in the real estate license application or in information given to the Commissioner of Commerce; representing membership in a real estate-related organization when no such membership exists; using inaccurate or misleading advertising concerning property, terms, value, policies, or services; giving an unlicensed person payment (in money or goods) for assistance in listing or selling property.

Disclosure of agency relationship. Minnesota regulations require that a salesperson conduct business only under the licensed name of and on behalf of the broker to whom he or she is licensed. An individual broker may conduct business only under his or her licensed name. A broker licensed to a corporation or partnership may conduct business only under the licensed corporate or partnership name. Salespersons must disclose the licensed name of the broker under whom they are authorized to do business, prior to conducting any real estate business.

Dual agency. As discussed in the text, a broker may sometimes have the opportunity to be compensated by both parties to a transaction. This situation, known as dual agency, is illegal in Minnesota unless the broker has informed and received the written consent of all parties to the transaction.

Broker-Salesperson Relationship

As prescribed by law, Minnesota real estate salespersons can work on behalf of only one licensed broker in the state at a time. When the salesperson is licensed, the broker receives his or her license; upon termination of the salesperson's association with the broker, the license is signed by the broker and mailed back to the Commissioner of Commerce. A salesperson never personally receives a license--it is always held by the supervising broker. While a salesperson may be employed by another broker in another state, the salesperson is limited to representing a broker in the jurisdiction in which he or she is licensed.

Throughout Minnesota, most brokers engage their salespersons as **independent contractors**, as explained in the text. However, a broker is responsible for the actions and real estate activities of his or her salespersons at all times, whether they are directly employed or engaged as independent contractors.

Antitrust Laws Applied to Real Estate Sales

As discussed in the text, the real estate industry is subject to federal and state antitrust laws. The most common antitrust violations that occur in the real estate business are price fixing and allocation of customers or markets.

The penalties for such acts are severe! Under the Minnesota Antitrust Law, persons fixing prices or allocating markets may be found guilty of a felony, punishable by one or more of the following penalties:

1. The licensee may lose his or her real estate license.

2. A court of law may set a criminal penalty of a maximum $50,000 fine or five years imprisonment.

3. A court may declare a maximum civil penalty of a $50,000 fine.

4. The attorney general may file suit to stop the guilty party from engaging further in the prohibited activities.

5. An aggrieved party who has suffered loss through the antitrust activities of the guilty party may recover triple damages from the broker plus attorney's fees and other costs.

Financial Planner Disclosure Rules

If a real estate salesperson or broker represents on advertisements, cards, signs, or in any other promotion that he or she is engaged in the business of financial planning services, counseling or advising (other terms may include but are not limited to investment counselor, estate planner, investment advisor, or financial consultant) a disclosure document must be signed by and given to the client. Failure to do so constitutes fraudulent, deceptive or dishonest practices.

The disclosure document must contain the following:
-the basis of fees, commissions or other compensation paid to the salesperson or broker for providing financial planning services

-the name and address of any firm or company that supplies the financial services or products offered

-the licenses held by the financial planner (real estate broker or salesperson, securities agent or broker/dealer, insurance agent, investment advisor)

-the products or services the person is authorized to sell via the license he or she holds.

QUESTIONS

1. A real estate broker is legally entitled to a commission when:

    a. he or she closes a sale.
    b. he or she presents the seller with a ready, willing, and able buyer.
    c. the buyer obtains financing.
    d. the seller receives payment for the property conveyed.

2. A person must be licensed as a real estate broker in Minnesota before he or she can legally perform all but which of the following for others and for a fee?

    a. appraising real estate
    b. buying real estate
    c. selling real estate
    d. dealing in real estate options

3. Real estate broker Juliette Jacobi is collecting a commission from both parties to a transaction she negotiated. Her dual agency is illegal in this situation unless she obtains the written permission of:

    I. the seller.
    II. the buyer.

    a. I only
    b. II only
    c. both I and II
    d. neither I nor II

4. Which of the following situations would not be considered a violation of state antitrust laws?

    a. Brokers Bernie Hobsen and Beauregard Nessen have their real estate offices on the same block in town. In order to "share the wealth," they agree that Hobsen will sell duplexes and triplexes, that Nessen will handle four- and six-unit buildings, and that they both will sell single-family houses.
    b. Brokers representing the Temple, ABC, and All-American Property Management Companies decide to de-escalate their current price war by charging more uniform rates.
    c. Salespersons Joe Black and Emma Marie Mitsubushi, working on behalf of XYZ Real Estate, agree that Black should seek listings only from the east side of town and that Mitsubushi should seek listings only from the west side of town.
    d. All of the above violate antitrust laws.

6

Listing Agreements

THE LISTING AGREEMENT

Minnesota brokers use the various types of listing agreements discussed in the text--open listings, exclusive-agency listings, exclusive-right-to-sell listings, and multiple-listing agreements. Net listings are not specifically prohibited by law, but, as explained in the text, their use should be discouraged.

The Minnesota Real Estate License Law specifically states that all listing agreements must be in writing in order to be enforceable through court action. This provision supersedes the Minnesota Statute of Frauds, which provides that some oral contracts may be enforced in court.

Rules adopted pursuant to the Minnesota Real Estate License Law provide that all listing agreements must include a definite expiration date; a description of the real property involved; the list price and any terms required by the seller; the amount of compensation or commission or the basis for calculating it; a clear statement explaining the events or conditions that will entitle a broker to a commission; information regarding an override clause, if applicable; and the following notice:

> Notice: The commission rate for the sale, lease, rental, or management of real property shall be determined between each individual broker and its client.

Listing agreements must not contain holdover clauses, automatic extensions or similar provisions, or override clauses that extend more than six months beyond the expiration date.

An override clause protects the broker in the event that a parcel of real estate is purchased after the expiration of a listing agreement by a person to whom the broker showed or negotiated the property while the listing agreement was in effect. The broker is entitled to his or her commission if the purchase agreement is signed within the period of time specified in the override clause. When an override clause is used in a listing agreement, the broker must, within 72 hours of the expiration of the listing agreement, furnish the seller with a "protective list" that includes the names and addresses of all prospective purchasers to whom the broker exhibited the property. The protective list must include the following notice in boldface type:

> IF YOU RELIST WITH ANOTHER BROKER WITHIN THE OVERRIDE PERIOD AND THEN SELL YOUR PROPERTY TO ANYONE WHOSE NAME APPEARS ON THIS LIST, YOU COULD BE LIABLE FOR FULL COMMISSIONS TO BOTH BROKERS. IF THIS NOTICE IS NOT FULLY UNDERSTOOD, SEEK COMPETENT ADVICE.

A copy of a typical Minnesota listing agreement is at the end of this chapter.

TRUTH-IN-HOUSING REPORT

Some municipalities in Minnesota, such as Minneapolis and Saint Paul, have enacted "truth-in-housing" ordinances for the purpose of consumer protection. Such an ordinance must be complied with before a purchase agreement may be executed on any used single- or two-family residence in the city. The broker must give a homebuyer a truth-in-housing report, prepared by a private evaluator who is licensed by the city, prior to the signing of a purchase agreement. The purchase agreement should indicate that the buyer has inspected the truth-in-housing report.

The report documents the condition of all interior and exterior features of the house, including the basement, plumbing, electrical service, upper floors, attic, and garage. Since the purpose of the report is consumer protection only, it may not be used as a basis for the enforcement of any building codes or ordinances. A certificate of compliance with all applicable city building codes, issued within a year of the date of the sale, may be substituted for this report. A truth-in-housing report is at the end of this chapter.

HOUSING STANDARDS AND WARRANTIES

Urea Formaldehyde Disclosure

Formaldehyde is a chemical used in the production of a variety of resins and plastics used in housing construction. Common building materials containing formaldehyde include plywood, particle board, and insulation. The federal Consumer Product Safety Commission prohibited the use of urea formaldehyde foam insulation in residences and schools completed after August 9, 1982. On April 7, 1983, this prohibition was overturned by the United States Circuit Court of Appeals.

Minnesota law and Minnesota Department of Health regulations require that all new mobile homes, single-family residences, multi-family residences, and health care facilities be tested, using prescribed testing procedures, to determine the level of formaldehyde emitted by building materials. At the time of sale, the air in newly constructed dwellings may not contain more than 0.5 parts formaldehyde per million parts of air. Furthermore, building material manufacturers and builders must provide the following written disclosure to the consumer of a product, or of a housing unit for sale or lease, containing urea formaldehyde:

WARNING: THIS PRODUCT (HOUSING UNIT) CONTAINS THE CHEMICAL FORMALDEHYDE. FOR SOME PEOPLE, FORMALDEHYDE MAY CAUSE HEALTH PROBLEMS, SUCH AS IRRITATION OF THE EYES, NOSE AND THROAT, SNEEZING, COUGHING, HEADACHES, SHORTNESS OF BREATH, OR CHEST OR STOMACH PAINS. CHILDREN UNDER THE AGE OF TWO, ELDERLY PEOPLE, PEOPLE WITH BREATHING PROBLEMS OR PEOPLE WITH ALLERGIES MAY HAVE MORE SERIOUS DIFFICULTIES. IF YOU HAVE QUESTIONS ABOUT PROBLEMS YOU MAY HAVE WITH FORMALDEHYDE, CONSULT A DOCTOR.

New-Home Warranty Legislation

New housing constructed for the purpose of sale is subject to certain warranties in favor of the purchaser. These warranties, which are intended for the subsequent buyers as well as for the initial purchaser, include the following points:

1. For a period of one year, the dwelling shall be free from defects caused by faulty workmanship and defective materials that result from noncompliance with building standards.

2. For a period of two years, the dwelling shall be free from defects caused by faulty installation of plumbing, electrical, heating, and cooling systems.

3. For a period of ten years, the dwelling shall be free from major construction defects.

The warranty period begins on the date the purchaser obtains title to the dwelling or on the date the purchaser first occupies the dwelling. Unless one of the specific exclusions set forth in the law is applicable, the purchaser may recover damages for breach of warranty. Damages are limited to the amount necessary to remedy the defect or to an amount measured by the difference between the value of the dwelling without the defect and the building with the defect.

Approved by the Greater Minneapolis Area Board of Realtors.

MINNEAPOLIS TRUTH-IN-SALE OF HOUSING DISCLOSURE REPORT
NOTICE — READ ENTIRE REPORT CAREFULLY

A.

ADDRESS OF EVALUATED DWELLING _____
OWNER'S NAME _____
OWNER'S ADDRESS _____
NUMBER OF DWELLING UNITS _____

This report is NOT VALID unless the following declarations are made and signed by the owner or owner's agent:

There are ____ are not ____ orders pending against this property from the City of Minneapolis.

The real estate taxes for this property payable in 19____ are:
   HOMESTEAD _____   PARTIAL HOMESTEAD _____   NON-HOMESTEAD _____

I declare to the best of my knowledge the following information regarding any flood damage, sewer backup or water seepage: _____

I declare to the best of my knowledge that no urea formaldehyde foam insulation, a potential health hazard, is installed in this property except as follows: _____

_____ Date _____
Signature of owner or owner's agent.

1. This report is NOT a warranty, expressed or implied by the City of Minneapolis or by the Evaluator of any building component or fixture.
2. This report will not be used by the Department of Inspections as a basis for enforcing Minneapolis Ordinances. Minimum standards for this Report are established in the Minneapolis Housing Maintenance Code.
3. The Ordinance requires and places the responsibility on the seller or agent to make sure that this report is publicly displayed on the premises when the house is shown to a prospective buyer. Also, the seller or agent must give a copy of this report to the buyer prior to the signing of a Purchase Agreement.
4. The evaluator is not required to ignite the heating plant, use a ladder to observe the condition of the roofing, disassemble items or evaluate inaccessible areas. This report covers only items visible at the time of evaluation.
5. The lender, FHA or VA may have different standards.
6. This report is valid for one year from the date of issue and only for the owner named on the report.
7. Any questions regarding this report should be directed to the Evaluator.
8. Any complaints regarding this report should be directed to the Review Evaluator, phone 348-7828, office hours 8:00-11:00 A.M., 300 Public Health Building, Mpls, MN 55415.

ZONING:
   Present Zoning District _____

   Present Occupancy: Conforming _____ Non-Conforming _____
   Reason for Non-Conforming Status _____

If the occupancy is indicated as being Non-Conforming, the owner shall provide the buyer prior to closing, settlement, or transfer of ownership, a written and signed verification as to the Zoning status by the City Zoning Administrator.

Evaluator _____ Date _____ Page ___ of ___

Revised 11/23/82

10 MINNESOTA SUPPLEMENT for Modern Real Estate Practice

Property Address _____ B.

If an item is non-existent the word "none" shall be indicated across the box; Items checked with a "C" will have a comment about that item; Items checked with a "B" are below minimum requirements and must have a comment about that item; Items checked with an "H" are Hazardous and must have a comment about that item; Any item marked "M" indicates no problems visible relating to that item at the time of evaluation. Additional comment sheets may be attached if needed.
This report covers only items visible at the time of the evaluation.

```
"M" = MEETS MINIMUM REQUIREMENTS
"B" = BELOW MINIMUM REQUIREMENTS
"H" = HAZARDOUS
"C" = COMMENTS
```

ITEM #   COMMENTS

1. Basement stairs _____ ____
2. Basement floor _____ ____
3. Foundation walls _____ ____
4. Evidence of dampness or staining
   a) on basement walls   YES ____ NO ____
   b) on basement floor   YES ____ NO ____
   c) (see owner's statement on page A)
5. Basement sleeping rooms,
   if yes, see page three (3C). YES ____ NO ____
6. First floor, floor system _____ ____
7. Columns and beams _____ ____
8. Floor drains _____ ____
9. Waste and vent piping _____ ____
10. Water piping _____ ____
11. Gas piping _____ ____
12. Water heater _____ ____
13. Water heater venting _____ ____
14. Basement plumbing fixtures _____ ____
15. Copper water line visible on the street side of water meter
    YES ____ NO ____
   Evaluator assumes no responsibility for copper water line being continuous to street.
16. Electrical service installation _____ ____
   The evaluator is not required to disassemble items or evaluate inaccessible areas.
17. Electrical service size at panel: _____
   AMPS _____ VOLTS _____
   60 amp suitable for one major 220 volt appliance.
18. Separate 20 amp kitchen circuit indexed at service panel
    YES ____ NO ____
19. Basement electrical outlets/fixtures _____ ____
20. Electrical outlet for laundry
   indexed at service panel   YES ____ NO ____
21. Heating plant installation _____ ____
   The evaluator is not required to ignite the heating plant.
22. Heating plant viewed in operation YES ____ NO ____
23. Heating plant combustion venting _____ ____
24. Auxiliary heating units   YES ____ NO ____
   a) Installation _____ ____
   b) Viewed in operation   YES ____ NO ____
   c) Combustion venting _____ ____

Evaluator _____ Date _____ Page ___ of ___

C.

Property Address _____

| | ITEM # | COMMENTS |

KITCHEN
25. Walls and ceiling components _____ ____
26. Evidence of dampness or staining   YES ___ NO ___
27. Floor condition _____ ____
28. Window size and openable area _____ ____
29. Window condition _____ ____
30. Electrical outlets & fixtures _____ ____
31. Plumbing fixtures _____ ____
32. Water flow _____ ____
33. Gas piping _____ ____

DINING/LIVING ROOM
34. Walls and ceiling components _____ ____
35. Evidence of dampness or staining   YES ___ NO ___
36. Floor area & ceiling height _____ ____
37. Floor condition _____ ____
38. Window size and openable area _____ ____
39. Window condition _____ ____
40. Electrical outlets & fixtures _____ ____

BATHROOM
41. Wall and ceiling components _____ ____
42. Evidence of dampness or staining   YES ___ NO ___
43. Floor condition _____ ____
44. Window size and openable area _____ ____
45. Window condition _____ ____
46. Electrical outlets & fixtures _____ ____
47. Plumbing fixtures _____ ____
48. Water flow _____ ____

HALLWAYS/STAIRWELLS
49. Wall and ceiling components _____ ____
50. Evidence of dampness or staining   YES ___ NO ___
51. Floor condition _____ ____
52. Window condition _____ ____
53. Electrical outlets & fixtures _____ ____
54. Stairs (upper floors) _____ ____

SLEEPING ROOM
55. Number of sleeping rooms _____ ____
56. Wall and ceiling components _____ ____
57. Evidence of dampness or staining   YES ___ NO ___
58. Floor area & ceiling height _____ ____
59. Floor condition _____ ____
60. Window size and openable area _____ ____
61. Window condition _____ ____
62. Electrical outlets & fixtures _____ ____

PORCH/SUNROOM
63. Wall and ceiling components _____ ____
64. Evidence of dampness or staining   YES ___ NO ___
65. Floor condition _____ ____
66. Window condition _____ ____
67. Electrical outlets & fixtures _____ ____

Evaluator _____ Date _____ Page ___ of ___

D.

Property Address _____

	ITEM #	COMMENTS

ATTIC SPACE (if visible)
68. Roof boards and rafters _____ ____
69. Evidence of staining or seepage   YES ____ NO ____
70. Electrical outlets/fixtures _____ ____

EXTERIOR This report covers only items visible at the time of the evaluation.
71. Foundation _____ ____
72. Basement windows _____ ____
73. Drainage (grade) _____ ____
74. Exterior walls _____ ____
75. Doors (frames/storms/screens) _____ ____
76. Windows (frames/storms/screens) _____ ____
77. Stoops _____ ____
78. Cornice and trim _____ ____
79. Roof covering and flashing. The evaluator is not required to use a ladder to observe the condition of the roofing. ____
80. Chimney _____ ____
81. Electrical outlets/fixtures _____ ____
82. Two family dwelling egress _____ ____

OPEN/UNHEATED TYPE PORCHES
83. Floor (structural) _____ ____
84. Wall (structural) _____ ____
85. Roof (structural) _____ ____
86. Doors/screens/windows _____ ____
87. Electrical outlets/fixtures _____ ____

GARAGE
88. Roof structure and covering _____ ____
89. Wall structure and covering _____ ____
90. Garage doors _____ ____
91. Electrical outlets/fixtures _____ ____

Informational Items: YES   NO
A. Fireplace damper _____ ____ ____
B. Attic/ceiling insulation _____ ____ ____
   Type of insulation _____
   Approx. number of inches _____
C. Attic ventilation _____ ____ ____
D. Weatherstripping
   Windows _____ ____ ____
   Doors _____ ____ ____
E. Caulking _____ ____ ____
F. Deadbolt lock _____ ____ ____
G. Smoke detector(s) _____ ____ ____
   Properly located _____ ____ ____

Evaluator not responsible for operation of smoke detector(s). Fireplaces, free standing fireplaces and air-conditioning units are not evaluated.

I hereby certify that this report is made in compliance with the Minneapolis Code of Ordinances, Chapter 248, and that I utilized care and diligence reasonable and ordinary for one meeting the Certification Standards. The report covers only those problems listed and reasonably visible at the time of my evaluation and does not warrant future useful life of any house component or fixture.

Evaluator _____ Date _____ Page ____ of ____
            Signature on line above
                    Evaluators phone number _____

QUESTIONS

1. Larry Fine is selling his Minneapolis home to Moe Howard. In order to comply with the Minneapolis truth-in-housing ordinance, Fine must supply Howard with a truth-in-housing report:

    a. before the initial offer is made.
    b. 30 days prior to sale.
    c. at the time of the sale.
    d. upon Howard's occupancy of the premises.

2. A broker who takes a net listing:

    I. has violated the state license law.
    II. is subject to civil and criminal action.

    a. I only
    b. II only
    c. both I and II
    d. neither I nor II

3. Broker Pete Hackel sold Roger Rambley's home, but did not secure a written listing agreement for the property. Broker Hackel:

    I. may not sue Rambley for his commission.
    II. has violated the Statute of Frauds.

    a. I only
    b. II only
    c. both I and II
    d. neither I nor II

4. An override clause:

    I. allows a broker to collect a commission on a sale that occurs after expiration of a listing agreement.
    II. may not extend more than six months beyond the expiration of the listing agreement.

    a. I only
    b. II only
    c. both I and II
    d. neither I nor II

7

Interests in Real Estate

ESTATES IN LAND

Freehold estates in fee simple absolute, fee defeasible (conditional or determinable fee), and life estates are all recognized by Minnesota statute. Leasehold estates for years, from period to period, at will, and at sufferance are also recognized by Minnesota statutes and will be discussed in Chapter 16 of the text and this Supplement. As discussed in the text, land estates are subject to encumbrances such as liens, restrictions, easements, encroachments, water rights, mineral rights, and air rights.

Defeasible Fee Estate

In a fee defeasible estate in Minnesota, all covenants, conditions, and restrictions created on or after April 27, 1937, and that at the time of examination are more than 30 years old, may be disregarded if the 30-year period ended before August 1, 1982. This standard does not apply to conservation restrictions or scenic, utility, drainage, access, or other easements. A defeasible fee estate may terminate when the original grantor dies and the property is probated, or when the conditional use is ended. Upon its termination, the estate may be reestablished by the grantor or his or her heirs if so desired.

Legal Life Estates

Dower and curtesy have both been abolished in Minnesota. These legal life estates have been replaced with statutory protections under the Minnesota law of descent. Descent will be covered in Chapter 12 of this Supplement.

Homestead

Minnesota homestead rights, as discussed in the text, provide homeowners with certain protection from unpaid creditors, as well as a special tax privilege for the family residence. Minnesota statutes provide that a homeowner is entitled to claim a homestead exemption from a court sale of property to pay his or her debts. Single persons or married couples may claim a homestead exemption on property they own (this includes condominiums and townhouses) by living there and occupying it as a principal residence.

The Minnesota homestead exemption is not limited on the basis of value. The entire value of the homestead property is exempted from a forced sale to satisfy an unsecured debt. For example, if the property is worth $30,000, then the homestead exemption is for $30,000; if the property is worth $100,000, the exemption is for $100,000, and so on. In addition, all proceeds from the sale of homestead property are exempt from debts and judgments for a period of one year after the date of sale. However, <u>homestead exemptions do not apply to loans secured by a parcel of real estate, such as mortgage debts, real estate tax liens, mechanics' and materialmen's liens</u> (debts incurred for work or materials furnished in the construction, repair, or improvement of the homestead property or for services performed by laborers or servants), income-tax liens, or medical assistance liens.

Note that under Minnesota law homestead property exempt from seizure and sale is limited to a maximum of one-half acre when located in a city, village, or borough. Rural homestead property is limited to a maximum of 80 acres.

Upon the death of the homeowner, homestead rights are inheritable by the surviving spouse and minor children if they occupy the property as their principal place of residence.

<u>Termination of homestead.</u> Minnesota homesteads may be terminated in one of three ways: when the owner or owners die; when the owner or owners cease to occupy the residence for six consecutive months without filing a declaration of homestead with the county assessor; or upon conveyance of the property. If the owner is married, both husband and wife must sign the instrument of conveyance in order to convey good title and to release all homestead rights.

<u>Homestead tax benefits.</u> In Minnesota, homestead property is given special real estate tax treatment. It is assessed at a reduced rate for tax purposes. In order to claim this special tax treatment, a homeowner must file a declaration of homestead with the county assessor each year. This form must indicate whether the property is to be considered a full or partial homestead. A **full homestead** exemption would be granted for owner-occupied single-family homes, duplexes, and triplexes, while a **partial homestead** exemption would be issued for an owner-occupied multiple-unit dwelling, such as a small apartment building. All other property would be considered nonhomestead realty. A partial homestead exemption would be limited to value corresponding to the portion of the building that the owner uses as a residence.

To qualify for a homestead exemption of either type, the owner must reside on the property. If a buyer takes possession of a property after January 1, he or she may file for a half year's homestead tax exemption. To prove ownership, new owners are required to present a deed or contract for deed when filing a homestead declaration. Homestead tax benefits will be discussed in detail in Chapter 10 of this Supplement.

EASEMENTS

Easement by Prescription

In Minnesota, a person may acquire an easement by prescription on the lands of another, provided that he or she had continuous and uninterrupted use of the land for a period of <u>15 years</u>. Such use must be open, so that the owner can easily know of it, and it must be hostile, that is, without the owner's permission. If the use begins with the owner's permission, it may become adverse if it continues after such permission is revoked.

Easement by prescription does not apply to Torrens property or to land owned by governmental bodies, railroads, utilities, and others having condemnation rights.

Air Rights

Air rights were introduced in Chapter 1 of the text. In Minnesota, the sale of air rights to a parcel of real estate is subject to building and zoning laws and ordinances, as well as state and federal regulations and easements.

18   MINNESOTA SUPPLEMENT for Modern Real Estate Practice

QUESTIONS

1. Residential property owned as a principal residence by either a single person or a married couple can be claimed as a homestead, except for:

   I. condominiums.
   II. townhouses.

   a. I only
   b. II only
   c. both I and II
   d. neither I nor II

2. In order to be eligible for special homestead property tax exemptions, a homeowner must file a homestead declaration:

   I. with the county assessor in the county where the property is located.
   II. every year.

   a. I only
   b. II only
   c. both I and II
   d. neither I nor II

3. In Minnesota, a person may acquire an easement by prescription in real estate owned by another person by using that property without the owner's permission for a period of:

   a. 5 years.
   b. 10 years.
   c. 15 years.
   d. 20 years.

4. Fred and Martha Gilhooley's homestead property has a market value of $50,000. Up to what value is their home protected against court judgments for payment of certain debts?

   a. $10,000
   b. $20,000
   c. $30,000
   d. $50,000

5. Grace Holley, a minor, just inherited her late parents' home. The homestead property is worth $40,000. On what amount of property value will Grace be expected to pay inheritance tax?

   a. nothing
   b. $20,000
   c. $30,000
   d. $40,000

8

How Ownership Is Held

Minnesota statutes permit estates in severalty and co-ownership (tenancy in common and joint tenancy). Note that ownership in trust, described in the text, is not recognized by Minnesota statutes.

CO-OWNERSHIP

According to Minnesota law, a conveyance of real estate to two or more persons automatically creates a tenancy in common unless the deed expressly creates a joint tenancy.

Tenancy by the entirety and community property ownership are not recognized in Minnesota. Similar survivorship rights may, however, be created by a joint tenancy.

Partition

Any joint tenant or tenant in common may file a suit for partition or for sale of the property if a partition cannot be done without great prejudice to the owners. If the land involved cannot be partitioned or divided with agreement among the owners, the court will appoint three referees to make the partition and divide the shares of the interest among the tenants, as determined by the court's judgment. Partition judgments, like other court decisions, may be appealed to the Minnesota Supreme Court.

ALIEN OWNERSHIP OF REAL ESTATE

Only citizens of the United States and permanent resident aliens can own an interest in Minnesota agricultural land. In addition, aliens can hold no more than 20 percent of the stock of any corporation or partnership that owns an interest in Minnesota land. These restrictions on alien ownership do not apply to:

1. agricultural land that is inherited;

2. land held as security for indebtedness or for the collection of debts or enforcement of a lien, provided that the land is disposed of within three years;

3. citizens of a foreign country whose rights to hold land are secured by treaty;

4. land used for transportation purposes by a common carrier;

5. land or interest in land acquired for use in connection with mining and mineral processing operations;

6. agricultural land operated for research or experimental purposes, whereby the ownership of such land is incidental to the research or experimental objectives and the total acreage does not exceed that owned on May 26, 1977;

7. a tract of land of 40 acres or less for facilities incidental to a pipeline operation.

CONDOMINIUMS

The original legislation authorizing the creation and regulation of condominiums in Minnesota was enacted in 1963. In 1980, Minnesota passed a version of the Uniform Condominium Act. The latter legislation applies to all condominiums created in the state after August 1, 1980. Condominiums created prior to that date continue to be governed by the original law, although some provisions of the newer uniform law, such as disclosure provisions necessary for resale, apply to them. The acts may be found in Minnesota Statutes, Chapters 515 and 515A.

Creation

A condominium is created when the owners or developers of the property execute and record a declaration. The declaration is filed for record in the county in which the property is located. The material to be included in or submitted with the declaration includes: the name and number of the condominium, the county in which it is located, a legal description, floor plans, the allocation of common elements to each unit, homeowners' association voting rights, operating expense allocation to each unit, maximum number of units, and occupancy and use restrictions. It is important to note that the developer can provide for a "flexible condominium" in the declaration, allowing the developer to change the number and size of the units and/or build additional units.

Ownership

Once the property is established as a condominium, each unit becomes a separate parcel of real estate that may be dealt with like any other parcel of real property. A condominium unit is owned in fee simple and may be held by one or more persons as a homestead in any type of ownership or tenancy that is recognized by Minnesota law.

Real estate taxes are assessed and collected on each unit as for an individual property. Default in the payment of taxes or a mortgage loan by one unit owner may result in a foreclosure sale of the owner's unit but does not affect the ownership interests of the other owners. In any instance in which a lien or debt becomes effective against two or more units or against the property as a whole, the owner of each unit involved may remove his or her unit from the lien by paying the proportion of the debt attributed to that unit.

Each unit owner also owns a specific undivided proportionate interest in the common elements. Whenever a unit is conveyed, leased, mortgaged, or otherwise encumbered or disposed of, the percentage of the common elements attached to the unit are automatically included. Common expenses of the condominium are usually apportioned among the unit owners according to the specific percentage of undivided interest in the common elements attached to each unit.

Operation and Administration

The condominium property is administered by a homeowners' association. The association must be organized as a corporation. It has the power to establish rules and regulations governing the condominium, adopt budgets, regulate and maintain the common areas, charge and collect assessments for common expenses, hire and terminate managing agents and/or employees, maintain property insurance on the condominium as well as liability insurance covering the common areas, and exercise the other duties conferred on it by state law, the declaration, or the association's bylaws.

Acting through its board of directors or officers, the association has the power to enter into contracts and to bring and defend suits. When a unit owner has not paid assessments for common expenses, the association can file a lien against that owner's unit. A lien may be foreclosed through litigation in the same manner as a mortgage is foreclosed.

Consumer Disclosure Requirements

The original and the Uniform Condominium acts adopted in Minnesota provide for the developer to disclose certain information to the original purchaser of each condominium unit. With respect to condominiums created prior to August 1, 1980, a disclosure report must be given to the purchaser at least 15 days prior to the closing of the sale of the unit. Thereafter, the purchaser has an unconditional right to cancel the purchase agreement at any time within five days after receiving the disclosure report. With respect to condominiums created after August 1, 1980, the declarant must provide the purchaser with a disclosure statement no later than the date of the purchase agreement. The purchaser has the unconditional right to cancel the purchase agreement at any time within 15 days after receiving the disclosure statement, except when a closing takes place within 15 days of the execution of the purchase agreement.

In addition, after August 1, 1980, if the owner of any condominium unit resells the unit, he or she must give certain documents to the purchaser prior to the execution of the purchase agreement. These documents include copies of the declaration, the bylaws, and the rules and regulations of the association, and a certificate no more than 90 days old containing information about fees, assessments, restrictions on alienation, budgets, insurance coverage, a capital improvement reserve statement and the disclosure of capital improvements approved by the association for the next two years, a current balance sheet and income and expense statement, a listing of any judgments against or suits pending upon the association, and other subjects of interest to a buyer. The association must provide the unit owner with the certificate no later than seven days after it was requested. The purchaser has the unconditional right to cancel the purchase agreement at any time within 15 days after receiving the documents. A Condominium Resale Disclosure Certificate is shown at the end of this chapter.

Flexible Condominiums

In a condominium declaration, a developer may reserve the right to make future changes in the size and number of units and/or the right to build additional units. This has several implications for a buyer. If changes are made, a shift in a unit's financial liability, use of the common elements, association voting rights, and physical appearance may change. A flexible condominium declaration requires the following:

1. an explicit reservation of any options to add or change units;

2. a time limit not to exceed seven years after the recording of the initial declaration, where the right to build additional units or change existing ones will expire, or these rights will lapse as a result of circumstances that would necessarily terminate the option before the set time limit;

3. legal descriptions of the additional real estate;

4. the timing and order of additional unit development;

5. the number of additional units allowed and the number restricted to residential use;

6. a statement that additional units will be compatible with the architectural style, construction, and material standards and size, or a statement that no assurances are made with respect to these factors;

7. a statement as to the use, occupancy and alienation provisions of additional units;

8. a description of all other improvements and common elements that may be created with additional units;

9. provisions made if no additional units are built.

Other Requirements

The Minnesota Statutes also set forth rules governing the conversion of buildings to condominium status. The declarant of a condominium conversion must give each tenant and subtenant in possession notice of an intent to convert the building at least 120 days before the declarant will require them to vacate. If at least one person living in a residential unit is a minor, over 62 years of age, or handicapped, the tenant may demand an additional 60 days in which to vacate.

The declarant must attach to the notice a form of the purchase agreement indicating the terms and conditions of the proposed sale of the unit. Thereafter the tenant has a 60-day option to purchase the unit on those terms and conditions. If the tenant fails to exercise the option, the declarant may not, during the following 180 days, offer to sell the unit at a price or on terms more favorable than those offered to the tenant. A tenant not wishing to exercise the option may terminate the lease during the notice period on 30 days' written notice. The law does not authorize the declarant to terminate any of the tenant's rights as stated in his or her lease agreement.

The Minnesota Statutes provide for both express and implied warranties by condominium developers for newly constructed and converted projects. In addition to building code warranties, express warranties are represented by the developer in writing and orally or by plans and models given to the consumer. Implied warranties provide coverage on faulty materials, workmanship, and building code compliance.

The Uniform Condominium Act contains several provisions giving unit owners greater flexibility with regard to their units. As long as the structural integrity or mechanical systems of the condominium are not impaired, an owner, after acquiring an adjacent unit and with the consent of the association, may remove any partitions between the units. In addition, the boundaries between adjoining units may be relocated by their owners if the association amends the declaration. To prohibit an amendment of this nature, the board must determine that the action is not in the best interest of the condominium. Also, if the declaration permits, a unit may be subdivided into two or more units. To effect such an action, the unit owner must prepare an amendment to the declaration.

24 MINNESOTA SUPPLEMENT for Modern Real Estate Practice

CONDOMINIUM RESALE DISCLOSURE CERTIFICATE

Name of Condominium: _____

Name of Owners' Association: _____

Address of Association: _____

Unit/Garage Unit Number(s): _____

The following information is furnished by the Owners' Association named above pursuant to Minnesota Statutes Section 515A.4-107.

1. There is no right of first refusal or other restraint on the free alienability of the above Unit(s) contained in the Declaration, By-Laws, Rules and Regulations, or any amendment thereof, except as follows: _____
_____
_____

2. The following common expense assessments are payable with respect to the above Unit(s):

    a. Annual assessment installments: $_____ Due:_____
    b. Special assessment installments: $_____ Due:_____
    c. Assessments currently due and payable:
       (1) Annual $_____
       (2) Special $_____

3. In addition to the amounts due under Paragraph 2 above, the following additional fees are payable by Unit Owners: _____
_____

4. The Association has not approved any capital expenditures for its current and next succeeding two fiscal years, except as follows: _____
_____

5. The Association has set aside the following aggregate amount of reserves for capital expenditures: _____. The following portions of those reserves have been designated by the Association for the following specified projects: _____
_____
_____
_____

6. There are no judgments against the Association, except as follows: _____
_____
_____

7. There are no pending lawsuits to which the Association is a party, except as follows (Identify and summarize status):_____
_____
_____
_____

(Form # MBR-330)

Approved by the Greater Minneapolis Area Board of Realtors. Note: This form is under revision; the revised form will be available in early 1985.

8. The Association provides the following insurance coverage for the benefit of Unit Owners: (Reference may be made to the specific sections of the Declaration or By-Laws, however, any additional coverages should be described in this space) _____
_____
_____
_____

9. A copy of the floor plans of the condominium and any amendments thereto are available in the office of the Association for inspection.

10. In addition to the foregoing statements and representations, the following documents are furnished with this Certificate pursuant to statute.

    a. The most recent regularly prepared balance sheet and income and expense statement, if any, of the Association.

    b. The current budget of the Association.

I hereby certify that the foregoing information and statements are true and correct as of _____.
                                      (Date)

                                        By: _____
                                                (Association Representative)

R E C E I P T

In addition to the foregoing information furnished by the Owner's Association, the Unit Owner is obligated to furnish to the buyer, a copy of the Declaration (Exclusive of the floor plans), the By-Laws and Rules and Regulations of the Association, and any amendments to these documents. Receipt of the foregoing documents, and the Disclosure Certificate, is hereby acknowledged by the undersigned buyer(s). In the event of cancellation of the purchase agreement, buyer(s) and selling agent agree to return all of the above documents and information to the listing company before disbursement of any earnest monies.

Date: _____   _____
                                                     (Buyer)

                                                            _____
                                                            (Buyer)

QUESTIONS

1. Ralph Waldo Estaban owns a unit in the Willowy Trails Condominium, but does not plan to live there for some time. Which of the following is(are) true?

    I. Since he is not going to be using any of the common areas, he needn't pay the owners' association for the upkeep of such facilities.
    II. He must still pay current real estate taxes.

    a. I only   c. both I and II
    b. II only   d. neither I nor II

2. Sean O'Hara is selling his Duluth apartment building. According to Minnesota law, a person (or persons) may purchase it and own the real estate:

    I. in severalty.
    II. in co-ownership as joint tenants.

    a. I only   c. both I and II
    b. II only   d. neither I nor II

3. Unless otherwise stated in the document, a deed granting title to a parcel of real estate to two or more persons automatically creates:

    a. a tenancy in common.   c. community property.
    b. a joint tenancy.   d. a tenancy by the entirety.

4. Bernice Grishelda, an apartment owner in the Golden Trails Condominium, hasn't paid her building maintenance assessment bills for the last four months. Who will probably file a lien against Grishelda's property and foreclose on it if she doesn't pay the assessments?

    a. the building developer
    b. the property manager acting as agent for the owners' association
    c. the condo owners' association
    d. the lending institution holding a prior lien on the unit

5. A condominium owners' association:

    a. must be organized as a corporation.
    b. must be organized as a partnership of all unit owners.
    c. has no legal authority to enter into contracts.
    d. must provide buyers with a detailed disclosure report.

6. Jayne Marie Kosinski has just signed a purchase agreement to buy a unit interest in the Sun Temple Acres Condominium. If she changes her mind about the deal, how long does she have to cancel the purchase agreement?

    a. two days prior to the closing of the deal
    b. three days after signing the purchase agreement
    c. 15 days after receiving the condo disclosure information
    d. one week after taking occupancy of the unit

9

Legal Descriptions

Minnesota land can be described by rectangular (government) survey, subdivision plat, and metes and bounds, as described in the text. In general, a Minnesota land description must be based on some recorded document, such as a subdivision plat, or it must sufficiently describe the property so that its exact location and size can be identified from the description alone. A mailing or street address is not an adequate legal description of real estate. If the purchase agreement fails to adequately describe the real estate, it violates the Statute of Frauds, and the parties may refuse to proceed with the transaction. A purchase agreement may sometimes contain the words "legal to govern." Such wording should be avoided because it is dangerously ambiguous.

RECTANGULAR SURVEY SYSTEM

Although Minnesota uses the rectangular survey system, neither a principal meridian nor a base line is located in the state (see the map on page 30). Rectangular survey descriptions in Minnesota are determined from the Fourth and Fifth Principal Meridians. The Fourth Principal Meridian begins near Beardstown, Illinois, and extends northward through Wisconsin to the Canadian border. Land in the eastern portion of Minnesota (also Wisconsin and the northwest portion of Illinois) is described as being a certain number of ranges west from the Fourth Principal Meridian, using an east-west base line that is the Illinois-Wisconsin state line. The Fifth Principal Meridian begins near the convergence of the Arkansas and Mississippi rivers and extends northwest through Missouri and Iowa. Surveys of land located in the western portion of Minnesota (also North Dakota, Iowa, Missouri, Arkansas, and the eastern half of South Dakota) are made from the Fifth Principal Meridian, using a base line that runs through the center of Arkansas. Thus, in Minnesota, <u>all property surveyed under the rectangular system lies west of its principal meridian and north of the base lines</u>.

SUBDIVISION PLATS

Description by subdivision plat is the predominant method of locating <u>urban</u> real estate and is also common for recreational properties in Minnesota. When a parcel of land is subdivided, the subdivider places a copy of the subdivision plat in the public record. The plat is given a name for identification purposes. Each recorded plat is a detailed map that shows the manner in which the land was subdivided--the size and shape of each lot are given, and numbers are assigned to each block and lot. In addition, the plat shows any of the land's distinguishing features, such as streets, alleys, sidewalks, easements, and wetlands. Each plat is also described by rectangular survey for exact location within the state. Subdivisions and subdividing will be discussed in detail in Chapter 19.

The following is a sample legal description for a parcel of urban Minnesota real estate:

"Lot six, block five, Ivy Falls addition to Mendota Heights, Dakota County, Minnesota, according to the recorded plat thereof."

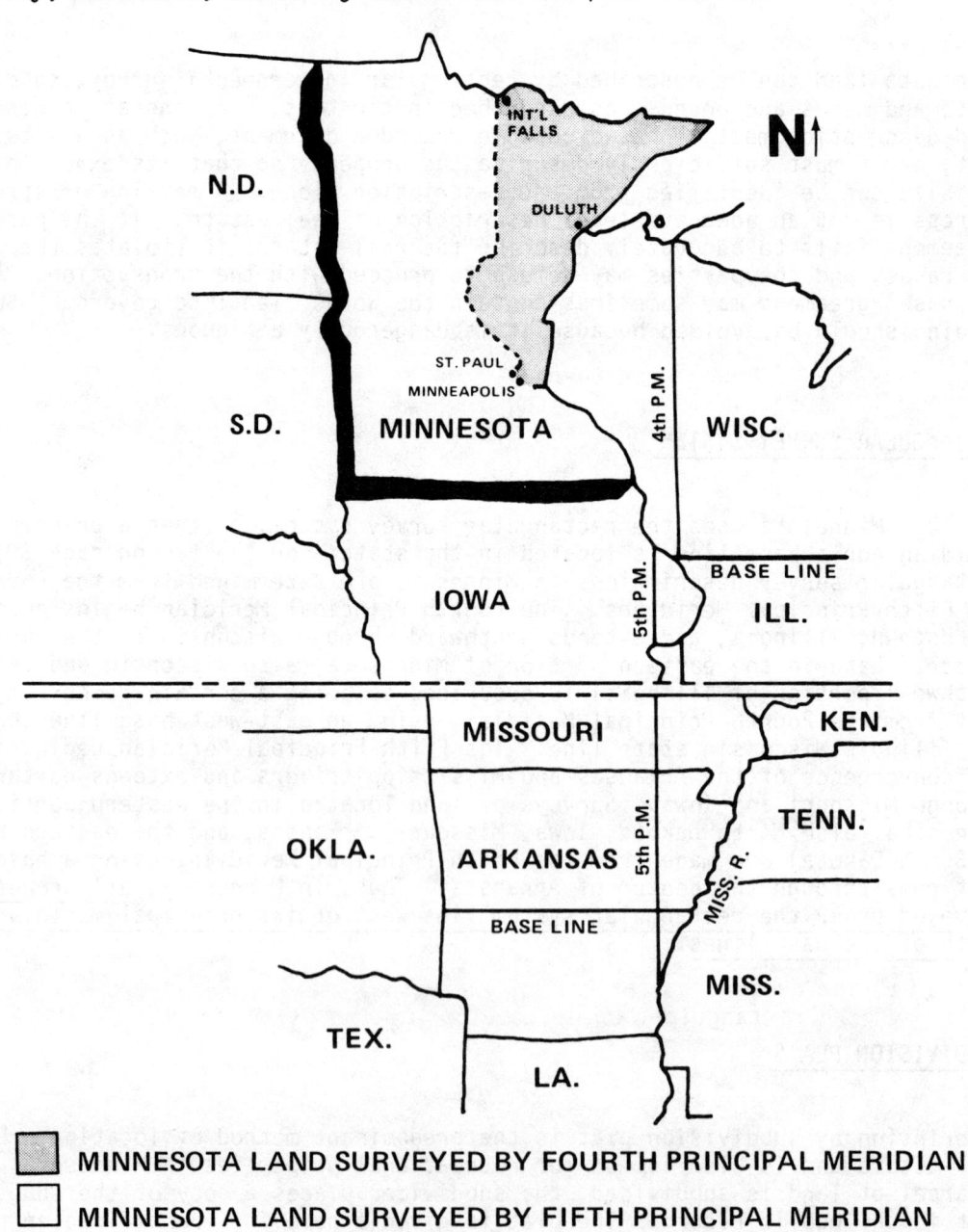

☐ MINNESOTA LAND SURVEYED BY FOURTH PRINCIPAL MERIDIAN
☐ MINNESOTA LAND SURVEYED BY FIFTH PRINCIPAL MERIDIAN

QUESTIONS

1. Rectangular surveys of land located in Duluth would be determined by the:

   I. Fifth Principal Meridian.
   II. Fourth Principal Meridian.

   a. I only
   b. II only
   c. both I and II
   d. neither I nor II

2. The base line for the Fourth Principal Meridian lies on:

   I. Illinois's northern border.
   II. Wisconsin's southern border.

   a. I only
   b. II only
   c. both I and II
   d. neither I nor II

3. Which of the following would not be an adequate legal description of Minnesota real estate?

   a. The N-1/2 of the SW-1/4 of the NW-1/4, Section 17, T136 N, R67 W.
   b. Lot 9, block 12, Sunny Acres, Cook County, Minnesota, according to the recorded plat thereof.
   c. The tract of land located at 2566 Wicker Avenue, lying in the county of Dakota in the state of Minnesota.
   d. That part of the NW-1/4 of the NW-1/4 of Section 3, T140 N, R59 W, bounded by a line described as follows: Commencing at Lake Fine, at a point 375 feet north of the NW-1/4 of the NW-1/4 of said section; thence due west, 300 feet; thence due north 500 feet; thence due east 289 feet to the shoreline of Lake Fine: thence following said shoreline south to the point of beginning.

4. Urban real estate in Minnesota is generally described by:

   a. metes and bounds.
   b. subdivision plats.
   c. rectangular survey.
   d. rectangular survey and metes and bounds.

5. Which of the following would appear on a subdivided plat?

   a. easements
   b. the numbers given to each individual block and lot
   c. the rectangular survey location of the plat
   d. all of the above

32   MINNESOTA SUPPLEMENT for Modern Real Estate Practice

Answer the following questions according to the information given in the plat of Honeysuckle Hills on page 33.

6. Which of the following statements is(are) true?

   I. Lot 9, Block A is larger than Lot 12 in the same block.
   II. The plat for the lots on the southerly side of Wolf Road between Goodrich Boulevard and Carney Street is found on Sheet 3.

      a. I only   c. both I and II
      b. II only   d. neither I nor II

7. Which of the following lots has the most frontage on Jasmine Lane?

      a. Lot 10, Block B   c. Lot 1, Block A
      b. Lot 11, Block B   d. Lot 2, Block A

8. "Beginning at the intersection of the east line of Goodrich Boulevard and the south line of Jasmine Lane and running south along the east line of Goodrich Boulevard a distance of 230 feet thence east parallel to the north line of Wolf Road a distance of 195 feet; thence northeasterly on a course N 22° E a distance of 135 feet; and thence northwesterly along the south line of Jasmine Lane to the point of beginning." Which lots are described here?

      a. Lots 13, 14 and 15, Block A
      b. Lots 9, 10 and 11, Block B
      c. Lots 1, 2, 3 and 15, Block A
      d. Lots 7, 8 and 9, Block A

9. On the plat, how many lots have easements?

      a. one   c. three
      b. two   d. four

PLAT OF HONEYSUCKLE HILLS SUBDIVISION
(SHEET 3 OF 4 SHEETS)

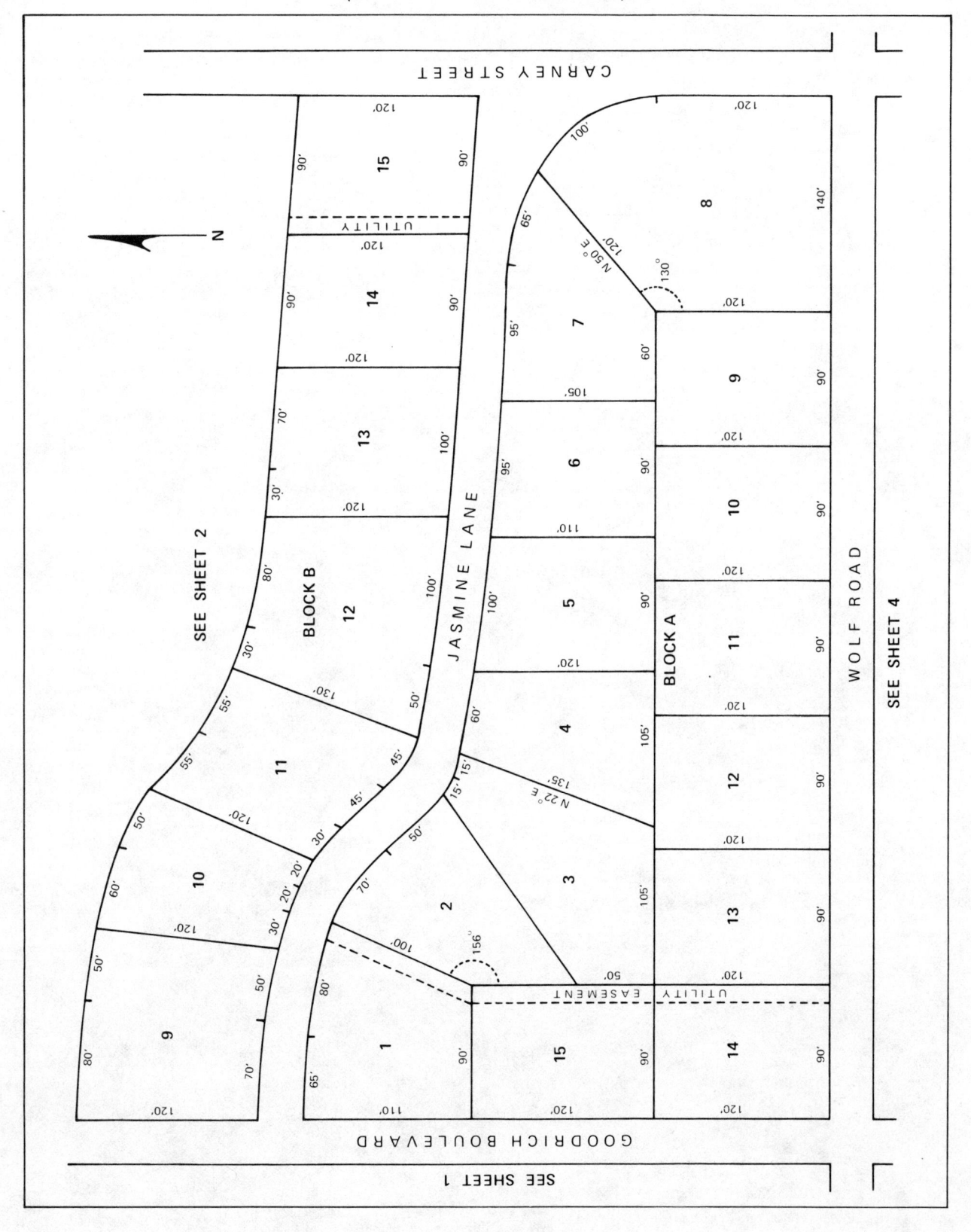

10

Real Estate Taxes and Other Liens

GENERAL (AD VALOREM) TAX

Minnesota property taxes are assessed and collected for the support of local and county governments and local school districts.

All Minnesota counties are required by law to employ county assessors appointed by the Board of County Commissioners with the approval of the state Commissioner of Revenue. The governing body of any township or city must appoint and employ an assessor who is licensed by the State Board of Assessors. Also, assessors of all cities with a population of 30,000 or more, including Minneapolis and Duluth, have the same powers and duties as the county assessor. Local assessors are under the jurisdiction of the county assessor. The Commissioner of Revenue has general supervision over the administration of all Minnesota tax laws.

Assessment

Real property is listed, and at least one-fourth of the parcels listed have to be appraised each year by the assessor with reference to their value on January 2 of that year. The law is designed to ensure that each parcel of real estate is appraised at maximum intervals of four years. Real property becoming taxable in any year is listed and assessed with reference to its value on January 2 of the year. Real estate is assessed for tax purposes at between five percent and 43 percent of its market value. The percentage applied to the market value of the property depends on how the assessor classified the property according to a classification system prescribed by law. Market value refers to the competitive selling price that could be obtained at a private sale, as opposed to a forced or auction sale.

Homestead tax benefits. As mentioned in Chapter 7, homestead property is eligible for special property tax treatment. The 1977 Omnibus Tax Bill provides that homestead property will be assessed at reduced rates. Currently a non-agricultural homestead property is assessed and valued at 17 percent for the first $30,000 of market value, 19 percent for the next $30,000 of market value, and 30 percent for the remaining market value.

Agricultural classification of farm land. To get the agricultural classification, the assessed land must be at least 10 contiguous acres in size and must have been used for agricultural purposes the year before. Agricultural land includes pasture, timber, waste, unusable wild land, and land included in federal farm programs. Real estate of less than 10 acres used mainly for raising poultry, livestock, fruit, vegetables, or other agricultural products is also considered agricultural land if it is not used principally for residential purposes. A farm homestead is taxed on the following basis: the first $60,000 of market value is valued and assessed at 14 percent, the additional market value at 19 percent.

Limited market value. After determining the market value of a property, the assessor is required to compare that value to the value of the property in the prior year. The amount of any increase from the 1984 to 1985 assessment cannot be more than 12-1/2 percent of the value without a refund being due. The refund is 50 percent of the tax increase over the specified amount of 12-1/2 percent for the 1984-1985 tax increases or 100 percent for increases over 20 percent for homestead property. Maximum increases and refunds for after 1984-1985 will be determined by the legislature.

Other exemptions and tax credits. Over the years, the Minnesota legislature has established various exemptions and property tax treatments. Generally, public burial grounds, schools, hospitals, churches, and other miscellaneous public properties are exempt. Details of these exemptions can be found in the Minnesota Statutes, Section 272.02.

Most homeowners are eligible for a cash refund of part of the property tax they have to pay. The refunds are intended to reduce the property burden of low-, middle-, and moderately high-income homeowners. The size of a homeowner's refund depends on the relationship between the amount of his or her income and the amount of his or her property tax. The maximum amount of property tax relief a homeowner can get is $800. However, this amount must be reduced by the amount of any state-paid homestead credit a homeowner already received on his or her property tax bill.

Appeals. Every citizen has the right to appeal an assessment. In Minnesota, there are a number of channels of assessment appeal. The first is through a local board of review or equalization. These boards meet between April 1 and June 30 each year to hear taxpayers' grievances. If the appeal is denied on a local level, the taxpayer can take the case to a county board of equalization. County boards of equalization convene each July. Appeal is then taken to the Tax Court of Appeals.

A taxpayer can also appeal an assessment after taxes are known and become payable by filing a petition with a tax court in Minnesota. A petition must be filed before June 1 of the year in which payment becomes due. An application for a petition will not be reviewed unless the first installment of the tax is paid before the filing of the petition.

Tax Rate

Minnesota property taxes are levied as so many mills for each $1.00 of assessed valuation. A mill is one-tenth of a cent ($.001), and there are 1,000 mills in one dollar. For example, a levy of 54.4 mills can be computed as 54.4 divided by 1,000, which is a tax of $.0544, or 5.44 cents, per dollar:

$$\frac{54.4}{1,000} = 1,000 \overline{)54.4000}^{.0544}$$

For an example of tax computation, consider a Minneapolis house that had a market value of $75,000 in 1984. To calculate the property tax, first determine the assessed valuation of the homestead:

```
        first $30,000 at 17%        = $ 5,100
        second $30,000 at 19%       =   5,700
        remaining market
          value of $15,000 at 30%   =   4,500
        total assessed value        = $15,300
```

The total assessed value is then multiplied by the mill rate, which, in this example, is assumed to be .113:

$$\$15,300 \times .113 = \$1,729$$

The total property tax, before any credit, is $1,729.

The mill rate is based upon the ratio of annual government expenditures to the assessed value of property in the tax area.

Tax Payment

The real estate tax in Minnesota becomes due on the first Monday in January following the year of assessment. Property is assessed as of January 2, and liens are established as of that date. If the property tax is more than $10, it can be paid to the county treasurer in two equal installments each year. The first installment, or any amount of tax less than $10, has to be paid no later than May 15, and the second installment has to be paid by October 15.

Delinquent Taxes--Redemption

Any owner or person holding an interest in tax-forfeited land can redeem the property at any time within the three- or five-year redemption period. The redemption period begins after the tax-forfeited land is entered into judgment. The property is entered into judgment on the second Tuesday in May following the year the taxes first became delinquent. The period of redemption for residential and agricultural homestead property or seasonal recreational property is five years. The period of redemption for nonhomestead and all other classifications of real estate is three years.

Property can be redeemed by paying all delinquent taxes plus interest (at a rate based upon the market yields of one-year United States Treasury Bills), along with all penalties and costs. If a type of property is classified and assessed at 40 percent or less of the market value, it can also be redeemed through a confession of judgment for delinquent taxes. This means an owner can enter into an agreement with local tax officials to pay back the delinquent tax in regular installments over a ten-year period. The owner also must agree to pay his or her current property taxes on time.

Tax Sales

Tax-delinquent property is entered into judgment, or "bid in for the state," in the year after the taxes or any part of them have not been paid. A property owner will lose his or her land if he or she does not redeem it or take action to retain equity within the three- or five-year forfeiture period that begins after the land is entered into judgment. The state acquires an absolute right to the title of the property after the period of redemption has expired and the county auditor has recorded a certificate of forfeiture.

All delinquent taxes, interest and penalties, and other costs are extinguished at the time the property is forfeited to the state. The county board of commissioners is responsible for the administration of the property after it has become tax forfeited. The county board can choose to transfer, sell, or hold the tax-forfeited land. Cities, townships, school districts, the county, and the state have priority over the acquisition of tax-forfeited land if they want it for an essential or dedicated public purpose.

If the county board decides to sell the tax-forfeited land, it must first review and classify the land and determine its most logical use. Then it must establish a minimum value at which the land can be sold. Sales of tax-forfeited land are normally held in each county between the months of July and November every year. All general sales must be published. The sales are held by the sheriff and the county auditor at the courthouse in each county seat. The tax-forfeited land cannot be auctioned for a price lower than the appraised value established by the county board in its official publication for the sale, nor can it be sold if only one individual submits an offer to purchase it.

If a property is not sold at the sale, it can normally be acquired through the county auditor's office for the amount of the appraised value established by the county board. If a property is not sold before the next annual sale occurs, the county board is responsible for the administration of the property. The county board can have the tax-forfeited property reappraised for a sale in a subsequent year.

Property purchased or acquired at a tax sale does not include the mineral rights to the land. The state retains the mineral rights to the land at the time it issues a state deed to the person acquiring the tax-forfeited land. The state deeds are issued to a purchaser by the Commissioner of Revenue after he or she receives a certificate of purchase from the county auditor who sold the tax-forfeited land. The state deed may constitute a marketable title to the property sold if it complies with the requirements of law. The state transfers all of its rights acquired through the forfeiture to the purchaser, except for the mineral rights.

MECHANICS' LIENS

A mechanic's lien is created by statute to protect the interests of persons who have performed work or furnished materials in the construction, repair, or remodeling of a building. Minnesota law includes architects, engineers, and surveyors in the class of those entitled to this protection. Monies owed to such persons become a lien against the real estate upon which the work is being performed as of the date the first labor was performed or materials furnished. In Minnesota, this includes the work of all mechanics and materialmen involved with the particular building, even though they may begin work at different phases of construction. In other words, all mechanics' liens stemming from a project attach (take effect) at the same time.

To perfect the lien, one must file a verified, written statement with the county recorder in the county where the property is located. This must be filed within 120 days of the last labor performed or materials furnished by anyone involved with the project. A mechanic or materialman must notify the property owner in writing that the liens have been filed. However, a mechanic or materialman need not notify the owner when work performed or materials furnished involved a five-or-more-unit residential property or other property having an area greater than 5,000 square feet of floor space.

An Example of Mechanics' Liens

Bonnie and Bill Daniels have decided to remodel the kitchen of their charming brownstone. They discuss their ideas with an architect from the firm Dooreit & Dudley. Their architect prepares her recommendations for structural work on September 15, 1983.

On October 17, carpenters and plumbers arrive and begin work on the Daniels' kitchen. Electricians start wiring several days later. The carpenters and plumbers complete their work on October 28, and the electricians finish two days later. The final painting is completed on November 10.

All mechanics' liens for the remodeling attach on September 15, the date the first labor was performed (in this case, by the architect). If any parties who performed the work wish to perfect a lien, they must file a statement with the county recorder before March 10, 1984 (120 days after the last work was completed). Thus, all mechanics' liens arising from remodeling the Daniels' kitchen attach on the same date, and the same time period for perfecting the liens applies to all the workers.

Notice of Nonresponsibility

Even though a person other than the landowner (a tenant, contract purchaser, etc.) orders work to be done on a specific parcel of real estate, the landowner is still considered by law to have authorized and consented to the work. The landowner can remedy this situation by posting a notice of nonresponsibility for the work in a conspicuous place on the property within five days after the first labor is performed or materials are furnished.

Subcontractors' Liens

As discussed in the text, a subcontractor is entitled to a mechanic's lien against the owner's property if the contractor is paid but has not, in turn, paid the subcontractor (the contractor in this instance would be guilty of theft). To be entitled to a mechanic's lien, a subcontractor must give the owner written notice that he or she may lose the property if the subcontractor is not paid. This notice must be delivered to the owner within 45 days after the work was begun or materials first furnished, and must advise the owner of what he or she must do to protect the property. However, such notice is not required in connection with large projects meeting certain statutory size requirements.

Minnesota law permits an owner to withhold from the contractor as much of the contract price as is necessary to pay the subcontractors and other lien claimants directly. In addition, the owner may withhold payment for 120 days

40   MINNESOTA SUPPLEMENT for Modern Real Estate Practice

following the completion of the improvement or project unless the contractor provides lien waivers signed by the subcontractors who had originally given the 45-day notice as described here.

JUDGMENTS

A court decree ordering money owed by a debtor-owner to be paid to a creditor becomes a judgment lien against the debtor's real property located in the county in which the judgment is rendered. The lien takes priority from the date on which the complaint stating the claim against the debtor was filed with the district court for that county. The judgment lien will then be in effect for the next ten years. The creditor can have a judgment lien attached to a debtor's real property located in any Minnesota county by filing a similar petition with the U.S. District Court for District of Minnesota.

Lis Pendens

Under Minnesota law, a notice of lis pendens may be filed in any action where title to an interest in or a lien upon real property is brought into question. The filing of the notice is intended to give purchasers and lenders notice of the rights of the party filing the notice.

QUESTIONS

1. Sam and Beth Halterston just received a notice of the tax assessment on their home. If they feel the assessment is too high, they must:

   I. first pay their taxes before appealing the assessment.
   II. file a complaint with District Court.

   a. I only   c. both I and II
   b. II only   d. neither I nor II

2. Which of the following may be entitled to a mechanic's lien?

   I. an architect
   II. a surveyor

   a. I only   c. both I and II
   b. II only   d. neither I nor II

3. Bruce Coary, a Minnesota homeowner, has just paid his current property tax bill. The txes he paid were actually levied:

   a. last year.   c. next year.
   b. this year.   d. the previous January 2.

10/Real Estate Taxes and Other Liens   41

4. Which of the following does <u>not</u> receive support from Minnesota real property taxes?

    a. local school districts   c. state governments
    b. county governments   d. local governments

5. Jane Peterson failed to pay the property taxes on her homestead, and they are delinquent. According to Minnesota law, how long does she have to redeem her property and thus retain ownership?

    a. about five years from the day the taxes became delinquent
    b. about seven years from the day the taxes became delinquent
    c. about nine years from the day the taxes became delinquent
    d. about ten years from the day the taxes became delinquent

6. Joseph English bought a parcel of real estate at a county tax sale. In exchange for his payment he receives:

    a. a deed to the property from the state.
    b. an assignment of title from the state.
    c. a declaration of homestead from the state.
    d. a clear title to the property in nine years.

7. Money judgments become a lien on an owner's real property in one specific county upon the date of the creditor's filing with:

    a. Minnesota District Court.
    b. U.S. District Court for District of Minnesota.
    c. municipal court.
    d. any court of competent jurisdiction.

8. Ralph Johnson, a general contractor, got an assignment to do some work on the old Silver mansion on August 15. He immediately hired and scheduled workers to do the repairs. The work was performed on the following days: exterior painting, September 11, 12, and 13; sidewalk repair, August 29; electrical service, September 2, 3, 4, and 5; and plumbing repair, September 9 and 10. On which of the following dates would any workers' mechanics' liens attach?

    a. August 15   c. September 9
    b. August 29   d. September 11

9. The Franklins' urban home has a market value of $47,000 (which includes a homestead base value of $15,000). What will its assessed value be for real estate tax purposes?

    a. $ 8,330   c. $15,651
    b. $13,656   d. $18,800

10. The assessed value of the Bergman residence is $19,640. How much real estate tax must the Bergmans pay for this year before receiving the state-paid homestead credit, if the tax levy is 32.4 mills per dollar of assessed valuation?

    a. $48.75
    b. $63.63
    c. $487.54
    d. $636.34

11

Contracts

REQUIREMENTS FOR A VALID CONTRACT IN MINNESOTA

The text describes four essential elements of a valid contract: offer and acceptance, consideration, legality of object, and competent parties. All of these are applicable in Minnesota. In addition, a contract for the sale of real estate in Minnesota must be in writing and signed, and it must contain a description of the property.

Capacity to Contract

Under Minnesota law, a person reaches majority and has the legal capacity to enter into a valid contract at the age of 18. A minor's contracts are not void, but they are voidable; the minor may disaffirm any such contract either before or within a reasonable time after he or she reaches majority (the legal age of 18). However, a minor who is not under the care of a parent or guardian is generally held responsible for contractrs to purchase items considered necessities.

Statute of Frauds

With respect to real estate, the Minnesota Statute of Frauds requires that agreements for the sale of or an interest in real property, as well as leases for a term of more than one year, must be in writing and signed by the parties. Any such agreements not in writing and signed are considered void and, as such, have no legal effect.

In addition, the parol evidence rule, in effect in Minnesota, provides that the terms of a written agreement may not be varied, contradicted, or altered by either prior or contemporaneous evidence (oral or written) unless there is a plea of fraud, duress, or mutual mistake in connection with the document. Thus, a party to a written agreement cannot normally argue that the terms he or she agreed to are not those actually represented in the contract. The rule does not, however, prevent the introduction of evidence to explain what was meant by the agreement, nor does it restrict evidence concerning matters not covered by the agreement or evidence introduced subsequent to the agreement.

Remember also that the Minnesota Real Estate License Law provides that a real estate licensee cannot bring any case before the courts regarding collection of a commission unless there is a written listing agreement for the property.

Statute of Limitations

The law allows a specific time limit during which parties to a contract may bring a legal suit to enforce their rights. In Minnesota, an injured party must bring a suit for performance within six years after the breach of contract.

Plain Language Contract Act

Effective on July 1, 1983, consumer contracts must be written in clear, plain, everyday language. A "consumer contract" is any written contract with a consumer except: (1) a contract where the price, excluding interest or finance charges, is more than $50,000; (2) a contract through which a consumer mortgages an interest in real estate or obtains money or credit to be used to purchase or refinance an interest in real estate; (3) a contract in which the sale of personal property is merely incidental to the sale of an interest in real estate. Accordingly, a real estate listing agreement must be in plain language form.

BROKER'S AUTHORITY TO PREPARE DOCUMENTS

Minnesota real estate brokers and salespersons must be able to prepare all documents for a real estate transaction. In addition, brokers and salespersons must be able to interpret to all involved parties the financial results or consequences of all clauses or conditions used in such documents. Licensees must thus be familiar with the state statutes that regulate the enforcement of contracts made in conjunction with real estate transactions, namely, the Statute of Frauds, Real Estate License Law, and Subdivided Land Sales Practices Act.

A broker or salesperson should not attempt to give a client legal advice, however--this is the job of an attorney. In addition, brokers and salespersons should use only forms that the Real Estate Commission has approved for use in Minnesota. Using a non-Minnesota contract can have unpredictable results.

CONTRACTS FOR THE SALE OF REAL ESTATE

In Minnesota, a real estate sales contract is known as an earnest money contract or more commonly, as a purchase agreement. The document contains the sales contract provisions as well as a receipt for the purchaser's earnest money deposit.

The actual contents of a purchase agreement may vary from office to office and form to form. Minnesota law does not require that any particular form be used; however, the broker should use a good, standard form that has been especially designed for selling specific types of property. Some forms typically used in Minnesota are included at the end of this chapter.

Rules adopted pursuant to the Minnesota Real Estate License Law provide that brokers must give copies of all records, instruments, and documents that are material to a transaction to the parties involved. They must also keep copies of these papers for their own records for a period of three years. In practice, the person making an offer to purchase should execute the original and at least three copies of the contract. The purchaser retains one copy as a receipt; the original and the other two copies are presented to the seller. Upon accepting the offer, the seller signs the original and the two copies. The seller retains one signed copy, one is delivered to the buyer, and the broker should retain one copy on file for three years, as required by law.

Receipt of Earnest Money

The amount of earnest money the broker accepts should be sufficient to compensate the seller if the contract is not consummated and the sale is not completed. In Minnesota residential real estate transactions, brokers collect either a flat amount, such as $500 or $1,000, or a percentage of the selling price. (Of course, this would not prevent either the seller or the broker from filing suit for damages if the amount of earnest money collected was not sufficient to cover damages incurred when a buyer defaulted on the transaction.) The amount of earnest money collected is usually greater in the sale of farm property.

The earnest money should be written out in words as well as figures in the document. There should also be an indication of whether the deposit was cash, a personal check, a promissory note, or some other form of payment in lieu of cash. If the manner of payment is not indicated, the seller can assume that the deposit was made in cash. For example, if the buyer forfeits the deposit by defaulting on the purchase agreement, the seller may then demand the money in cash (unless otherwise provided in the contract). If the buyer is to deposit additional earnest money, the contract should provide a definite date for such payment. Note that a salesperson should never write up an earnest money contract without collecting earnest money; likewise, a salesperson should not collect earnest money without completing an earnest money agreement. Earnest money _must_ be deposited in the broker's trust account by the next business day _after_ the offer is accepted unless both parties have given written permission not to do so.

Personal Property

Most contract forms also include a paragraph that lists and describes any items of personal property included in the sale price. If this provision is acceptable to the buyer, the broker should make out a separate bill of sale for the personal property when the transaction is closed.

Alterations in the Contract

The negotiation process in a real estate transaction involving offers and counteroffers is described in the text. If the seller wishes to make minor changes in the contract, the broker or salesperson will have the seller and purchaser approve them in writing, either by executing a separate amendment or by initialing the changes in the margin of the contract. If the seller's alterations are more extensive, the best practice is to prepare a new contract according to the seller's proposed terms and have both parties sign this agreement if it is acceptable.

Out-of-Town Seller

If the seller is out of the area when an offer is made to purchase the property, the buyer should send the seller a telegram describing the exact terms of the offer and advising the seller to wire an acceptance or rejection of the offer. The broker should retain copies of this telegram and of the agreement. If the seller accepts the offer, these telegrams should be attached to the earnest money contract. Note that these telegrams should be sent personally by the buyer and seller.

HANDLING EARNEST MONEY DEPOSITS (TRUST ACCOUNTING)

Minnesota law sets forth specific requirements for the handling of earnest money deposits and other funds entrusted to a real estate broker. Failure to account for trust funds properly is a basis for suspension or revocation of the broker's license. A broker must immediately deposit all funds entrusted to him or her in a special trust account established for this purpose (unless the parties to the transaction sign an express, written agreement directing the funds to be used in some other way--for example, the purchase of a certificate of deposit). The trust account must be a demand deposit or checking account in any Minnesota bank or trust company or out-of-state bank that authorizes scrutiny of such accounts by the Commissioner of Commerce. By law, anything of value other than cash used as a down payment in a real estate transaction must be held by an authorized escrow agent. Remember, brokers must retain copies of all documents and records pertaining to a real estate transaction for three years from the date of closing (or the date of listing, should a transaction not be consummated). Earnest money deposit requirements will be discussed in detail in Chapter 14 of this Supplement.

INSTALLMENT CONTRACTS

In Minnesota, installment contracts, as described in the text, are known as contracts for deed. Contracts for deed will be discussed in Chapter 15 of this Supplement.

ESCROW AGREEMENTS

The escrow procedure of closing a transaction, as described in the text, is rarely used in Minnesota. Absolute delivery of the title to the purchaser is much more common.

DISCLOSURE REGARDING REPRESENTATION OF PARTIES

As of August 1, 1985 Minnesota law requires that a written statement be furnished to all parties of a real estate transaction by a real estate salesperson or broker identifying which party the salesperson or broker represents. The law, (Minnesota Statutes, Section 82.19) requires that this disclosure be in at least six-point bold type on the purchase agreement and that it must be made prior to any offer being made to or accepted by the buyer. Furthermore, if events occur that change the initial disclosure or make it incomplete, misleading or inaccurate a new disclosure must be made in writing by the salesperson or broker involved. (see purchase agreement)

Example:

_____ stipulates that he/she is representing _____ in this
agent/broker   buyer/seller

transaction.

Listing agent or broker stipulates that he/she is representing the seller in

this transaction.

STANDARD PURCHASE AGREEMENT

Form Approved By Greater Minneapolis Area Board of REALTORS® REVISED, JULY 1985

1. _____, Minnesota _____, 19 ___
2. RECEIVED OF _____
3. the sum of _____ Dollars ($ _____)
4. by ___CHECK CASH NOTE State Which___ as earnest money to be deposited the next business day after acceptance in trust account of listing broker
5. (unless otherwise specified in writing) and in part payment for the purchase of the premises legally described as _____
6. _____
7. _____
8. located at (Street Address) _____,
9. City of _____, County of _____, State of Minnesota,
10. including all plants, shrubs and trees, all storm windows and/or inserts, storm doors, screens, awnings, window shades, blinds, curtain-
11. traverse-drapery rods, attached lighting fixtures with bulbs, plumbing fixtures, water heater, heating system, humidifier, central air conditioning,
12. electronic air filter, automatic garage door opener with controls, water softener, cable television outlets and cabling, BUILT-INS to include:
13. dishwasher, garbage disposal, trash compactor, oven(s), cooktop stove, microwave oven, hood-fan, intercom, installed carpeting, IF ANY,
14. located on the premises which are the property of Seller and also the following personal property: _____
15. _____
16. _____
17. all of which property Seller has this day sold to Buyer for the sum of: $ _____
18. _____ Dollars,
19. _____
20. which Buyer agrees to pay in the following manner: Earnest money of $ _____ and
21. $ _____ cash on or before _____, the date of closing, and the balance
22. of $ _____ by financing as follows: _____
23. _____
24. _____
25. _____
26. _____
27. _____
28. _____
29. _____
30. _____
31. **Attached are** _____ addendums which are made a part of this agreement.
32. **SUBJECT TO** performance by Buyer, Seller agrees to execute and deliver a _____ Warranty Deed,
33. to be joined in by spouse, if any, conveying marketable title to the premises subject only to the following exceptions:
34. (1) Building and zoning laws, ordinances, State and Federal regulations. (2) Restrictions relating to use or improvement of the premises without
35. effective forfeiture provision. (3) Reservation of any minerals or mineral rights to the State of Minnesota. (4) Utility and drainage easements
36. which do not interfere with present improvements. (5) Rights of tenants, if any.

37. **REAL ESTATE TAXES** Seller agrees to pay _____ / 12ths and Buyer agrees to pay _____ / 12ths of taxes due and payable in the year
38. 19 ___ . Seller agrees to pay _____ / 12ths and Buyer agrees to pay _____ / 12ths of annual installment of special assessments due
39. and payable in the year 19 ___ . __(BUYER/SELLER)__ agrees to __(PAY/ASSUME)__ on the date of closing all special assessments levied and pending.
40. Buyer shall pay taxes due and payable in the year 19 ___ and any unpaid installments of special assessments payable therewith
41. and thereafter. Seller warrants that taxes due and payable in the year 19 _____ will be __(FULL PART NON State Which)__ homestead
42. classification. Neither Seller nor Seller's Agent makes any representation concerning the amount of future real estate taxes.
43. **WARRANTIES** Seller warrants that buildings, if any, are entirely within the boundary lines of the premises. Seller warrants that all
44. appliances, heating and air conditioning, wiring and plumbing used and located on the premises are in proper working order on date of closing.
45. Buyer has right to inspect premises prior to closing. Buyer shall satisfy himself/herself at his/her expense that all appliances, heating and air
46. conditioning, wiring and plumbing are in proper working order before closing. Seller warrants that the premises are connected to: city sewer
47. ☐ yes - ☐ no; city water ☐ yes - ☐ no. If the premises are destroyed or substantially damaged by fire or any other cause before the
48. closing date, this agreement shall become null and void at Buyer's option, and the earnest money shall be refunded to Buyer.
49. **POSSESSION** Seller agrees to deliver possession not later than _____ closing.
50. All interest, city water and sewer charges, electricity and natural gas charges, fuel oil and liquid petroleum gas shall be pro-rated between the
51. parties as of _____ . Seller agrees to remove all debris and all personal property not included herein from the
52. premises before possession date.
53. **TITLE & EXAMINATION** Seller shall, within a reasonable time after acceptance of this agreement, furnish an Abstract of Title, or a
54. Registered Property Abstract, certified to date to include proper searches covering bankruptcies, State and Federal judgments and liens. Buyer
55. shall be allowed 10 business days after receipt for examination of title and making any objections, which shall be made in writing or deemed
56. waived. If any objection is so made, Seller shall be allowed 120 days to make title marketable. Pending correction of title, payments hereunder
57. required shall be postponed, but upon correction of title and within 10 days after written notice to Buyer, the parties shall perform this
58. agreement according to its terms. If title is not corrected within 120 days from the date of written objection, this agreement shall be null and
59. void, at option of Buyer, neither party shall be liable for damages hereunder to the other, and earnest money shall be refunded to Buyer.
60. **DEFAULT** If title is marketable or is corrected within said time, and Buyer defaults in any of the agreements herein, Seller may terminate this
61. agreement, and on such termination all payments made hereunder shall be retained by Seller and Agent, as their respective interests may appear,
62. as liquidated damages, time being of the essence hereof. This provision shall not deprive either party of the right of enforcing the specific performance
63. of this agreement, provided this agreement is not terminated and action to enforce specific performance is commenced within six months after
64. such right of action arises.
65. **ACCEPTANCE** Buyer understands and agrees that this sale is subject to acceptance by Seller in writing. Agent is not liable or responsible
66. on account of this agreement, except to return or account for the earnest money.
67. **AGENCY DISCLOSURE** _____(NAME OF AGENT OR BROKER)_____ stipulates he or she is representing the _____(BUYER SELLER)_____
68. in this transaction. The listing agent or broker stipulates he or she is representing the seller in this transaction.

69. I, the owner of the premises, accept this agreement and   I agree to purchase the premises for the price and on the terms and
70. the sale hereby made.   conditions set forth above.

SELLER _____   BUYER _____

SELLER _____   BUYER _____

Delivery of all papers and monies shall be made at the office of:

Company _____   Selling Agent _____

Address _____   City _____ Zip _____

THIS IS A LEGALLY BINDING CONTRACT. IF NOT UNDERSTOOD, SEEK COMPETENT ADVICE.   MBR-312

50 MINNESOTA SUPPLEMENT for Modern Real Estate Practice

Purchase Agreement Addendum
Form Approved By Greater Minneapolis Area Board of REALTORS® December, 1985

CONVENTIONAL

1 This is an addendum to the Standard Purchase Agreement dated _____ (date of Std. P.A.) pertaining
2 to the sale of real estate at _____ (address) _____.

3 ☐ **CASH TO NEW PRIVATELY INSURED LOAN OR CONVENTIONAL MORTGAGE.**

4 Earnest money herein paid, $_____ and $_____ cash on or before, _____, the date of
5 closing, $_____ by Buyer placing at his expense a (Insert correct type: Privately insured or Conventional
6 loans) mortgage in at least this amount amortized monthly over a period of not less than _____ years with
7 interest at no more than _____ percent per annum. Application for mortgage is to be made immediately upon
8 acceptance of this purchase agreement by Seller. Buyer agrees to use best efforts to secure a commitment for
9 such financing and to execute all documents required to consummate said financing. In the event the Buyer
10 cannot secure a commitment for such mortgage on or before _____, this agreement shall become null
11 and void on said date, and the earnest money paid herein shall be refunded to Buyer. Seller agrees to pay not
12 more than $_____ to the lender at the time of closing to assist Buyer in obtaining said mortgage.

13 ☐ **CASH TO ASSUME EXISTING MORTGAGE OR CONTRACT FOR DEED**

14 $_____ by assuming and agreeing to pay according to its terms and conditions a balance of
15 approximately this amount on the existing _____ (hereinafter referred to as underlying debt). Exact
16 balance(s) shall be determined at time of closing and the difference shall be adjusted in cash so the purchase
17 price will remain the same. Said underlying debt to be current as of closing date, to be evidenced by a written
18 statement from the lender. This purchase agreement is contingent upon purchaser being allowed to assume said
19 loan with no change being made in the terms or conditions of the loan as originally made. The Buyer agrees to
20 pay assumption fee(s) of approximately $_____ required by the holder of the underlying debt. This
21 agreement is subject to the holder of the underlying debt(s) approving the assumption(s), if required, and if not
22 approved, this agreement is null and void and earnest money shall be refunded to the Buyer.

23 BUYER _____ SELLER _____

24 BUYER _____ SELLER _____

25 FIRM _____ AGENT _____

MBR-311

Purchase Agreement Addendum
Form Approved By Greater Minneapolis Area Board of REALTORS® December, 1985

FHA/VA

1 This is an addendum to the Standard Purchase Agreement dated ____(date of Std. P.A.)____ pertaining to the
2 sale of the real estate at ____(address)____.
3 ☐   FHA insured mortgage ____(program type)____
4 ☐   VA guaranteed mortgage ____(program type)____

5 $_____ by Buyer placing at own expense a mortgage in this amount plus applicable mortgage insurance
6 premium (MIP or funding fee). The Buyer shall make application for said mortgage immediately.

7 The ____(Buyer/Seller)____ agrees to pay the loan placement fee (discount points) not to exceed _____% of
8 the mortgage amount including applicable MIP or funding fee). If the discount points are to be floating, it shall be
9 the sole discretion of the ____(Buyer/Seller)____ to "lock-in" the discount points.

10 In the event Buyer is unable to secure a commitment for said mortgage by _____, this agreement shall
11 become null and void, and the earnest money refunded to Buyer.

12 "It is expressly agreed that, notwithstanding any other provisions of this contract, the purchaser shall not be
13 obligated to complete the purchase of the property described herein or to incur any penalty by forfeiture of
14 earnest money deposits or otherwise (1) in the case of an FHA loan, unless the Seller has delivered to the
15 purchaser a written statement issued by the Federal Housing Comissioner setting forth the appraised value of the

16 property (excluding closing costs) of not less than $_____ which statement the Seller hereby agrees
17 to deliver to the purchaser promptly after such statement is made available to the Seller, or (2) in the case of a VA
18 loan, if the contract purchase price or cost exceeds the reasonable value of the property established by the
19 Veterans Administration. The purchaser shall, however, have the privilege and option of proceeding with the
20 consummation of this agreement without regard to the amount of the aforementioned valuation."
21 THE APPRAISED VALUATION IS ARRIVED AT TO DETERMINE THE MAXIMUM MORTGAGE THE
22 DEPARTMENT OF HOUSING AND URBAN DEVELOPMENT WILL INSURE. HUD DOES NOT WARRANT THE
23 VALUE OR THE CONDITION OF THE PROPERTY. THE BUYER SHOULD EXAMINE THE PROPERTY
24 CAREFULLY TO DETERMINE THE PRICE AND THE CONDITION OF THE PROPERTY ARE ACCEPTABLE.
25 FHA DOES NOT APPROVE FINANCIAL ASSISTANCE IN CONNECTION WITH MAKING NEEDED REPAIRS.

26 BUYER_____   SELLER_____

27 BUYER_____   SELLER_____

28 FIRM_____   AGENT_____

MBR-308

Purchase Agreement Addendum

Form Approved By Greater Minneapolis Area Board of REALTORS® December, 1985

CONTINGENCIES

1 This is an addendum to the Standard Purchase Agreement dated _____(date of Std. P.A.)_____ pertaining to the
2 sale of the real estate at _____(address)_____.
3
4 ☐   _____ Hour Contingency
5 This agreement is contingent upon the Buyer(s) entering into a valid purchase agreement for the sale of the
6 Buyer(s) real estate located at: _____ on or before _____, 19____. In the
7 event said real estate is not sold by the date mentioned, this agreement is null and void and the earnest money will
8 be refunded to the Buyer(s). The Seller(s) and/or their agent(s) reserve the right to continue to offer the real
9 estate at _____ for sale unless this contingency has been removed in writing by
10 Buyer. Seller may demand removal of this contingency at anytime, by service of written notice upon the Buyer. If
11 Buyer does not comply with this demand within _____ hours of receipt of notice then, in that event, this
12 agreement shall be null and void and the earnest money herein paid shall be immediately refunded to Buyer. THE
13 _____ HOURS SHALL START WHEN THE CONTINGENCY REMOVAL NOTICE IS SERVED UPON THE
14 SELLING REAL ESTATE COMPANY, accepted, dated and timed by ANY LICENSED AGENT in the company and
15 it is the selling company's responsibility to deliver the papers to the Buyer(s) for their immediate consideration. If
16 said contingency is not removed, this purchase agreement shall become null and void. THE BUYER(S) AGREE
17 TO SIGN CANCELLATION PAPERS IMMEDIATELY AND THE EARNEST MONEY WILL BE RETURNED.
18 It is understood by the Buyer(s) and Seller(s) that the Buyer(s) can remove this contingency only in the event
19 there is a binding purchase agreement on their home or they have written evidence satisfactory to Seller they are
20 capable of performing on this contract without the sale or closing of their home.
21
22 BUYER_____ SELLER_____
23 BUYER_____ SELLER_____
24
25 AGENT_____ AGENT_____

26 ☐   **NOTICE TO PURCHASER**
27 TO PURCHASER: _____
28   _____
29 Pursuant to the purchase agreement and supplement dated _____, 19____ between you and the
30 undersigned, you are hereby notified the undersigned has, subject to your rights under the CONTINGENCY
31 AGREEMENT, accepted a written offer for the purchase of the real estate. Unless you are able to meet the
32 conditions for removal outlined in the CONTINGENCY AGREEMENT with respect to the sale of your real estate
33 commonly known as _____ within the time specified in the
34 CONTINGENCY AGREEMENT, the purchase agreement shall be null and void.

35 DATED:_____, 19____ TIME:_____ SELLER:_____
36 RECEIVED BY
37 BUYER/AGENT:_____ DATED:_____, 19____ TIME:_____

38 ☐   **REMOVAL OF CONTINGENCY**
39 Buyer hereby removes the _____ hour contingency clause from the above cited purchase agreement and
40 agrees to proceed with the closing according to the terms and conditions of said Purchase Agreement. Buyer
41 represents that Buyer has entered into a valid purchase agreement, not contingent on the sale of other real estate,
42 for the sale of Buyer's real estate, a copy of which is attached hereto, or Buyer represents that Buyer is financially
43 able and capable of performing Buyer's obligations under the terms of this Purchase Agreement without the sale
44 of Buyer's real estate and the evidence substantiating Buyer's representation is attached hereto. Seller hereby
45 acknowledges the receipt and sufficiency of such evidence and hereby agrees to the removal of the contingency.
46 SELLER_____ BUYER_____
47
48 SELLER_____ BUYER_____

49 ☐   **CANCELLATION OF PURCHASE AGREEMENT**
50 The undersigned agree that a purchase agreement dated _____, 19____ relating to the real
51 estate described above is hereby cancelled and terminated and Buyer hereby release all rights to said real estate
52 to Seller. The earnest money in connection with said agreement shall be disposed of as follows:
53 _____. The parties hereto hereby mutually release the other
54 from all rights, covenants, conditions and obligations in said agreement.
55 SELLER_____ BUYER_____
56
57 SELLER_____ BUYER_____
58 DATED_____ DATED_____
59   PREPARED BY:_____, AGENT

MRR-310

Purchase Agreement Addendum

Form Approved By Greater Minneapolis Area Board of REALTORS® December, 1985

CONTRACT FOR DEED

1 This is an addendum to the Standard Purchase Agreement dated _____(date of Std. P.A.)_____ pertaining to the
2 sale of the real estate at _____.

3 ☐ **CASH TO CONTRACT FOR DEED.**

4 Earnest money herein paid, $_____ and $_____ cash on or before, _____, the
5 date of closing. $_____ with interest thereon at _____% per annum, by a contract for deed (MN
6 Uniform Blank) payable in monthly installments of $_____ commencing on the _____ day of
7 _____, 19_____, and on the _____ day of each and every month thereafter until the full principal balance
8 together with all accrued interest shall have been paid. Interest shall run from and including _____.
9 Payments shall be credited first to interest and remainder to principal. All or any part of the principal balance
10 hereof may be prepaid at any time without penalty.

11 ☐ **CASH TO CONTRACT FOR DEED BALLOON PAYMENT.**

12 Earnest money herein paid, $_____ and $_____ cash on or before, _____, the date of closing.
13 $_____ with interest thereon at _____% per annum, by a contract for deed (MN Uniform Blank) payable in
14 monthly installments of $_____ commencing on the _____ day of _____, 19_____, and on the _____
15 day of each and every month thereafter until _____, 19_____, when the entire unpaid balance of this
16 contract for deed along with all accrued interest shall be due and payable. Interest shall run from and including
17 _____. Payments shall be credited first to interest and remainder to principal. All or any part of the
18 principal balance hereof may be prepaid at any time without penalty.

19 ☐ **STRAIGHT CONTRACT FOR DEED SALE IF THERE IS A MORTGAGE AND/OR CONTRACT FOR DEED**
20 **WHICH THE BUYER DOES NOT ASSUME.**

21 It is understood and agreed by and between the parties there is now a mortgage/contract of record in favor of
22 _____ encumbering the premise with an approximate balance of $_____, which
23 encumbrance Buyer does not assume nor agree to pay, but is to be paid according to its terms and conditions by
24 the Seller.

25 ☐ **RESERVATION BY SELLER TO ENCUMBER.**

26 Seller reserves the right at any time to place a mortgage on said premises in an amount not exceeding the
27 principal balance then due on this contract for deed, bearing a rate of interest no greater than specified in this
28 contract for deed and providing for the payment of monthly installments not exceeding those required to be paid
29 under the terms of this contract for deed. Buyer covenants and agrees that Buyer and all parties claiming any
30 interest in said premises under Buyer, shall join in the execution of all mortgages and other documents necessary
31 or incidental to the placing of such mortgage. All expenses incurred in placing such mortgage, including
32 discount fees, shall be paid by Seller and Seller agrees to pay the mortgage according to its terms and conditions.

33 ☐ **TAXES AND/OR INSURANCE TO BE PAID WITH C/D PAYMENT.**

34 The Buyer agrees there shall be added to each monthly payment required hereunder, an amount estimated by
35 Seller to be reasonably sufficient to enable Seller to pay, at least thirty days before taxes/insurance become due,
36 all premiums for the renewal of insurance policies required hereunder, and all real estate taxes, special
37 assessments, and other similar charges against the above described premises, which the Seller agrees to pay
38 when due. Such additional payments are not considered "trust funds" and may be commingled with the general
39 funds of Seller, and no interest shall be payable in respect thereto. Upon demand by Seller, Buyer shall deliver to
40 Seller such additional monies as are necessary to make up any deficiency in the amount necessary to enable
41 Seller to pay the foregoing items. Upon demand by Buyer, Seller shall deliver to Buyer any excess funds after
42 payment of the foregoing items together with an accounting of receipts and disbursements.

43 ☐ **CREDIT REPORT AUTHORIZATION.**

44 This purchase agreement is subject to Buyer, at own expense, delivering to Seller a credit report satisfactory to
45 Seller within _____ working days of the acceptance of this purchase agreement by Seller. Seller agrees to
46 accept or reject this purchase agreement in writing within _____ days after receipt of the credit report. If such
47 credit report is not satisfactory to Seller, this purchase agreement shall be null and void, and earnest money paid
48 herein shall be returned to Buyer. Agent is not responsible for findings of others in connection with said credit
49 report or with the contents thereof.

50 **NOTE: THE MINNESOTA UNIFORM BLANK CONTRACT FOR DEED DOES CONTAIN ADDITIONAL**
51 **CLAUSES REGARDING INSURANCE AND DEFAULTS.**

52 BUYER _____ SELLER _____
53 BUYER _____ SELLER _____
54 FIRM _____ AGENT _____

MBR-309

QUESTIONS

1. Meryl Kleiman is selling her Minnesota home to her good friend James Adam for $68,000 cash. Since they are such good friends, Adam and Kleiman are not executing a written contract for the sale. Because of this:

   I. the sale is valid between the parties.
   II. the agreement is voidable at the seller's option.

   a. I only
   b. II only
   c. both I and II
   d. neither I nor II

2. George Bronstone is selling his house to Artemus E. Choke with everything from the rugs on the floor to the pictures on the wall. Regarding the items of personal property included in the transaction, Bronstone's broker should:

   I. list these articles in the earnest money contract.
   II. draw up a separate bill of sale for the personal property.

   a. I only
   b. II only
   c. both I and II
   d. neither I nor II

3. By law, Minnesota brokers must give copies of all documents used in a real estate transaction to the:

   I. buyer.
   II. seller.

   a. I only
   b. II only
   c. both I and II
   d. neither I nor II

4. Ronald and Marcia McAllister contracted with Bill and Georgia Beaner to purchase the Beaners' home for $36,000. The Beaners, however, decided not to sell after all and broke the contract with the McAllisters. If the McAllisters decide to sue the Beaners for breaching the contract, how much time do they have to bring legal action against them?

   a. two years from the day the contract was broken
   b. four years from the day the contract was broken
   c. six years from the day the contract was broken
   d. eight years from the day the contract was broken

5. The amount of earnest money customarily deposited with Minnesota brokers in residential real estate transactions is:

   a. 10 percent of the total purchase price of the real estate.
   b. between $500 and $1,000.
   c. at least $1,000.
   d. the amount of commission the broker will receive when the transaction is closed.

6. Broker Phil Franklin has just closed another real estate transaction. He must keep copies of all the documents to the transaction in his records for the next:

    a. one year.
    b. two years.
    c. three years.
    d. four years.

12

Transfer of Title

In Minnesota, title to real property can be transferred through voluntary alienation (by sale, gift, will, marriage, or dedication) and involuntary alienation (through descent, public grant, adverse possession, eminent domain, or accretion), as described in the text.

VOLUNTARY ALIENATION--DEEDS

Deeds generally used in Minnesota include **warranty deeds, quitclaim deeds,** and **special warranty (limited warranty) deeds**, as described in the text. In Minnesota, deeds of conveyance must be signed by the grantor (and his or her spouse, if married, to release homestead rights). Other requirements include: the name and address of the person preparing the deed; for tax statements, the name and address of grantee; and the use of standard forms, which may be changed by the Commissioner of Commerce. In Minnesota, a deed is considered to be valid even if it is not witnessed or acknowledged. Seals, as described in the text, are not required on deeds executed by individuals in Minnesota. (Corporate deeds, however, must bear the corporation's seal, if the corporation has one.)

A deed that uses the words "convey and warrant" includes all covenants of general warranty that the grantor, his or her heirs, and personal representatives are obliged to perform, just as if they were actually written into the deed. The five covenants of general warranty are listed in the text.

A quitclaim deed containing the words "conveys and quitclaims" conveys all existing legal and equitable rights of the grantor, if any, held at the time of delivering such a deed.

A sample warranty deed and a sample quitclaim deed appear at the end of this chapter.

Signature of Grantor

In Minnesota, a married person may not give his or her spouse a power of attorney for the purpose of selling or transferring real estate.

State Deed Tax

To complete a valid transfer of title, the seller must pay the Minnesota State Deed Tax at the closing. He or she must purchase tax stamps from the county treasurer in the county where the real estate is located. The tax stamps are affixed to the deed itself and must be cancelled to prevent their reuse. The seller or closer cancels the stamps by initialing them in ink.

Proceeds from the sale of tax stamps go into the county's general fund. Any unused stamps may be resold or kept for future use at the owner's discretion.

The State Deed Tax is $1.10 per $500 of consideration or fraction thereof, less the value of any assumed liens and encumbrances and the value of any personal property included in the transaction. There is a minimum charge of $2.20 per conveyance. For example, if a seller is conveying a house for $49,000 and the buyer is assuming the seller's mortgage of $25,000, the transfer tax for the transaction would be computed as follows:

Full actual consideration	$49,000
Less amount of assumed mortgage	-25,000
Net taxable consideration	$24,000
Amount of tax to be paid	$24,000 ÷ $500 = 48
	48 x $1.10 = $52.80

In this case, the seller is required to purchase $52.80 worth of state deed tax stamps.

Executory contracts--that is, contracts in which full performance is not yet completed--are exempt from the tax, as are mortgages and their assignments, extensions, partial releases, or satisfactions. In addition, wills, plats, leases, cemetery lot deeds, and deeds conveyed by public officials while performing their official duties are exempt from the tax.

INVOLUNTARY ALIENATION--ADVERSE POSSESSION

Adverse possession for 15 years defeats legal title to Minnesota real estate. Legal title by adverse possession cannot be obtained if the land is public property or is registered under the Torrens system of land registration. Torrens will be discussed in Chapter 13 of this Supplement.

Minnesota requires adverse claimants to pay the property taxes on the property in question for five consecutive years, except in cases of boundary disputes.

TRANSFER OF A DECEASED PERSON'S PROPERTY

Descent and Distribution

The Minnesota laws of descent and distribution can be found in the Probate Code, Minnesota Statutes 1974, Chapter 525. The descent laws provide for the distribution of Minnesota real estate and personal property owned by a person who has died without leaving a valid will (intestate).

Distribution of homestead property. Homestead property owned by a person who dies intestate is distributed as follows:

1. If there is a surviving spouse, but no surviving children or descendants of deceased children, the homestead property descends to the spouse.

2. If there are a surviving spouse and one or more surviving children or descendants of children, the spouse receives a life estate in the homestead property, while the surviving children (or their descendants if they are deceased) divide the remainder by right of representation (that is, equally among themselves).

3. If there is no surviving spouse, the homestead property descends in the same manner as nonhomestead property.

Distribution of nonhomestead property. Nonhomestead property owned by a person who dies intestate is distributed as follows:

1. If the deceased left children or descendants of deceased children, the surviving spouse takes one-third interest in each parcel of real estate. The children or their descendants will share the remaining two-thirds equally. If the deceased left only one child or descendants of same, the surviving spouse and child each take a one-half interest in the real estate. If the deceased left no children or descendants of same, the surviving spouse takes full possession of the real estate. Note that the law provides that descendants of a deceased heir (child, brother, or sister) divide that heir's share equally among themselves. (This is known as the right of representation.)

   When there are two or more heirs to distributed property, such heirs take ownership as tenants in common.

2. If there is no surviving spouse and the deceased left one or more children, the children share the estate equally among themselves.

3. If there is no surviving spouse or child (as in the case of an unmarried person), the estate is divided between parents, brothers, and sisters, first to the parents or surviving parent, then to the brothers and sisters and to the children of deceased brothers and sisters.

4. If there are no such surviving heirs, the estate is divided between other next of kin, beginning with the closest blood relatives.

5. If the deceased left no surviving spouse, kindred, or heirs, the real estate escheats to the state.

Debts, liens, and judgments of the deceased person must be settled before the estate is distributed to the heirs or devisees.

Wills

Minnesota law provides that any person of sound mind and legal age (18) can make a will. A will must be in writing and signed and declared by the maker (testator) to be his or her last will and testament. In addition, the document must be signed by two competent witnesses. Holographic wills (wills that are handwritten, dated, and signed by the testator with no witnesses) are not recognized as legally binding in Minnesota.

Upon the death of the testator, the will must be filed in the probate court located in the county where the deceased person resided. The court appoints a personal representative, and the testator's assets are inventoried. After hearing all claims and renouncements (if any) against the will, the court will order distribution of the estate. As stated earlier, all debts, liens, and judgments of the deceased must be settled before distribution takes place.

The surviving spouse of the deceased may renounce the will in probate court within nine months after the death of the testator, or within six months after the probate of the will, and claim one of the following interests:

1. If the deceased left no surviving child or descendants of children, the spouse may claim one-half of the estate.

2. If the deceased left descendants, the spouse may claim one-third of the estate, or one-half if only one child or the descendants of one child survive.

12/Transfer of Title 61

Form No. 1-M—WARRANTY DEED   Minnesota Uniform Conveyancing Blanks (1978)   Miller-Davis Co., Minneapolis
Individual(s) to Individual(s)

No delinquent taxes and transfer entered; Certificate of Real Estate Value ( ) filed ( ) not required
Certificate of Real Estate Value No. _____
_____, 19 ____

_____
County Auditor

by _____
Deputy

(reserved for recording data)

STATE DEED TAX DUE HEREON: $ _____

Date: _____, 19 ____

FOR VALUABLE CONSIDERATION, _____
_____, Grantor(s),
(marital status)

hereby convey(s) and warrant(s) to _____
_____, Grantee(s),

real property in _____ County, Minnesota, described as follows:

(if more space is needed, continue on back)
together with all hereditaments and appurtenances belonging thereto, subject to the following exceptions:

Affix Deed Tax Stamp Here

STATE OF MINNESOTA }
                    } ss.
COUNTY OF _____ }

The foregoing instrument was acknowledged before me this _____ day of _____, 19____,
by _____, Grantor(s).

NOTARIAL STAMP OR SEAL (OR OTHER TITLE OR RANK)

SIGNATURE OF PERSON TAKING ACKNOWLEDGMENT

Tax Statements for the real property described in this instrument should be sent to (Include name and address of Grantee):

THIS INSTRUMENT WAS DRAFTED BY (NAME AND ADDRESS)

Form No. 27-M — QUIT CLAIM DEED Minnesota Uniform Conveyancing Blanks (1978) Miller-Davis Co., Minneapolis
Individual(s) to Individual(s)

No delinquent taxes and transfer entered; Certificate of Real Estate Value ( ) filed ( ) not required Certificate of Real Estate Value No._____
_____, 19_____

_____
                                County Auditor

by _____
                                        Deputy

STATE DEED TAX DUE HEREON: $ _____

Date: _____, 19 ____

(reserved for recording data)

FOR VALUABLE CONSIDERATION, _____
_____, Grantor(s),
                                        (marital status)
hereby convey(s) and quitclaim(s) to _____
_____, Grantee(s),
real property in _____ County, Minnesota, described as follows:

(if more space is needed, continue on back)
together with all hereditaments and appurtenances belonging thereto.

Affix Deed Tax Stamp Here

STATE OF MINNESOTA
                    } ss.
COUNTY OF _____

The foregoing instrument was acknowledged before me this _____ day of _____, 19____,
by _____, Grantor(s).

NOTARIAL STAMP OR SEAL (OR OTHER TITLE OR RANK)

_____
SIGNATURE OF PERSON TAKING ACKNOWLEDGMENT

Tax Statements for the real property described in this instrument should be sent to (Include name and address of Grantee):

THIS INSTRUMENT WAS DRAFTED BY (NAME AND ADDRESS):

QUESTIONS

1. Rick H. Felski, a wealthy Minneapolis entrepreneur who died unexpectedly, left his entire estate of nonhomestead property to his wife and three children. However, it was later learned that his will was invalid. In this situation, the Minnesota laws of descent and distribution dictate that:

   I. Felski's wife will receive a one-fourth share of his estate.
   II. Felski's children will share the estate with his wife equally.

   a. I only
   b. II only
   c. both I and II
   d. neither I nor II

2. Which of the following are exempt from the Minnesota state deed tax?

   I. leases
   II. quitclaim deeds

   a. I only
   b. II only
   c. both I and II
   d. neither I nor II

3. Ruth Jackson was left out of her husband Jack's will. Since they had no children, Jack left all his money and property to charity. By renouncing the will in probate court, Ruth Jackson will be entitled to:

   a. all of her husband's estate.
   b. two-thirds of her husband's estate.
   c. one-half of her husband's estate.
   d. one-third of her husband's estate.

4. In order to be valid in Minnesota, a will must be in writing, signed by the testator, and:

   a. written in English.
   b. notarized.
   c. witnessed by two competent persons.
   d. filed with the county registrar.

5. Legal title to real property can be acquired through adverse possession which is open, notorious, and hostile after:

   a. 5 years of continuous use.
   b. 10 years of continuous use.
   c. 15 years of continuous use.
   d. 20 years of continuous use.

6. Barry and Sylvia Brewster are selling their home to Brian and Georgia McInerney for $33,500. The McInerneys are assuming the Brewsters' existing mortgage of $12,350. How much state deed tax will the Brewsters be required to pay?

    a. $84.60
    b. $47.30
    c. $42.30
    d. $40.00

13

Title Records

RECORDING DOCUMENTS

Any instrument that affects title to or possession of real estate may be docketed (recorded) or registered in the county where the land is located. In Minnesota, the abstract method of recordation and the Torrens system of land registration--both described in the text--are used. To be recorded or registered, an instrument must be acknowledged (signed before a notary public) and notarized. Also, the document must include the name and address of the person or corporation responsible for drafting it.

Any deed or contract for deed presented for recording or registration must be accompanied by a certificate of real estate value executed by the buyer and seller or their agents. Contracts for deed executed after January 1, 1984, must be recorded within six months. If they are not recorded within this time, a penalty of $.15 per $100 is assessed.

Local real estate records are held by the county recorder. The registrar of titles works in the county recorder's office with the county property registered under the Torrens system.

In Minnesota, unrecorded documents, including deeds, are valid between the parties to the transaction; however, they will not protect such persons against claims by subsequent purchasers or lenders who do not have actual notice and cannot learn of such claims by inspecting the public records or the premises. Actual, visible possession of real property constitutes legal notice to everyone of an interest in the property.

Recording Fees

Fees for recordation in Minnesota are $1 per page, with a $5 minimum charge per document.

Foreign Language Documents

Minnesota law makes no special provision for documents written in a foreign language. The registrar will accept any document for recording if it is properly acknowledged and accompanied by the appropriate fees.

TITLE EVIDENCE

In most real estate transactions that take place in Minnesota, the seller is required to furnish evidence of his or her good title to the property being sold. In Minnesota, the abstract of title, or registered property abstract, and attorney's opinion, as described in the text, are usually acceptable evidence of the title. The "chain of title" in Minnesota can be traced to the original land grants by the U.S. government. The purchaser's attorney prepares an opinion of the title or ownership rights based upon this history of recorded documents affecting the title.

Title Insurance

In some cases, title insurance is used in Minnesota because of the greater protection it offers potential real estate buyers. The text discusses title insurance policies in detail.

Torrens System

The Torrens system of land registration, which is generally described in the text, was adopted for use in Minnesota in 1905. The terms Torrens property and registered property are used interchangeably, although the original statute uses the term registered land. Registration of land (which should not be confused with recording a deed or other document) creates an absolute (judicial) determination of the status of the title as to the time of the registration.

Registration. Any real estate owner can register his or her property under the Torrens system by filing an application with the district court in the county in which the property is located. The court will refer the application to an examiner of titles, who searches the chain of title and all factors that could affect its validity. The examiner then files a report with the court, recommending the persons who should be given notice of the proceedings.

The court issues a summons directing all persons who have or claim to have an interest in or against the real estate to appear at a special hearing. At the hearing, if the court finds that the applicant has a title proper for registration, the court will issue a decree confirming the applicant's title and ordering its registration. The decree is then registered with the county recorder (register of titles), who will retain the original and all subsequent certificates of title.

An owner of registered property receives an owner's duplicate certificate of title. This duplicate certificate must be presented to a buyer as title evidence upon sale of property. A purchaser of such property must register both his or her deed and the duplicate certificate with the registrar. The registrar will cancel the old certificate and issue a new certificate in the new owner's name.

Registered title protection. According to Minnesota law, title to registered property can never be acquired by prescription or through adverse possession. Also, any court judgment against an owner of registered property is not a lien against that property unless a certified copy of the judgment is registered on the certificate of title. This gives an owner of registered land added protection against third-party claims.

Torrens assurance fund. A registered owner who sustains damage or loss because of any error, omission, or misdescription in the registration of his or her title may file a claim against the registrar in the district court of the county in which the land is located. An assurance fund is maintained through registration fees to cover any such claims.

UNIFORM COMMERCIAL CODE

Minnesota has adopted the Uniform Commercial Code, which is described in the text.

QUESTIONS

1. For the last 16 years, Joe Don Kurek has been living in a hand-made shack located on registered land owned by Jim Schmanski. Schmanski has known of Kurek's occupancy ever since it began, and has ignored the entire situation. According to Minnesota law:

    I. Kurek can now obtain title to the land through his adverse possession of it.
    II. Kurek must go to court to obtain title to the land.

        a. I only
        b. II only
        c. both I and II
        d. neither I nor II

2. Ronald Berringer is selling a parcel of real estate to Morris Philips. The abstract of title that Berringer will give Philips as title evidence should be previously examined and evaluated by:

        a. the purchaser's attorney.
        b. the broker who has negotiated the transaction.
        c. the County Recorder.
        d. the County Registrar of Titles.

3. To be eligible for recording in Minnesota, a document must be:

        a. written in English.
        b. registered under the Torrens system.
        c. valid against third-party claims.
        d. none of the above

4. Jerry Powers wants to register the title to his home. He must complete a Torrens application and file it with:

        a. the district court of the county in which he resides.
        b. the register of deeds of the county in which he resides.
        c. the register of titles of the county in which he resides.
        d. the examiner of titles of the county in which he resides.

14

Real Estate License Law

The Minnesota Real Estate License Law can be found in Minnesota Statutes, Chapter 82. The law was enacted in 1955 and rewritten in 1973 and is administered by the Department of Commerce, Securities Division.

The license law regulates those who act as agents for others in real estate and business opportunity transactions. The system of regulation consists of the law and rules adopted by the Commissioner of Commerce. The rules elaborate on the basic law and provide additional standards for Minnesota real estate licensees. The summaries of the Minnesota Real Estate License Law and the rules presented in this chapter are intended to acquaint you with their general provisions.

Every real estate office is required to have a copy of the Real Estate Laws, Minnesota Statutes, Chapters 82 and 83 and the Commerce Department Real Estate Broker and Licensing Rules. Copies of both publications may be obtained from the State Register and Public Documents Division, Department of Administration, 117 University Avenue, Saint Paul, MN 55155. A verbatim copy of the license law and the rules appears at the back of this supplement.

WHO MUST BE LICENSED

Under Section 82.19, it is illegal for any person to act, advertise, or represent him- or herself as a real estate broker or salesperson unless licensed. Any person violating the provisions of the license law is guilty of a gross misdemeanor (Section 82.32).

In addition, no person engaged in the real estate business can file a court suit for collection of payment for the performance of professional services unless that person can prove he or she was licensed at the time the services were performed (Section 82.33).

Definitions

Real estate broker (Section 82.17, Subd. 4). A real estate broker is defined as any person who, for another and for compensation or the promise of compensation, directly or indirectly performs any of the following activities with regard to real estate, business opportunities, or an interest in either:

1. lists;
2. sells;
3. exchanges;
4. buys;
5. rents;
6. manages;
7. offers or attempts to negotiate a sale, option, exchange, purchase, or rental;
8. advertises or holds him- or herself to be engaged in any of these activities;
9. negotiates or offers or attempts to negotiate a loan secured by a mortgage or other encumbrance on real estate;
10. offers, sells, or attempts to negotiate the sale of property subject to the Minnesota Subdivision Law, Minnesota Statutes, Chapter 83;
11. charges in advance fee or contracts to promote the sale of real estate by listing it in a publication designed for such purpose;
12. establishes a pattern of real estate sales (being engaged as principal in five transactions during any 12-month period, whether or not as the owner of the property);
13. sells or rents a business opportunity or its good will, inventory, etc.

Real estate salesperson (Section 82.17, Subd. 5). A real estate salesperson is defined as any person who acts on behalf of a real estate broker in the performance of any of the activities just listed.

The word person, as used throughout the license law, refers to an individual, firm, partnership, corporation, or association. In addition, the definition of real estate, as used throughout the law, includes manufactured (mobile) homes that are affixed to land.

Manufactured home (Section 82.17, Subd. 8). Also known as a mobile home, a manufactured home is a factory-built structure equipped with the necessary service connection that allows it to be used as a dwelling unit though it is also readily movable. The license law qualifies a manufactured home as real estate when it is affixed to the land. A manufactured home may be considered affixed to the land when it is set upon a special pad or other supportive device connected to local electric, water, and sewer systems. When the unit is sold under circumstances suggesting that the next occupant will reside in the mobile home on its present location, it is considered affixed to the land. When it appears that a mobile home sold from a lot will be used in the future in another location, it is, in all probability, not affixed to the land.

A real estate agent must follow the Minnesota statutes for mobile home sales. These statutes generally require that a dealer in manufactured homes have a license from the Commissioner of Administration. However, licensed real estate brokers and salespersons who broker the sales of used manufactured homes are exempt from this requirement. Any real estate broker or salesperson who violates a provision of the statutes for mobile home sales is considered to have violated a provision of the real estate license law.

Exceptions (Section 82.18)

The Minnesota Real Estate License Law does not apply to:

1. licensed attorneys acting solely as an incident to their practice;

2. receivers, trustees, administrators, guardians, executors, or other persons appointed by or acting under the judgment or order of any court;

3. persons owning and operating a cemetery and selling lots solely for use as burial plots;

4. persons employed by the owner or manager of a residential building (such as custodians or janitors) who lease residential units in the building; managers of industrial and commercial property are not exempt from the license law;

5. any bank, trust company, savings and loan association, public utility, land mortgage association, or farm loan association, when acting under the scope of its corporate powers;

6. public officers or their employees while performing their official duties;

7. bonded auctioneers while engaged in the performance of their professional duties;

8. any person who acquires real estate in connection with the business of constructing residential, commercial, or industrial buildings for the purpose of resale (for up to 25 transactions per 12-month period) when such person complies with all trust account requirements of the license law;

9. any person who offers to sell or sells an interest or estate in real estate that is a security registered under the Minnesota Securities Law;

10. any person who sells or offers to sell a business opportunity that is a registered franchise under the Minnesota Franchise Act (limited to the sale of the franchise only; if the transaction involves the sale or lease of an interest in real estate, such person must be licensed);

11. any person who contracts with or solicits on behalf of a providor or contracts with a resident or prospective resident to provide continuing care in a registered continuing care facility.

COMMISSIONER OF COMMERCE (Sections 82.28-29)

The Commissioner of Commerce of the Department of Commerce administers the Minnesota Real Estate License Law. The commissioner has the authority to promulgate rules and regulations necessary to enforce the provisions and purpose of the license law. In addition, the commissioner may publish information to educate and protect the public from fraudulent, deceptive, or dishonest practices in the real estate industry.

Licensees must notify the commissioner within ten days of a change in the information contained in the license application, of an adverse court ruling in a case in which the licensee was a defendant, of the suspension or revocation of the licensee's real estate or other occupational license, and of any charge of a felony or of a gross misdemeanor alleging fraud, misrepresentation, conversion of funds, or similar violation of any real estate licensing law.

LICENSING PROCEDURE

Applications and Requirements (Section 82.20)

An application for a Minnesota real estate license must be made in writing, on forms prepared and furnished by the commissioner. Each application must be signed and sworn by the applicant and must be accompanied by the appropriate fees. An applicant must be at least 18 years of age and must not have had a real estate license revoked in any state within two years of the date of application.

In addition, an applicant for a real estate broker's license must have worked as a licensed real estate salesperson for two years within the previous five years prior to application. The commissioner may, however, reduce or eliminate this requirement, based on the applicant's educational background or practical experience.

Specifically, an applicant may obtain a waiver of the salesperson licensing requirement if able to provide evidence of the following: (1) successful completion of 90 quarter credits or 270 classroom hours of real estate-related studies; (2) a minimum of five consecutive years of real estate-related practical experience; or (3) successful completion of 30 credits or 90 classroom hours and three years' practical experience in real estate-related areas. If the applicant receives a waiver for the two years' experience as a real estate salesperson, he or she must successfully complete the real estate broker's examination within one year.

In practice, a candidate for licensing makes two applications. The first is an application to take the examination; the second is an application for a license, which is made after passing the exam.

Licensing requirement (Section 82.22, Subd. 6). As of 1984, applicants for a salesperson's license must successfully complete 30 hours of instruction in the real estate field before they may take the examination, plus 30 more hours of instruction before they can become licensed. The course of study approved by the commissioner includes Courses I, II, and III. Applicants must pass the licensing examination within one year after completing Course I. Anyone who fails to do so must retake Course I. Applicants must take Course II after passing the exam and before being licensed. Within one year of being licensed, each salesperson must successfully complete an additional 30 hours of approved instruction in real estate (Course III).

Examinations (Section 82.22). Each license applicant must also successfully pass a written examination conducted under the auspices of the commissioner. Exams are given every 45 days at various locations throughout Minnesota; consult the bulletin of information given to license applicants for these locations. Both the salesperson and broker licensing exams consist of two sections--a uniform and a state exam. The uniform exam consists of 80 questions, while the state section consists of 40 questions; applicants will be given four and one-half hours to complete both sections. A score of 75 percent or better on both individual sections of the test is necessary to pass the exam. (Cheating on an examination is grounds for denial of a license application.)

Application for licenses (Section 82.22, Subd. 3). Upon receiving a passing grade, an applicant has one year from the date of passing the exam to apply for the appropriate license. Any applicant who fails to apply (or to remain active as a licensed salesperson in the case of a broker applicant) within this time must pass another examination before a license will be issued.

Issuance of Salesperson's License (Section 82.20, Subd. 6)

The salesperson's license is mailed directly to the licensed broker with whom he or she will be associated. The broker holds the salesperson's license until the salesperson terminates his or her association with the broker. A salesperson is licensed under a specific broker and may not represent any other broker at the same time.

Limited Broker's License (Section 82.20, Subd. 13)

The commissioner has the authority to issue a limited broker's license, whereby an individual is authorized to act in transactions as principal only. This license is a means of regulating the activities of individuals who are not professionally engaged in the real estate brokerage business and requires no examination. The holder of a limited license may not employ salespeople on his or her behalf. An officer of a corporation or a partner of a partnership licensed as a limited broker may act on behalf of the firm without having to obtain an individual license.

Licensure of Corporations and Partnerships (Section 82.20, Subd. 4)

A corporation or partnership may obtain a broker's license if an officer of the firm is properly licensed to act as broker for the firm. In this instance, the firm itself is authorized to act as broker; however, each officer or partner who intends to engage in real estate activities for the firm must obtain an individual broker's license. When a corporation or partnership is licensed as a limited broker, no partner or officer of that firm may apply for a real estate salesperson's license.

The commissioner must be notified in writing whenever a partner or officer ceases or intends to cease acting as his or her firm's licensed broker.

Fees (Section 82.21)

Each license applicant must pay a license fee as set by law when filing an application with the commissioner. Licenses expire annually on June 30 and must be renewed by July 1. If the renewal application is filed by June 15, in acceptable form and accompanied by the appropriate fee, and no notice of denial has been received, the license will be deemed renewed.

The following is a schedule of Minnesota real estate license fees:

	Initial License	Renewal
Broker	$90	$30
Salesperson	$65	$15
Corporation/Partnership	$90	$30
Limited Broker	$90	$30

There is a $10 fee for license transfers. Upon submission of an application for examination, candidates must pay a $17.50 fee to Educational Testing Service of Princeton, New Jersey.

In addition, each licensee must pay an initial fee of $40, and a renewal fee of $5, toward the Real Estate Education, Research, and Recovery Fund, which will be discussed later in this chapter. Fees received by the state licensing department are deposited in the state treasury (Section 82.21, Subd. 3) and are accounted for in the commissioner's annual report (Section 82.34, Subd. 15 and 19).

Nonresidents--Reciprocity (Section 82.22, Subd. 12)

Residents of North Dakota, South Dakota, and Iowa may obtain Minnesota real estate brokers' and salespersons' licenses upon compliance with all the provisions of the law. These are the only states with which Minnesota has license reciprocity. Where a reciprocal agreement is in effect, the commissioner may waive the examination requirements for nonresidents under the following conditions:

1. The applicant is licensed in his or her state.
2. The state's licensing requirements are "substantially similar" to Minnesota's.

Reciprocity does not mean that licensing is automatic. A nonresident who wishes to act as a broker or salesperson must apply for a Minnesota license.

Nonresident applicants must appoint the commissioner as their agent for service of process, against whom all Minnesota legal actions or proceedings may be served. Such an appointment becomes effective when the nonresident's license is issued and is considered irrevocable.

REAL ESTATE EDUCATION, RESEARCH, AND RECOVERY FUND

Minnesota's Real Estate Education, Research, and Recovery Fund was created to protect the public against losses sustained through fraudulent, deceptive, or dishonest acts or the conversion of trust funds by a licensee in connection with a real estate transaction. Every licensee must pay a $40 fee into the fund at the time of the initial licensing. Thereafter, at the time of renewal, the licensee will pay an additional $5 to the fund. This annual charge is in addition to other fees paid for the renewal of the license.

If the portion of the fund designated for recovery purposes falls below $400,000, each licensee may be required to pay an amount not to exceed $35 at the time of license renewal. The commissioner is authorized to make an assessment to replenish the fund in the event it is depleted through the payment of claims.

Sums in excess of $400,000 are available to the commissioner for educational and research purposes.

Recovery Procedure

After a judgment is obtained against a licensee, a court (upon receipt of a verified application) may direct recovery of the amount of actual and out-of-pocket loss that remains unpaid upon the judgment, up to the sum of $20,000. The law specifies that the fund shall not be liable for more than $20,000 per transaction. The maximum amount of liability to all persons for all losses is $25,000 for any one licensee.

To collect from the fund, an aggrieved person must first obtain a final judgment against the defendant licensee in any court of competent jurisdiction. After all appeals, the aggrieved person may file a verified (under oath) application with the court, asking the court to direct payment of the judgment from the fund. Copies of this application are then served upon the commissioner and the defendant licensee.

The court must hold a hearing and act on the application within 30 days. At the hearing, the aggrieved party must show that he or she has obtained a proper judgment and complied with all requirements concerning the fund. Such person must also show that all possible legal steps have been taken to collect the judgment from the licensee and that he or she does not have sufficient funds to satisfy it. In addition, the aggrieved party must prove that he or she is not the licensee's spouse or personal representative.

The commissioner may intervene at any time and defend the fund through presentation of evidence, cross-examination of witnesses, and so on.

If the court determines that the person seeking recovery has a "valid cause of action" and has complied with the provisions of the act, it will order payment of the judgment out of the fund.

Automatic Suspension

When recovery is granted from the fund as a result of a licensee's actions, his or her license is automatically suspended. The license will not be reinstated until the licensee repays twice the amount recovered from the fund plus 12 percent inerest and obtains a surety bond in the amount of $40,000. A licensee cannot avoid suspension of his or her license by filing for bankruptcy.

GENERAL OPERATION OF A REAL ESTATE BUSINESS

Broker's Responsibilities

Every real estate brokerage in Minnesota must be operated by and in the name of a licensed real estate broker. If an individual broker maintains more than one place of business, each place of business must be under the broker's direction and supervision. If a partnership or corporate broker maintains more than one place of business, each must be under the direction and supervision of an individual broker licensed to act on behalf of the partnership or corporation.

Records (Section 82.23). Licensed real estate brokers must retain copies of all listings, deposit receipts, purchase-money contracts, cancelled checks, trust account records, and other records related to a real estate transaction for three years from the date of closing (or the date of listing, should a transaction not be consummated). The commissioner may inspect a broker's records at any time necessary to enforce the provisions of the license law.

Brokers are responsible for the preparation, accuracy, and safekeeping of all real estate contracts and documents, although the broker may assign such duties to another person.

Complaints. Brokers must investigate and attempt to resolve complaints made with regard to any individual licensed to them. The broker must maintain for each such individual a complaint file containing all material relating to written complaints for a three-year period.

Disclosure of information. Brokers may not allow any unlicensed person to disclose information regarding a listed property, except its address and whether it is available for sale or lease.

Broker-salesperson relationship (Sections 82.20, Subd. 5 and 82.19, Subd. 4). Each broker is responsible for the actions of all licensees acting on his or her behalf. Likewise, each officer or partner of a firm licensed as a real estate broker has the same responsibility regarding the firm's salespeople. In all transactions, a salesperson must disclose the name of the broker to whom he or she is responsible. No real estate licensee should engage or authorize any person to act as a broker or salesperson unless such person is licensed in accordance with the license law.

Renewal (Section 82.20, Subd. 3, 8, and 10). As discussed earlier, licenses are renewed each July 1. A licensee who fails to make a timely application (before June 15) and does not receive his or her new license by July 1 is considered unlicensed until the new license arrives. No examination is required for the renewal of a real estate license; however, a re-examination is required if the licensee was suspended or the license has lapsed for one year or more. No examination is required for failure to renew while the licensee is on active duty with the armed forces.

Salesperson continuing education (Section 82.22, Subd. 6 and 13). All real estate salespersons are required to successfully complete 45 hours of real estate education, either as students or as lecturers, in courses of study approved by the commissioner. This educational requirement must be completed within three years after the licensee's annual renewal date. A Course III may be applied to this requirement if the licensee has not previously taken a course on that subject.

Termination and transfers (Section 82.20, Subd. 9 and 10). When a salesperson terminates activities on behalf of a broker, his or her license immediately becomes ineffective. The broker must notify the commissioner in writing and return the salesperson's license to the commissioner within ten days of the termination. The salesperson may apply for transfer of his or her license to another broker at any time within the remainder of the current license year. Upon receiving a transfer application and payment of the transfer fee, the commissioner may, at his or her discretion, issue a 45-day temporary license. However, an application for a new license must be filed if the transfer is not made within the current license period (that is, after July 1).

A salesperson who terminates his or her activity on behalf of one broker in order to begin association with another broker within five days may have his or her license transferred automatically. The transfer becomes effective either upon mailing a $10 fee and the executed documents by certified mail or upon personal delivery of the fee and documents to the commissioner's office. If the licensee holds a subdivided land license, it must be transferred at the same time, and there is an additional $10 fee.

When a broker's license is suspended or revoked, the licenses of all salespeople working on the broker's behalf automatically become ineffective. The salespersons may, however, apply for a transfer to another licensed broker.

Real Estate Contracts and Documents

The Minnesota Real Estate License Law includes specific provisions regarding the documents involved in real estate transactions.

Documents furnished to parties. Real estate licensees must furnish true and accurate copies of the following documents to all involved parties the time the documents are signed or agreements entered into:

- listing forms or agreements;
- earnest money receipts;
- purchase agreements;
- contracts for deed;
- option agreements;
- closing statements;
- truth-in-housing reports;
- all other records, instruments, or documents material to the transaction
- which are in the licensee's possession.

Listing agreements. All listing agreements must provide for specific expiration dates and other information and must not contain holdover clauses, automatic extensions, or similar provisions. Listing agreements must not contain override clauses or similar provisions that extend beyond six months of the expiration date.

In addition, when an override clause is used in a listing agreement, the seller must be furnished with a protective list of the names and addresses of prospective purchasers to whom the broker exhibited the property. The seller must receive this list within 72 hours of the expiration of the listing agreement.

Requirements for listing agreements are covered more fully in Chapter 6.

Closing statements. At the time of closing a transaction, the listing broker must deliver to the seller a complete and detailed closing statement. The broker must also deliver a statement to the buyer. Closing statements are discussed in Chapter 23.

Care and Handling of Funds

Trust funds (Section 82.24). A broker must immediately deposit all funds entrusted to him or her in a special trust account (unless the parties to the transaction sign an express written agreement for the broker to do otherwise). This account must be a demand deposit or checking account in any Minnesota bank or trust company or any out-of-state bank that authorizes scrutiny of such accounts by the commissioner. The account provides security for all parties to a transaction.

At the time of application for a license, a broker must notify the commissioner of the names of the banks and the numbers of the trust accounts that he or she will be using. A broker must immediately report any change in trust account status to the commissioner. Furthermore, a broker may not close an existing trust account without giving the commissioner ten days' written notice.

Upon a buyer's written request, a broker may hold a check without depositing it in a trust account, pending acceptance or rejection of an offer. Upon acceptance, the check must be deposited in the broker's trust account (or any other neutral escrow depository) on the next business day following acceptance of the offer, unless the parties to the transaction sign a written agreement to let the broker continue to hold the check. If the offer is rejected, the broker must return the check to the buyer on the next business day after rejection. The broker may also hold the check provided that it is not negotiable by him or her, that is, if it is not made out to the broker. Unless otherwise agreed upon, the listing broker is entrusted with all funds to be deposited.

Commingling funds (Section 82.24, Subd. 4). A licensee must not commingle trust funds received in connection with a real estate transaction with his or her own personal funds in a trust account. However, a maximum of $100 in personal funds may be deposited in a trust account to cover service charges. Such deposits must be specifically indentified in all records as being used for these purposes.

Nondepositable items (Section 82.24). Anything of value received by a licensee in lieu of cash as earnest money or down payment in a real estate transaction must be deposited with an authorized escrow agent. The buyer must obtain a receipt for the value of the deposit. In the event that the broker acts as the escrow agent, he or she must obtain written authority from both the buyer and seller to hold such deposits. In addition, all involved parties must be notified of the details relevant to the deposit, and the broker must record such deposits in his or her trust account records.

Licensee acting as principal (Section 82.24, Subd. 2). When a licensee acts as principal in the sale of real estate, he or she must place in his or her trust account all payments, received on contracts, that are necessary to meet amounts due on mortgages, contracts for deed, or other conveying instruments. Reserve for taxes, insurance payments, or other encumbrances must also be deposited in the account. The licensee must maintain all deposits until the proper disbursements are made and give proper accounting to all entitled parties.

Trust account records. Every licensed broker must keep records of all trust funds received. All records are subject to inspection at any time by the commissioner or his or her agent. Such records must state the following:

- the date the funds were received;
- from whom they were received;
- the amount received;
- the date of deposit in a trust account;
- the check number or date of any disbursed funds;
- a monthly balance of the trust account.

Each broker must also maintain a formal trust-receipts journal and a formal disbursements journal in accordance with generally accepted accounting principles. In addition, brokers must keep, for each transaction, separate records accounting for all funds deposited in the trust account. These records must sufficiently identify the transaction and the parties involved. They must also set forth the date and amount of each deposit, as well as the date, check number, amount, and description of each disbursement.

Disclosure

Advertising. Licensees must identify themselves as either a broker or an agent in any advertising for the purchase, sale, lease, or other disposition of real property.

Financial interests of licensee. Prior to the negotiation or consummation of any transaction, the licensee must disclose to the owner of real property that he or she is a real estate broker or agent, and in what capacity he or she is acting, if the licensee directly or through a third party purchases or intends to acquire an interest in or option to purchase the owner's property him- or herself.

Material facts. A licensee must disclose to any prospective purchaser all material facts pertaining to the property, of which the licensee is aware, that could adversely and significantly affect use of the property.

Nonperformance of any party. If a licensee is made aware that any party to a real estate transaction will not perform in accordance with the terms of a purchase agreement, the licensee must immediately disclose that fact to the other party or parties to the transaction. The licensee should notify the nonperforming party of his or her intent to give such notice.

Guaranteed sales programs. A broker who advertises a guaranteed sales program, in which the broker will purchase real property if unable to sell it within a specified period of time, must provide to the seller a written disclosure clearly setting forth the terms under which the broker agrees to purchase the property and what will happen to the profit from the sale. The broker must make this disclosure prior to the execution of a listing agreement.

Other Provisions and Ethical Considerations

A real estate licensee must always obtain the consent of the owner or his or her duly authorized agent before offering real property for sale or lease. A licensee must not attempt to represent a property owner in any real estate transaction if he or she knows that the owner has with another broker a valid, written exclusive-agency agreement for the property in question. The licensee must ask whether such an agreement exists. A licensee may not induce any party to a contract of sale or lease to break it in favor of substituting a new contract with another principal, nor may the licensee discourage prospective parties to a transaction from seeking the services of an attorney.

All written offers to purchase or lease must be promptly submitted in writing to the seller or lessor. A licensee may not disclose the terms of an offer to another prospective buyer before presenting the offer to the seller. Finally, licensees may not promise or guarantee buyers future profits from resale of real property unless promises or guarantees are fully disclosed in the contract, purchase agreement, or similar document.

Commissions (Sections 82.19 and 82.33, Subd. 2)

As discussed earlier in this chapter, a person must be licensed as a real estate broker before he or she is entitled to collect a commission for engaging in real estate activities. A licensee may therefore receive a commission only from his or her broker. Section 82.19, Subd. 3 makes it illegal for a licensee to offer, pay, or give anything of value to an unlicensed person in connection with a real estate transaction. Also, the law provides that a licensee cannot bring any case before the courts regarding collection of a commission unless able to prove that he or she has a written listing agreement for the property. A licensee may not receive any undisclosed commission.

If, through no fault of the buyer, the seller fails to consummate a real estate transaction, the listing broker may not claim any part of the trust funds, unless such an agreement was made with the buyer.

ADVERTISING

In all advertising, the licensee must clearly state that he or she is in the real estate business and must not use any trade name or insignia of membership of any organization unless he or she is actually a member. In addition, a licensee must obtain the consent of the owner or the owner's agent before listing or placing a sign on any property for sale or rent.

The following are examples of the most common violations of the Minnesota Real Estate License Law regulations regarding real estate advertising:

1. Failure by a real estate broker or salesperson to disclose in all advertising that he or she is acting in a principal capacity in the offer for sale of real property. All advertising by a real estate licensee who is also acting as principal must contain the words, "owner-agent" or similar language.

2. Failure by a real estate salesperson to disclose in all advertising the name of the broker to whom the salesperson is licensed. Brokers also fail to use the correct name in which their licenses are issued. An individual broker (sole proprietor) may use a trade name if the trade name is properly registered and appears on the license issued to the broker. An officer/partner broker is additionally required to disclose in all advertising the name of the corporation or partnership in which a broker's license is issued.

Failure to comply with these standards constitutes grounds for suspension or revocation of a real estate license or for censure of a licensee.

DENIAL, SUSPENSION, AND REVOCATION OF LICENSES (Sections 82.25 and 82.27)

The Minnesota Commissioner of Commerce may investigate the actions of a licensee at any time that reasonable evidence indicates that any provision of the license law has been or is about to be violated. To aid in the enforcement of the law, the commissioner may undertake public or private investigations within or outside of the state.

The commissioner must make two findings before taking disciplinary action against a licensee. First, he or she must determine that such disciplinary action would be in the public interest. Second, he or she must find that an applicant for a new license or a present license directly or indirectly engaged in one or more of the following activities:

1. filed an incomplete license application or one containing false or misleading statements;

2. has been permanently or temporarily enjoined by any court from conducting real estate business;

3. did not reasonably supervise his or her brokers or salespeople and thus caused harm or injury to the public;

4. violated or failed to comply with any provision of the license law;

5. engaged in a fraudulent, deceptive, or dishonest practice.

Minnesota regulations further define fraudulent, deceptive, or dishonest practices as the following:

1. acting on behalf of more than one party to a transaction without the knowledge and consent of all parties;

2. acting in the dual capacity of licensee and undisclosed principal in any transaction;

3. receiving funds, while acting as principal, that would constitute trust funds if received by a licensee acting as an agent, unless the funds are placed in a trust account or all parties to the transaction specify a different disposition of the funds;

4. violating any state or federal law concerning discrimination;

5. making a material misstatement in a license application or in any information furnished to the commissioner;

6. procuring or attempting to procure a real estate license by fraud, misrepresentation, or deceit;

7. representing membership in any real estate-related organization in which the licensee is not a member;

8. advertising properties, terms, values, policies, or services in a misleading or inaccurate manner;

9. making any material misrepresentation or permitting another to do so;

10. making or permitting another to make false or misleading statements likely to influence or induce consummation of a real estate transaction;

11. failing within a reasonable time to account for or remit any money that belongs to another;

12. commingling trust funds with the licensee's own money or property;

13. demanding from a seller a commission the licensee knows he or she is not entitled to;

14. paying an unlicensed person for any assistance or information relating to procuring a listing or a prospective buyer;

15. failing to maintain a trust account;

16. engaging in an anticompetitive activity with respect to the offer, sale, or rental of real estate.

Legal Actions--Injunctions (Section 82.26)

When it appears to the commissioner that any licensee has engaged or is about to engage in any violation of the law, the commissioner may bring action in district court in the state's name in order to stop the licensee from performing any acts or practices that are in violation of the license law and to force compliance with the law. Upon proper showing, the court may grant a permanent or temporary injunction, restraining order, or other appropriate relief. The matter may also be turned over to the state attorney general.

QUESTIONS

1. When an applicant passes the salesperson licensing examination:

    I. he or she will be issued a license.
    II. the applicant's license will be mailed to his or her supervising broker.

    a. I only
    b. II only
    c. both I and II
    d. neither I nor II

2. All involved parties to a real estate transaction agree to let Jerry Chase hold a stock portfolio as a down payment instead of the unusual earnest money deposit. To legally do this for buyer and seller, Chase must be:

    I. a licensed real estate broker.
    II. an authorized escrow agent.

    a. I only
    b. II only
    c. either I or II
    d. neither I nor II

3. Businessman Charles Rudolph Hertz wants to sell 17 of his Minnesota real estate holdings. He is not in the regular business of selling real estate, yet if he personally sells all 17 parcels of land this year:

    I. he must obtain a real estate broker's license.
    II. he must place the title to the land in escrow until sold.

    a. I only
    b. II only
    c. both I and II
    d. neither I nor II

4. When a corporation holds a real estate broker's license, all officers of the firm who intend to take an active part in the real estate business must be individually licensed as:

    I. real estate brokers.
    II. real estate salespersons.

    a. I only
    b. II only
    c. both I and II
    d. neither I nor II

5. Broker Jack Stevens's close friend Paul Ihlen helped him secure a listing that netted Stevens a large commission. To show his appreciation, Stevens gave his friend a new color TV set. In this situation:

    I. Stevens has violated the license law.
    II. Stevens has committed a gross misdemeanor.

    a. I only
    b. II only
    c. both I and II
    d. neither I nor II

6. Which of the following situations is(are) in violation of the license law?

   I. Word quickly spreads around town that Phil Everlast is about to sell his palatial home. Broker Joe Huckster, recognizing the house as a "hot property," sends one of his top-notch salespersons over to see Everlast and secure a listing agreement with him. Everlast finally decides to sign an exclusive-agency agreement with another broker. The next day, Huckster's salesperson returns with a prospective buyer for Everlast's house.
   II. Broker Jill Hester is a member of the local board of Realtors®, but does not display this fact on any of her signs or advertising.

   a. I only
   b. II only
   c. both I and II
   d. neither I nor II

7. When Minnesota real estate broker Fred Miller sold a house to Barney Burnside, he neglected to tell Burnside about the rotted timbers and the termites that infested the house. It cost Burnside nearly $13,000 to repair the house, and he now wishes to recover the loss from the Real Estate Education, Research, and Recovery Fund. What must Burnside do before he can collect?

   I. prove that the loss resulted from a fraudulent, deceptive, or dishonest act on the part of broker Miller
   II. sue broker Miller and obtain a judgment against him

   a. I only
   b. II only
   c. both I and II
   d. neither I nor II

8. When a broker's license is suspended, his or her salespeople must immediately:

   I. apply for new licenses.
   II. stop selling and listing.

   a. I only
   b. II only
   c. both I and II
   d. neither I nor II

9. Which of the following persons need not be licensed as a real estate broker or salesperson?

   a. John Walters, who negotiates a mortgage loan for a friend and receives a fee for his services
   b. Jack Carver, who manages several apartment buildings on behalf of their owners
   c. Laurie Gripe, who auctions off several homes on behalf of the state at a tax sale
   d. Chris Taylor, who arranges for the exchange of two parcels of real estate for a negotiating fee

10. Upon the expiration of a listing agreement, a broker must furnish a seller with a protective list of all the persons to whom he or she showed a particular parcel of real estate:

    a. within 24 hours.
    b. within 48 hours.
    c. only if the listing agreement included an override clause.
    d. only if the listing agreement included a holdover clause.

11. The Minnesota Real Estate License Law is administered by:

    a. the Commissioner of Securities.
    b. the Commissioner of Commerce.
    c. the Chairman of the Real Estate Advisory Council.
    d. the Commissioner of Securities and Real Estate.

12. Buyer Keven Rosehips gives Broker Calvin College a check for $750 in earnest money. College does not have to deposit the check in his trust account if:

    a. it is made out to him.
    b. the buyer authorizes him in writing not to deposit it.
    c. the offer has already been accepted by the seller.
    d. all of the above

13. A licensed broker may close an existing trust account:

    a. at any time.
    b. provided that he or she gives the commissioner 10 days' written notice prior to the closing.
    c. provided that the commissioner first reviews the account records.
    d. only when his or her license comes up for renewal.

14. When Broker Jack Harrison completes a real estate transaction, he must keep all records and receipts regarding the transaction for the next:

    a. one year.   c. three years.
    b. two years.   d. four years.

15. The maximum judgment per transaction that may be paid out of the Real Estate Education, Research, and Recovery Fund is:

    a. $20,000.   c. $100,000.
    b. $30,000.   d. $200,000.

16. John Burgher wishes to purchase and operate a "Chicken Lickin's Finger Pickin' Chicken" franchise. He is purchasing this interest through Wally Fry, who is not a licensed broker. Fry is charging Burgher a four percent commission for negotiating the sale. This practice is legal insofar as the license law is concerned if:

    a. it is a registered franchise.
    b. it is a registered franchise, and the sale includes all necessary buildings and fixtures.
    c. the seller acts as principal in six or more such transactions per year.
    d. Burgher registers his franchise with the Commissioner of Commerce after the transaction is closed.

17. A newly licensed salesperson must complete an approved 30-hour course of real estate study within:

    a. one year of the date that his or her license was first issued.
    b. three years from the date of his or her first license renewal.
    c. two years from the date of application for a license.
    d. his or her first full license period.

18. Broker Sal Santelli and Jack Russell have been good friends for years --such good friends that when Santelli sold Russell's house, he didn't bother to get a written listing agreement. The two have had a bit of a falling out because of the transaction, however, and now Russell refuses to pay Santelli's commission. What can Santelli legally do to collect a commission from Russell?

    a. nothing
    b. take Russell to court and obtain a judgment against him
    c. enforce his broker's lien for commission on Russell's real and personal property
    d. attempt to collect his money from the Real Estate Education, Research, and Recovery Fund

15

Real Estate Financing

MORTGAGE LOANS

With regard to mortgage loans, Minnesota is considered to be a lien theory state. State statutes hold that a mortgage is only a lien against the real property involved, not a transfer of title, regardless of its terms or wording.

Mortgages in Minnesota generally carry the **power of sale**. This means that the documents provide for the mortgagee's speedy and nonjudicial sale of mortgaged lands in the case of a mortgagor's default. General provisions of mortgage loans are described in the text.

Junior Mortgages

Minnesota statutes allow banks and trust companies to make junior mortgages (those secured by real estate other than as a first lien), if the total unpaid aggregate of all outstanding liens against the real estate does not exceed 80 percent of its appraised value. Before the loan is made, the value of the property must be determined by appraisal.

Mortgage Commitments

Minnesota law provides that some conventional loans and contracts for deed may carry an interest rate that is different from the one originally agreed upon. If the loan or contract for deed is based upon a commitment made prior to July 31, 1983, the lender or contract vendor may change the interest rate specified in the commitment, when the loan document or contract for deed is executed. This is true even if the maximum lawful rate of interest declined to a level below the rate specified in the commitment during the period between the issuing of the commitment and the execution of the loan documents or contract for deed. An executed purchase agreement in which a seller agrees to finance all or part of a purchase price with a contract for deed is considered a commitment for a contract for deed.

Recording

Minnesota mortgages must be executed and recorded as a deed is: that is, filed with the county recorder in the county in which the land is located. Such recording by the mortgagor protects all persons involved against third-party claims and gives the loan priority over any subsequent liens. In addition, at the time and place of recording, the mortgagor must pay the Minnesota mortgage registration tax of $.15 per $100, or fraction thereof, of the principal amount secured by the loan. (The mortgagee, however, may agree to pay this amount.) The mortgage registration tax does not apply to contract-for-deed financing or to co-owners partitioning property.

Discount Points

Conventional loans may contain provisions permitting discount points as long as the discount points will not result in a loan yield that is usurious.

Assumption of Mortgage

When the purpose of a conventional loan in Minnesota is to enable a borrower to purchase a one- to four-family dwelling as his or her primary residence, the lender must allow the existing borrower to transfer the real estate if he or she continues to be obligated for repayment. The lender must release the existing borrower if the transferee meets certain credit standards and if the transferee executes an agreement assuming the loan obligations. In the assumption of a conventional mortgage, the lender may charge a fee that does not exceed one-tenth of one percent of the remaining unpaid principal balance when the existing borrower continues to be obligated, or not more than one percent of the remaining unpaid principal balance when the existing borrower is released from the obligation.

No conventional loan made on or after May 28, 1977, may contain a provision authorizing the imposition of a penalty if the loan is prepaid.

Due-on-Sale Clauses

In Minnesota, alienation clauses are generally referred to as due-on-sale clauses. The trend has been for lending institutions to enforce these clauses and for the courts to uphold their right to do so. However, due-on-sale clauses are not enforceable for conventional mortgages originated between June 1, 1979, and May 8, 1981. Lenders must allow an assumption, provided that the assuming party meets standards of credit worthiness and executes with the lender an agreement to assume the existing mortgage obligations.

TRUST DEEDS

Trust deeds (deeds of trust), as described in the text, are rarely used to finance real estate in Minnesota.

FORECLOSURE

In Minnesota, mortgages in default may be foreclosed by either judicial or nonjudicial foreclosure, as described in the text. Whether or not a mortgage may be foreclosed in a nonjudicial manner depends upon its carrying a power of sale, as described earlier in the chapter.

Nonjudicial Foreclosure--Foreclosure by Advertisement

When a borrower defaults on a loan secured by a mortgage, and the mortgage contains the power of sale, the lender may foreclose by advertisement and sell the mortgaged property without lengthy legal action. A loan in default may be foreclosed by advertisement if the original mortgage and any assignments were recorded and the lender is not suing the borrower to collect on the debt.

To foreclose, the mortgagee publishes once each week for 60 days a notice of the foreclosure. The notice is printed in a publication of general distribution that is either printed or distributed in the county where the land is located. After the notice is published, the land may be sold at a foreclosure sale.

The mortgagee must provide the property's occupant with a notice of default, served like a civil summons, at least eight weeks before the land is to be sold. Such notices must contain the following information:

1. the name of the mortgagor and mortgagee (or the assignee, if the mortgage was assigned);

2. the date the mortgage was executed and the date and place of recording (or registration, if the property is under Torrens);

3. the amount currently due on the mortgage loan, including any taxes the mortgagee may have paid as of the date of the notice;

4. a description of the mortgaged premises;

5. the time and place of the mortgage sale;

6. the time allowed by law for the mortgagor's redemption of the real estate after the mortgage sale.

Judicial Foreclosure--Foreclosure by Action

In cases where the mortgage does not contain a power of sale, the mortgagee forecloses by action. A foreclosure by action is a civil suit; the mortgagee serves a summons and complaint (which is then filed with a Minnesota district court for the county in which the land is located), seeking a judgment against the mortgagor for the amount due on the mortgage, together with an order directing sale of the real estate. The court may, in certain rare cases, appoint a receiver to collect rents, pay taxes, and make repairs on the property when the mortgagor is financially insolvent and is committing waste by not maintaining the property.

Foreclosure Sale

Foreclosure sales--whether the property is foreclosed by action or advertisement--are conducted at an auction by the county sheriff or in the county in which the property is located, between 9:00 A.M. and sunset. The real estate is sold to the highest bidder.

A purchaser of land at a foreclosure sale receives a **sheriff's certificate of sale**, stating the following information:

1. a description of the mortgage;

2. a description of the property sold;

3. the price paid for the land;

4. the time and place of the sale;

5. the name of the purchaser;

6. the amount of time allowed by law for redemption by the mortgagor.

The purchaser must record this certificate within 20 days of the foreclosure sale. When the mortgagor's redemption period expires, the certificate operates as a deed, granting the purchaser the interest in the property that the mortgagor owned at the time the mortgage was executed.

When property is sold by court order, the court reviews the sale and may approve or reject the sale. If the sale is approved, the court clerk enters a satisfaction of judgment in the judicial record for the amount paid and executes the certificate of sale. If the sale is denied--for example, because the court believes the terms are unjust--a new sale is ordered. That sale must be conducted in like manner and is subject to the same discretionary power to approve or reject the result of the action.

Redemption

In Minnesota, redemption takes two forms--equitable redemption and statutory redemption.

Equitable redemption. During the course of a foreclosure proceeding, but prior to the foreclosure sale, the mortgagor or any person having an interest in the real estate may pay the lender the amount currently due, plus costs, and thus reinstate the mortgage. All foreclosure proceedings will be terminated. The text refers to this procedure as equitable redemption. If some person other than the mortgagor redeems the property, the mortgagor's interest, if any, will be subject to the interest acquired by that other person.

Statutory redemption. A mortgagor has six months from the date of the foreclosure sale in which to redeem the foreclosed real estate. The redemption period is extended to 12 months, however, if one or more of the following conditions apply:

1. The mortgage was executed prior to July 1, 1967.

2. The amount currently due on the mortgage is less than two-thirds of the original principal secured by the loan.

3. The mortgaged land is more than 10 acres in size.

Note that Minnesota statutes also provide for redemption of defaulted property by creditors whose liens are subordinate to the mortgage lien if the defaulted mortgagor does not redeem within either the 6- or 12-month period. The creditor having the lien of highest priority may redeem within five days of the expiration of that period. At the expiration of this five-day period, the holder of the lien with the next highest priority may redeem within five days, and so on, until all junior lienholders have been given an opportunity to redeem. In redeeming the property, a lienholder must pay the mortgage sale purchaser the amount for which the property was sold, and he or she must pay off all prior liens against the property. Any creditor wishing to redeem foreclosed property must file a prior notice of intent to do so, within the statutory redemption period of the mortgagor, with the county recorder of the county in which the land is located.

Deficiency

If the proceeds from a foreclosure sale are not sufficient to satisfy the mortgage debt, interest, and other costs, a mortgagee may seek a deficiency judgment against the mortgagor, as described in the text.

This remedy, however, is only available when the foreclosure procedure allows a 12-month redemption period. When the redemption period is six months, the remedy of deficiency judgment is not available to the mortgagee against the mortgagor. Satisfaction of the loan is limited to the proceeds from the sale of the foreclosed property.

Surplus

Any surplus funds from a foreclosure sale that remain after satisfaction of the mortgage debt plus all costs are given to the defaulted mortgagor.

Attorney's Fees

Attorney's fees in a foreclosure by advertisement are regulated by statute. Attorney's fees in a foreclosure by action suit may be set by the court.

INTEREST

Usury

Minnesota usury law differentiates between first and second mortgage liens. There is no ceiling on the interest rate that may be charged on _first liens_; the rate was negotiated between buyer and seller. The rate for _junior liens_ is set each month by the State Commission of Banking, and has been based upon the monthly index of the Federal National Mortgage Association auction yields. Since these auctions have been discontinued, the state must now seek to establish an alternative index.

Loans that provide for an interest rate that is usurious (greater than the interest ceiling for the month in which the contract was executed) are void. As a general rule, persons aggrieved by usurious contracts may bring an action to

recover the full amount of all interest charges paid, plus costs. If the
lender of the usurious loan is a financial institution regulated by certain
sections of the Minnesota statutes, the lender forfeits all interest, and the
aggrieved person may recover up to twice the amount of interest paid, if action
is commenced within two years from the date of the transaction.

In the event a contract for deed is usurious, the contract is not unenforceable. However, persons who have paid usurious interest may recover an amount
not to exceed five times the usurious portion of the interest paid under the
contract, plus attorney's fees.

FHA-insured and VA-guaranteed loans are exempted from state usury regulations
by statute. The VA periodically sets an interest rate ceiling for the loans
it administers.

Statutory Interest Rate

Minnesota law sets a statutory rate of interest of 6 percent. This interest
rate is applicable when a contract does not specify the rate of interest to
be charged.

OTHER FINANCING TECHNIQUES

Renegotiable Rate Mortgages

In 1980 Minnesota authorized savings banks and savings and loan associations
to offer renegotiable rate notes secured by a long-term mortgage. Under this
arrangement the note may not exceed 95 percent of the appraised value of the
security, and the term of the mortgage covering the security may not exceed 30
years. A renegotiable rate note must have a term of three to five years and
must be repayable in equal monthly installments of principal and interest that
will amortize the loan over the life of the mortgage.

The loan is automatically renewable at the option of the borrower. At the
expiration of a note term, a new note is issued. The new note bears interest
at the then-current rate of interest and has a term of approximately the same
length as the preceding note. Thus, the interest note may be changed and can
fluctuate periodically during the course of the loan. There are, however,
restrictions on the amount that a lender may require interest rates to change.

Graduated Payment Mortgages

The graduated payment home loan is a conventional loan, made by a financial
institution, in which the initial periodic payments are lower than those under
a standard conventional loan. The periodic payments gradually rise to a predetermined point before becoming constant. Restrictions are imposed on the
amount and frequency of changes in the periodic payments. The periodic payments may not be increased after the tenth year of the loan, and borrowers
retain the right to convert the graduated payment mortgage to a standard
nongraduated payment mortgage at any time without penalty.

Reverse Mortgage Loans

A reverse mortgage loan, made by certain financial institutions to borrower, is one in which installments are paid to the borrower over a period of time. The loan is secured by a mortgage on the borrower's residential property and is due upon the occurrence of one of the following:

1. the lender's final payment to the borrower;

2. the borrower's sale of the property;

3. the borrower's termination of use of the property as a principal residence, and thus, the loss of homestead status;

4. the death of the last surviving borrower.

The reverse mortgage loan allows a homeowner who has substantial equity in his or her home to make use of this equity without selling the property.

Contracts for Deed

Chapter 11 of the text describes a method of purchasing real estate under a land contract, known in Minnesota as a contract for deed. Minnesota law does not provide for a statutory redemption period during which a buyer can redeem contract-for-deed property after foreclosure.

The interest rate charged under a contract for deed (called the **contract rate**) must be within the same legal limits as prescribed for a conventional mortgage loan.

Assuming a contract for deed. Occasionally, real estate is sold with the new buyer assuming an existing contract for deed from the original buyer. When a buyer assumes an existing contract for deed, he or she must obtain two instruments:

1. an **assignment of contract** from the original seller still holding the contract;

2. a **quitclaim deed** from the original buyer, conveying his or her equitable interest in the property.

As with any conveying instrument, both documents should be recorded in the county where the real estate is located.

Default--termination of the contract. Minnesota law permits a more prompt and abrupt remedy for a default under a contract for deed than is allowed for a second mortgage. When a purchaser defaults in payment on a contract for deed, the seller may terminate the contract by serving notice of the default on the buyer or his or her representative, in the manner of a civil summons. The notice must specify the conditions in which the default occurred and state that the contract will terminate at a specified time. With contracts for deed executed prior to May 1, 1980, the specified times are as follows:

1. 30 days if the purchaser has paid less than 30 percent of the sale price;

2. 45 days if the purchaser has paid 30 percent to 50 percent of the sale price;

3. 60 days if the purchaser has paid more than 50 percent of the sale price.

The specified times for termination of contracts for deed executed on or after May 1, 1980, are as follows:

1. 30 days if the purchaser has paid less than 10 percent of the sale price;

2. 60 days if the purchaser has paid 10 percent to 25 percent of the sale price;

3. 90 days if the purchaser has paid more than 25 percent of the sale price.

Reinstatement. To redeem a pre-May 1, 1980, contract for deed the buyer must cure the default described in the notice and pay certain costs required by statute (for example, the amount due at the time of the notice). To redeem a contract for deed executed on or after May 1, 1980, the buyer must pay all amounts owed through the date of making the curative payment, in addition to paying certain specified costs.

15/Real Estate Financing

Mortgage Deed.
Individual to Individual.

Form No. 41-M.

Miller-Davis Co., Minneapolis
Minnesota Uniform Conveyancing Blanks (Revised 1976)

This Indenture, Made this 15th day of March, 19 84, between Mark and Helen Time, husband and wife as joint tenants

of the County of Hennepin and State of Minnesota, mortgagors, and First American Federal Savings and Loan, Cherryvale, Minnesota

of the County of Hennepin and State of Minnesota, mortgagee,

Witnesseth, That the said mortgagors, in consideration of the sum of Twenty-nine thousand, three hundred, sixty-seven and no/100 ($29,367.00) DOLLARS, to Them in hand paid by the said mortgagee, the receipt whereof is hereby acknowledged, do hereby Grant, Bargain, Sell, and Convey unto the said mortgagee, heirs and assigns, Forever, all the tract or parcel of land lying and being in the County of Hennepin and State of Minnesota, described as follows, to-wit:

Lot 27, Block 8, Secnic Heights Addition to Cherryvale, Hennepin County, Minnesota, According to the plat thereof on file and of record in the office of the Registrar

To Have and To Hold the Same, Together with the hereditaments and appurtenances thereto belonging to the said mortgagee, heirs and assigns, forever. And the said mortgagors, for their heirs, administrators, executors and assigns, do covenant with the said mortgagee, heirs and assigns, as follows: That They lawfully seized of said premises and have good right to sell and convey the same; that the same are free from all incumbrances,

that the mortgagee, their heirs and assigns, shall quietly enjoy and possess the same; and that the mortgagor will Warrant and Defend the title to the same against all lawful claims not hereinbefore specifically excepted.

Provided, Nevertheless, That if the said mortgagor, heirs, administrators, executors or assigns, shall pay to the said mortgagee, heirs or assigns, the sum of Twenty-nine thousand, three hundred, sixty-seven and NO/100 ($29,367.00) Dollars, according to the terms of principal promissory note of even date herewith due and payable,

Twenty years from date hereof

with interest thereon at the rate of 12 per cent per annum

executed by the said mortgagors, and payable to the order of said mortgagee at its office in the city of Cherryvale, Minnesota

and shall repay to said mortgagee, heirs or assigns, at the times and with interest as hereinafter specified, all sums advanced in protecting the lien of this mortgage, in payment of taxes on said premises, insurance premiums covering buildings thereon, principal or interest on any prior liens, expenses and attorney's fees herein provided for and sums advanced for any other purpose authorized herein, and shall keep and perform all the covenants and agreements herein contained, then this deed to be null and void, and to be released at the mortgagor's expense.

AND THE MORTGAGORS, for Their heirs, administrators and executors, do hereby covenant and agree with the mortgagee, heirs and assigns, to pay the principal sum of money and interest as above specified; to pay all taxes and assessments now due or that may hereafter become liens against said premises at least ten days before penalty attaches thereto; to keep any buildings on said premises insured by companies approved by the mortgagee against loss by fire for at least the sum of Forty thousand and NO/100 ($40,000.00) Dollars and against loss by windstorm for at least the sum of Forty thousand and NO/100 ($40,000.00) Dollars, and to deliver to said mortgagee the policies for such insurance with mortgage clause attached in favor of said mortgagee or assigns; to pay, when due, both principal and interest of all prior liens or incumbrances, if any, above mentioned, and to keep said premises free and clear of all other prior liens or incumbrances; to commit or permit no waste on said premises and to keep them in good repair; to complete forthwith any improvements which may hereafter be under course of construction thereon, and to pay any other expenses and attorney's fees incurred by said mortgagee........, ...its...heirs or assigns, by reason of litigation with any third party for the protection of the lien of this mortgage.

In case of failure to pay said taxes and assessments, prior liens or incumbrances, expenses and attorney's fees as above specified, or to insure said buildings and deliver the policies as aforesaid, the mortgagee......., ...heirs or assigns, may pay such taxes, assessments, prior liens, expenses and attorney's fees and interest thereon, or effect such insurance, and the sums so paid shall bear interest at the highest rate permitted by law from the date of such payment, shall be impressed as an additional lien upon said premises and be immediately due and payable from the mortgagor.S...... ....heirs or assigns, to said mortgagee......., ...heirs or assigns, and this mortgage shall from date thereof secure the repayment of such advances with interest.

In case of default in any of the foregoing covenants, the mortgagor.S...confer........upon the mortgagee.........the option of declaring the unpaid balance of said principal note and the interest accrued thereon, together with all sums advanced hereunder, immediately due and payable without notice, and hereby authorize and empower said mortgagee......., ... heirs and assigns, to foreclose this mortgage by judicial proceedings or to sell said premises at public auction and convey the same to the purchaser in fee simple in accordance with the statute, and out of the moneys arising from such sale to retain all sums secured hereby, with interest and all legal costs and charges of such foreclosure and the maximum attorney's fee permitted by law, which costs, charges and fees the mortgagor...S..herein agree........ to pay.

In Testimony Whereof, the said mortgagor S ha ve hereunto set their hand S the day and year first above written.

State of Minnesota, } ss.
County of Hennepin

The foregoing instrument was acknowledged before me this 15th day of March, 19 84,

by ....
(NAME OF PERSON ACKNOWLEDGED)

....
(SIGNATURE OF PERSON TAKING ACKNOWLEDGMENT)

....
(TITLE OR RANK)

THIS INSTRUMENT WAS DRAFTED BY
E.P. Burnside, BROKER
5111 Maple Drive (Name)
Cherryvale, MN 55123 (Address)

Doc. No. 3012467

MORTGAGE DEED
Individual to Individual

Mark and Helen Time
TO
First American Federal

Office of County Recorder
State of Minnesota
County of Hennepin

I hereby certify that the within Mortgage was filed in this office for record on the 15th day of March 19 84, at 3:27 o'clock P.M., and was duly recorded in Book 904 of Mortgages, page 37 or
☐ Copied ☐ Microfilmed and was duly recorded as instrument No. 147216

R.W. Stevens
County Recorder.
By ....Deputy.

March 15, 1984, No. 147216
Registration tax hereon of Forty four and 10/100 ($44) Dollars paid.
Bernard M. Milsap
County Treasurer
By ....Deputy
Countersigned:
Bernard W. Wilson
County Auditor
By ....Deputy

Tax statements for the real property described in this instrument should be sent to:
Mark and Helen Time
2111 North Banana Avenue
Cherryvale, MN 55123
Name Address

CONTRACT FOR DEED   Form No. 54-M   Minnesota Uniform Conveyancing Blanks (1978, Miller Davis Co., Minneapolis)
Individual Seller

No delinquent taxes and transfer entered;
Certificate of Real Estate Value
( )filed   ( )not required
_____, 19___.

_____
County Auditor

By _____
Deputy

(reserved for mortgage registry tax payment data)

(reserved for recording data)

MORTGAGE REGISTRY TAX DUE HEREON:

$ __64.50__

Date: __March 15__, 19__84__

THIS CONTRACT FOR DEED is made on the above date by __Maurice W. Armbuster__ and __Mabel C. Armbuster__, __husband and wife__
(marital status)

Seller (whether one or more), and __Mark T. Time and Helen B. Time__

__husband and wife, as joint tenants__, Purchaser (whether one or more).

Seller and Purchaser agree to the following terms:

1. PROPERTY DESCRIPTION. Seller hereby sells, and Purchaser hereby buys, real property in __Hennepin__ County, Minnesota, described as follows:

   Lot 27, Block 8, Scenic Heights Addition to Cherryvale,
   Hennepin County, Minnesota, According to the plat thereof
   on file and of record in the office of the Register of
   Deeds in and for the said county and state.

   together with all hereditaments and appurtenances belonging thereto (the Property).

2. TITLE. Seller warrants that title to the Property is, on the date of this contract, subject only to the following exceptions:
   (a) Covenants, conditions, restrictions, declarations and easements of record, if any;
   (b) Reservations of minerals or mineral rights by the State of Minnesota, if any;
   (c) Building, zoning and subdivision laws and regulations;
   (d) The lien of real estate taxes and installments of special assessments which are payable by Purchaser pursuant to paragraph 6 of this contract; and
   (e) The following liens or encumbrances:

   NONE

3. DELIVERY OF DEED AND EVIDENCE OF TITLE. Upon Purchaser's prompt and full performance of this contract, Seller shall:
   (a) Execute, acknowledge and deliver to Purchaser a __Warranty__ Deed, in recordable form, conveying marketable title to the Property to Purchaser, subject only to the following exceptions:
      (i) Those exceptions referred to in paragraph 2(a), (b), (c) and (d) of this contract;
      (ii) Liens, encumbrances, adverse claims or other matters which Purchaser has created, suffered or permitted to accrue after the date of this contract; and
      (iii) The following liens or encumbrances:

   ; and

   (b) Deliver to Purchaser the abstract of title to the Property or, if the title is registered, the owner's duplicate certificate of title.

4. PURCHASE PRICE. Purchaser shall pay to Seller, at __901 East Lake Street,__
   __Minneapolis, Minnesota 55123__, the sum of
   __Fifty-three thousand and No/100__ ($ __53,000.00__),
   as and for the purchase price for the Property, payable as follows:
   Ten thousand and No/100 ($10,000.00) dollars cash and

   Forty-three thousand and No/100 ($43,000.00) in the following manner:
   one payment of three hundred, thirty-one dollars and eighty-nine
   cents ($331.89) per month, due on the 25th day of each month, for
   twenty-five years from the month herein, which includes payment of
   8% annual interest.

5. PREPAYMENT. Unless otherwise provided in this contract, Purchaser shall have the right to fully or partially prepay this contract at any time without penalty. Any partial prepayment shall be applied first to payment of amounts then due under this contract, including unpaid accrued interest, and the balance shall be applied to the principal installments to be paid in the inverse order of their maturity. Partial prepayment shall not postpone the due date of the installments to be paid pursuant to this contract or change the amount of such installments.

6. REAL ESTATE TAXES AND ASSESSMENTS. Purchaser shall pay, before penalty accrues, all real estate taxes and installments of special assessments assessed against the Property which are due and payable in the year 19 85 and in all subsequent years. Real estate taxes and installments of special assessments which are due and payable in the year in which this contract is dated shall be paid as follows:

   Seller herein shall pay $119.33 and buyers herein shall pay $596.67

   Seller warrants that the real estate taxes and installments of special assessments which were due and payable in the years preceding the year in which this contract is dated are paid in full.

7. PROPERTY INSURANCE.
   (a) INSURED RISKS AND AMOUNT. Purchaser shall keep all buildings, improvements and fixtures now or later located on or a part of the Property insured against loss by fire, extended coverage perils, vandalism, malicious mischief and, if applicable, steam boiler explosion for at least the amount of Fifty-three thousand and No/100 ($53,000.00). If any of the buildings, improvements or fixtures are located in a federally designated flood prone area, and if flood insurance is available for that area, Purchaser shall procure and maintain flood insurance in amounts reasonably satisfactory to Seller.
   (b) OTHER TERMS. The insurance policy shall contain a loss payable clause in favor of Seller which provides that Seller's right to recover under the insurance shall not be impaired by any acts or omissions of Purchaser or Seller, and that Seller shall otherwise be afforded all rights and privileges customarily provided a mortgagee under the so-called standard mortgage clause.
   (c) NOTICE OF DAMAGE. In the event of damage to the Property by fire or other casualty, Purchaser shall promptly give notice of such damage to Seller and the insurance company.

8. DAMAGE TO THE PROPERTY.
   (a) APPLICATION OF INSURANCE PROCEEDS. If the Property is damaged by fire or other casualty, the insurance proceeds paid on account of such damage shall be applied to payment of the amounts payable by Purchaser under this contract, even if such amounts are not then due to be paid, unless Purchaser makes a permitted election described in the next paragraph. Such amounts shall be first applied to unpaid accrued interest and next to the installments to be paid as provided in this contract in the inverse order of their maturity. Such payment shall not postpone the due date of the installments to be paid pursuant to this contract or change the amount of such installments. The balance of insurance proceeds, if any, shall be the property of Purchaser.
   (b) PURCHASER'S ELECTION TO REBUILD. If Purchaser is not in default under this contract, or after curing any such default, and if the mortgagees in any prior mortgages and sellers in any prior contracts for deed do not require otherwise, Purchaser may elect to have that portion of such insurance proceeds necessary to repair, replace or restore the damaged Property (the repair work) deposited in escrow with a bank or title insurance company qualified to do business in the State of Minnesota, or such other party as may be mutually agreeable to Seller and Purchaser. The election may only be made by written notice to Seller within sixty days after the damage occurs. Also, the election will only be permitted if the plans and specifications and contracts for the repair work are approved by Seller, which approval Seller shall not unreasonably withhold or delay. If such a permitted election is made by Purchaser, Seller and Purchaser shall jointly deposit, when paid, such insurance proceeds into such escrow. If such insurance proceeds are insufficient for the repair work, Purchaser shall, before the commencement of the repair work, deposit into such escrow sufficient additional money to insure the full payment for the repair work. Even if the insurance proceeds are unavailable or are insuffficient to pay the cost of the repair work, Purchaser shall at all times be responsible to pay the full cost of the repair work. All escrowed funds shall be disbursed by the escrowee in accordance with generally accepted sound construction disbursement procedures. The costs incurred or to be incurred on account of such escrow shall be deposited by Purchaser into such escrow before the commencement of the repair work. Purchaser shall complete the repair work as soon as reasonably possible and in a good and workmanlike manner, and in any event the repair work shall be completed by Purchaser within one year after the damage occurs. If, following the completion of and payment for the repair work, there remain any undisbursed escrow funds, such funds shall be applied to payment of the amounts payable by Purchaser under this contract in accordance with paragraph 8 (a) above.

9. INJURY OR DAMAGE OCCURRING ON THE PROPERTY.
   (a) LIABILITY. Seller shall be free from liability and claims for damages by reason of injuries occurring on or after the date of this contract to any person or persons or property while on or about the Property. Purchaser shall defend and indemnify Seller from all liability, loss, costs and obligations, including reasonable attorneys' fees, on account of or arising out of any such injuries. However, Purchaser shall have no liability or obligation to Seller for such injuries which are caused by the negligence or intentional wrongful acts or omissions of Seller.
   (b) LIABILITY INSURANCE. Purchaser shall, at Purchaser's own expense, procure and maintain liability insurance against claims for bodily injury, death and property damage occurring on or about the Property in amounts reasonably satisfactory to Seller and naming Seller as an additional insured.

10. INSURANCE, GENERALLY. The insurance which Purchaser is required to procure and maintain pursuant to paragraphs 7 and 9 of this contract shall be issued by an insurance company or companies licensed to do business in the State of Minnesota and acceptable to Seller. The insurance shall be maintained by Purchaser at all times while any amount remains unpaid under this contract. The insurance policies shall provide for not less than ten days written notice to Seller before cancellation, non-renewal, termination or change in coverage, and Purchaser shall deliver to Seller a duplicate original or certificate of such insurance policy or policies.

11. CONDEMNATION. If all or any part of the Property is taken in condemnation proceedings instituted under power of eminent domain or is conveyed in lieu thereof under threat of condemnation, the money paid pursuant to such condemnation or conveyance in lieu thereof shall be applied to payment of the amounts payable by Purchaser under this contract, even if such amounts are not then due to be paid. Such amounts shall be applied first to unpaid accrued interest and next to the installments to be paid as provided in this contract in the inverse order of their maturity. Such payment shall not postpone the due date of the installments to be paid pursuant to this contract or change the amount of such installments. The balance, if any, shall be the property of Purchaser.

12. WASTE, REPAIR AND LIENS. Purchaser shall not remove or demolish any buildings, improvements or fixtures now or later located on or a part of the Property, nor shall Purchaser commit or allow waste of the Property. Purchaser shall maintain the Property in good condition and repair. Purchaser shall not create or permit to accrue liens or adverse claims against the Property which constitute a lien or claim against Seller's interest in the Property. Purchaser shall pay to Seller all amounts, costs and expenses, including reasonable attorneys' fees, incurred by Seller to remove any such liens or adverse claims.

13. **DEED AND MORTGAGE REGISTRY TAXES.** Seller shall, upon Purchaser's full performance of this contract, pay the deed tax due upon the recording or filing of the deed to be delivered by Seller to Purchaser. The mortgage registry tax due upon the recording or filing of this contract shall be paid by the party who records or files this contract; however, this provision shall not impair the right of Seller to collect from Purchaser the amount of such tax actually paid by Seller as provided in the applicable law governing default and service of notice of termination of this contract.
14. **NOTICE OF ASSIGNMENT.** If either Seller or Purchaser assigns their interest in the Property, a copy of such assignment shall promptly be furnished to the non-assigning party.
15. **PROTECTION OF INTERESTS.** If Purchaser fails to pay any sum of money required under the terms of this contract or fails to perform any of Purchaser's obligations as set forth in this contract, Seller may, at Seller's option, pay the same or cause the same to be performed, or both, and the amounts so paid by Seller and the cost of such performance shall be payable at once, with interest at the rate stated in paragraph 4 of this contract, as an additional amount due Seller under this contract.

    If there now exists, or if Seller hereafter creates, suffers or permits to accrue, any mortgage, contract for deed, lien or encumbrance against the Property which is not herein expressly assumed by Purchaser, and provided Purchaser is not in default under this contract, Seller shall timely pay all amounts due thereon, and if Seller fails to do so, Purchaser may, at Purchaser's option, pay any such delinquent amounts and deduct the amounts paid from the installment(s) next coming due under this contract.
16. **DEFAULT.** The time of performance by Purchaser of the terms of this contract is an essential part of this contract. Should Purchaser fail to timely perform any of the terms of this contract, Seller may, at Seller's option, elect to declare this contract cancelled and terminated by notice to Purchaser in accordance with applicable law. All right, title and interest acquired under this contract by Purchaser shall then cease and terminate, and all improvements made upon the Property and all payments made by Purchaser pursuant to this contract shall belong to Seller as liquidated damages for breach of this contract. Neither the extension of the time for payment of any sum of money to be paid hereunder nor any waiver by Seller of Seller's rights to declare this contract forfeited by reason of any breach shall in any manner affect Seller's right to cancel this contract because of defaults subsequently occurring, and no extension of time shall be valid unless agreed to in writing. After service of notice of default and failure to cure such default within the period allowed by law, Purchaser shall, upon demand, surrender possession of the Property to Seller, but Purchaser shall be entitled to possession of the Property until the expiration of such period.
17. **BINDING EFFECT.** The terms of this contract shall run with the land and bind the parties hereto and their successors in interest.
18. **HEADINGS.** Headings of the paragraphs of this contract are for convenience only and do not define, limit or construe the contents of such paragraphs.
19. **ASSESSMENTS BY OWNERS' ASSOCIATION.** If the Property is subject to a recorded declaration providing for assessments to be levied against the Property by any owners' association, which assessments may become a lien against the Property if not paid, then:
    (a) Purchaser shall promptly pay, when due, all assessments imposed by the owners' association or other governing body as required by the provisions of the declaration or other related documents; and
    (b) So long as the owners' association maintains a master or blanket policy of insurance against fire, extended coverage perils and such other hazards and in such amounts as are required by this contract, then:
        (i) Purchaser's obligation in this contract to maintain hazard insurance coverage on the Property is satisfied; and
        (ii) The provisions in paragraph 8 of this contract regarding application of insurance proceeds shall be superceded by the provisions of the declaration or other related documents; and
        (iii) In the event of a distribution of insurance proceeds in lieu of restoration or repair following an insured casualty loss to the Property, any such proceeds payable to Purchaser are hereby assigned and shall be paid to Seller for application to the sum secured by this contract, with the excess, if any, paid to Purchaser.
20. **ADDITIONAL TERMS:**

SELLER(S)　　　　　　　　　　　　　　PURCHASER(S)
Maurice W. Armbuster　　　　　　　Mark T. Time
Mabel C. Armbuster　　　　　　　　Helen B. Time

State of Minnesota } ss.
County of __Hennepin__

The foregoing instrument was acknowledged before me this **15** day of **March**, **1984**, by **Maurice W. Armbuster and Mabel C. Armbuster, husband and wife and Mark T. Time and Helen B. Time, husband and wife**.

NOTARIAL STAMP OR SEAL (OR OTHER TITLE OR RANK)

SIGNATURE OF NOTARY PUBLIC OR OTHER OFFICIAL

State of Minnesota } ss.
County of _____

The foregoing instrument was acknowledged before me this ____ day of _____, 19___, by _____.

NOTARIAL STAMP OR SEAL (OR OTHER TITLE OR RANK)

SIGNATURE OF NOTARY PUBLIC OR OTHER OFFICIAL

Tax Statements for the real property described in this instrument should be sent to

THIS INSTRUMENT WAS DRAFTED BY (NAME AND ADDRESS)

FAILURE TO RECORD OR FILE THIS CONTRACT FOR DEED MAY GIVE OTHER PARTIES PRIORITY OVER PURCHASER'S INTEREST IN THE PROPERTY.

QUESTIONS

1. With regard to real estate financing:

    I. Minnesota is a title theory state.
    II. trust deeds are rarely used in Minnesota.

    a. I only
    b. II only
    c. both I and II
    d. neither I nor II

2. The maximum interest rate Minnesota lenders may charge their customers on long-term loans:

    I. varies each month.
    II. is equal to the rate of return on long-term U.S. treasury bonds.

    a. I only
    b. II only
    c. both I and II
    d. neither I nor II

3. Reggie Slumbers is behind in his mortgage loan payments, and the Fresh Air Mortgage Company has instituted foreclosure proceedings. If Slumbers raises enough money to cover the amount due Fresh Air, plus costs before the foreclosure sale:

    I. the foreclosure proceedings will be abandoned.
    II. the mortgage will continue as before.

    a. I only
    b. II only
    c. both I and II
    d. neither I nor II

4. Usurious lending contracts in Minnesota are considered to be:

    a. void.
    b. voidable.
    c. unenforceable.
    d. ineffectual.

5. The McClanahans recently took out a mortgage loan on their new home. The lender told them that the mortgage contained a power of sale clause. This means:

    a. the McClanahans can sell the real estate at any time.
    b. the lender may sell the mortgage to an investor in the secondary mortgage market.
    c. the sale of the land does not affect the status of the mortgage.
    d. should the McClanahans default on the mortgage, the lender may sell the property after a reasonable time to recover all monies owed.

6. John and Emily Fishbein bought a house just outside of Duluth for $29,000, taking out a mortgage on the property for $22,000. When they record the mortgage with the county registrar, how much mortgage registration tax will they have to pay?

   a. $20.00
   b. $22.00
   c. $33.00
   d. $36.50

7. Which of the following is not a prerequisite for foreclosure by advertisement?

   a. The mortgagor must be in default.
   b. No legal action must be currently pending on the debt by the mortgagee.
   c. The mortgage must have been recorded.
   d. A summons and complaint must be filed with district court, seeking payment of the debt and the sale of the property.

8. Today, Ralph Baxter bought a parcel of land at a foreclosure sale. In return for the money he paid for the land, he will receive:

   a. a state deed.
   b. a certificate of sale.
   c. clear title to the real estate.
   d. a quitclaim deed to the property.

9. Jeannie Sill defaulted in payment on her mortgage. As Jeannie had obtained the loan last year, she had only paid off a small portion of the principal. The lender, Titanic Savings and Loan, has since foreclosed on the mortgage and the property was sold today at a foreclosure sale. How long does Sill have to redeem the real estate?

   a. six months
   b. twelve months
   c. six years
   d. seven years

10. In the case of Jeannie Sill's foreclosed mortgage lien in question 9, if the proceeds from the foreclosure sale were not sufficient to settle the debt and pay off all costs, what can Titanic Savings and Loan legally do to recover the unpaid portion?

    a. nothing
    b. sue Sill for the deficiency
    c. force Sill to take out another loan to cover the deficiency
    d. enforce a lien on all of Sill's personal and/or other real property

11. George Bernard Kowalski is purchasing a condominium under a contract for deed executed on August 15, 1982. This morning, the seller served him with a notice of default on the contract. How much time does Kowalski have in which to pay all monies owed before the contract is terminated?

    a. 30 days if he has paid less than 10 percent of the sales price
    b. 45 days if he paid 30 to 50 percent of the sales price
    c. 60 days if he paid more than 50 percent of the sale price
    d. 90 days if he paid 75 percent of the sale price

12. Juanita O'Brian is buying Brian McIlhenny's house. O'Brian is assuming McIlhenny's existing contract for deed on the real estate, originally issued to him by Cyrus and Eloise Friedman, the original owners. What must O'Brian do concerning this transaction?

    a. obtain a quitclaim deed from McIlhenny, conveying his equitable interest in the property
    b. obtain an assignment of mortgage from the Friedmans and record it with the county recorder
    c. obtain an assignment of contract from McIlhenny, transferring all rights and obligations under the original instrument to her
    d. pay off McIlhenny's contract in full before the transaction can be completed

16

Leases

LEASEHOLD ESTATES

Minnesota law recognizes the four types of leasehold estates described in the text--estates for years, estates from period to period, tenancy at will, and tenancy at sufferance.

STANDARD LEASE PROVISIONS

A lease is a valid contract between the lessor (landlord) and lessee (tenant), and, like any other contract, it should include all the terms and conditions of the agreement. The essentials of a valid lease are discussed in the text.

Under the Minnesota Statute of Frauds, leases for more than one year must be in writing, express consideration for the lease, and be signed by the lessor or his or her agent. In addition, leases for longer than three years must be executed like a deed and can be recorded. The recording of such leases gives constructive notice of the long-term rights of the lessee and thus makes the lease valid against third-party claims.

Landlord-Tenant Provisions

Rent. Minnesota laws do not recognize a statutory landlord's lien--that is, the right to have a delinquent debt related to rent collection paid out of the proceeds of a court sale of the debtor's property, except in the instance of unlawful detainer proceedings, which will be discussed later in this chapter.

Automatic renewals. An automatic renewal clause provides that a lease will be automatically renewed for another full leasing period unless the tenant gives the landlord a notice of termination prior to the expiration/renewal date of the document. Such clauses are void in Minnesota unless the landlord notifies the tenant of the effect of the clause by personal service or certified or registered mail, no more than 30 nor less than 15 days prior to the date that notice or intent to vacate is required.

Landlord information disclosure. Tenants must be informed of the names and addresses of all owners and property managers of their leased property. In addition, a typewritten notice of such information must be on display in a conspicuous place on the property at all times. No landlord can take legal action for rent collection unless this is done. Also, when a lease involves residential property, all interested parties must have access to the landlord's records involving violations of any state, county, or city health, housing, building, fire prevention, or housing maintenance codes.

Notice of absence from premises. A tenant who intends to vacate leased premises for any reason between November 15 and April 15 must give his or her landlord three days' notice. Such notice must be given to prevent damage due to the freezing of water, steam, or other pipes during the winter months. A tenant's failure to give such notice will make him or her guilty of a misdemeanor.

Security Deposits

Landlord-held security deposits must be returned to the tenant, along with five and one-half percent simple interest, within three weeks of termination of tenancy and receipt of the tenant's mailing address or delivery instructions regarding where the deposit is to be sent.

In a legal action involving recovery of a security deposit, the bad faith retention of such funds can subject a landlord to up to $200 in punitive damages along with actual damages. The landlord, however, may legally withhold any part of the deposit necessary to restore the premises to their original condition, excluding normal wear and tear. Any part of the security deposit may be withheld to cover the cost of rents or other costs due the landlord.

LEGAL PRINCIPLES OF LEASES

Destruction of Leased Premises

Common law required the tenant to continue to pay rent if the property were destroyed. Minnesota statutes, however, state that destruction (that makes the premises uninhabitable) terminates the obligation to pay rent.

Termination of Tenancy

Either the landlord or the tenant may terminate estates at will by one party serving written notice on the other at least three months, the rental interval, or 14 days (in the cse of neglect or default in the rent payment), whichever is less, before the termination date of the lease. Estates from year to year may be terminated by either the landlord or the tenant serving a written termination notice on the other party at least three months prior to the end of the second and subsequent years. Landlord or tenant may terminate tenancy from period to period by giving one month's notice. There is no implied tenancy for longer than the rent interval.

Landlord's Remedies

When a tenant remains in possession of leased premises without paying rent due or after termination of tenancy, the landlord has the right to recover possession of the premises through the quasi-criminal action of forcible entry and unlawful detainer. In this legal action, the landlord obtains a court order directing the tenant to return possession of the property to the landlord. If the tenant fails to move out within 24 hours after being served with such an order, he or she will be evicted by an officer of the court. In addition, the landlord will have a <u>lien on the tenant's property</u> still on the premises and may sell the property at public sale after 60 days in order to recover rent and other costs.

If, however, the tenant pays all rent owed plus costs and attorney's fees while being sued by the landlord for nonpayment of rent, the legal action will be dismissed, and the tenancy will continue as prescribed in the lease.

If a landlord recovers possession of leased premises through a court action and the lease was recorded, he or she must file a certified copy of the court judgment with the register of deeds or registrar of titles in the county where the property is located. If the possession of such property was recovered through a tenant's abandonment or surrender of the premises, the landlord must file an affidavit setting forth such facts in a similar manner.

When the term of the lease is longer than 20 years, the landlord must give the tenant, as well as all creditors and other persons claiming an interest to the property, 30 days' notice prior to eviction. After eviction, a tenant in such action can redeem the lease within six months of the eviction date upon payment of all rent due plus interest and costs.

Tenants' Rights

A tenant has the legal right to sue his or her landlord for the recovery of premises the tenant was evicted from if he or she was evicted wholly as a penalty for attempts either to enforce his or her rights as stated in the lease or to report violations of health, safety, housing, or building laws. In addition, if the tenant was evicted for nonpayment of rent, he or she may sue the landlord for recovery upon proof that the rent was increased or services decreased as a penalty for the activities previously mentioned.

In the event that the landlord does not pay his or her real estate taxes and the tenant is forced to do so, the tenant may file a lien notice with the registrar of titles or county register of deeds in the county in which the land is located, giving the tenant a lien on the landlord's property for the amount paid.

A useful source of information on this subject is the <u>Tenants' Rights Handbook</u>, published by the Minnesota Public Interest Research Group, Minneapolis.

QUESTIONS

1. Jackson and Emily Spratt are leaving their St. Paul apartment to vacation in sunny Florida for the winter. The landlord was not notified of their plan to be away. In the event that, during their absence, the water pipes in their apartment freeze and break:

    I. the Spratts would be considered guilty of a misdemeanor.
    II. the Spratts' lease would be automatically cancelled.

    a. I only
    b. II only
    c. both I and II
    d. neither I nor II

2. The lease on the Rudolphs' apartment contains an automatic renewal clause, and the renewal date is approaching. If the Rudolphs' landlord wishes to renew the lease, he must:

    I. do nothing, since the lease will be renewed automatically.
    II. give notice of the intent to renew within 15 to 30 days prior to the renewal date.

    a. I only
    b. II only
    c. both I and II
    d. neither I nor II

3. Landlord-held security deposits must be returned to a tenant:

    a. on the day of the termination of the tenancy.
    b. within one week of the termination of the tenancy.
    c. along with five and one-half percent simple interest.
    d. regardless of the condition of the property upon termination of the tenancy.

4. Jane Crawley has never learned the true identity of the owner of the building in which she leases an apartment. Until she is informed of the owner's name and address, the owner cannot legally:

    a. collect rent from Crawley.
    b. raise Crawley's rent.
    c. take Crawley to court and sue her for nonpayment of rent.
    d. be considered a landlord.

5. Ralph J. McCabe, Jr. lost his job recently, and, as a result, has been unable to pay the rent on his apartment for the last two months. His landlord, Harry Hiss, is growing impatient and wants to take action to collect his money from McCabe. Legally, Landlord Hiss can:

    a. throw McCabe off the property.
    b. sell McCabe's property to satisfy the debt.
    c. take McCabe to court and obtain a judgment against him.
    d. give McCabe and his other creditors 30 days' prior notice before evicting him.

18

Real Estate Appraisal

RESIDENTIAL MARKET VALUE

Chapter 18 in the text discusses real estate appraisal from the professional real estate appraiser's point of view. This supplementary chapter, in contrast, will deal with the role of the real estate salesperson in determining a property's fair market value at the time of listing, a subject touched upon in Chapter 6 of the text.

Value Estimates

As discussed in the text, there are three approaches to estimating real estate value:

1. the market comparison approach, an estimate of value based on comparisons of houses that have been sold recently, those put on the market recently, and those unsold after an extended period of time.

2. the cost approach, determined by computing the cost of reproducing the physical property, less physical, functional, and/or economic depreciation;

3. the income approach, figured by calculating the cost of acquiring income property that would generate income equal to that of the property being appraised and at the same risk.

The cost and income approaches are generally used by professional appraisers and real estate investment specialists. Their reconciliation of data is long and detailed, based upon a complete and thorough examination of the subject property, its history, the neighborhood, and so on.

The market comparison approach, however, is a relatively simple, quick approach to value (assuming adequate comparable data exist). Therefore, it is often used by real estate salespersons when obtaining listing agreements.

MARKET COMPARISON

A market comparison depends largely on the collection, organization, and analysis of information about the seller's competition--comparable houses either sold recently or currently on the market.

Market Data

The competitive property analysis includes data on a number of comparable houses--those currently on the market, those sold recently, and those remaining unsold. A broker's listings and/or MLS files are a prime source for researching these facts. Note that the more comparable the properties a salesperson selects for use in the analysis, the more accurate the market comparison appraisal will be.

FHA/VA appraisals. A salesperson should record the results of any FHA or VA appraisals that may have been taken on comparable properties and that may be available in his or her brokerage's files.

Buyer appeal. The salesperson should identify and calculate the effect certain features of the home may have on its competitive market value. Each of the following five elements is rated at 0 percent to 20 percent--the maximum total rating for any property being 100 percent.

A property's location rating would probably be 20 percent if, for example, it is located in a fine neighborhood and close to schools, stores, and transportation.

A property with highly rated extras might include a swimming pool, landscaping, family room, paneled den with woodburning fireplace, and so on. Such extras may or may not dramatically increase the selling price of the home, but they are excellent purchasing points.

Special financing can represent a possible assumption of the seller's mortgage at a low interest rate or the buyer's willingness to accept a low down payment or take back a purchase-money mortgage or contract for deed.

Appeal usually represents the property's esthetic qualities as well as its general physical makeup.

The seller's willingness to sell under market price warrants either a 20 percent (yes) or 0 percent (no) rating. This rating may or may not be determined until the analysis is brought to the seller for his or her approval. If the total of the other four appeals is below 50 percent, a salesperson may try to convince the seller to convey the property at less than its market value in order to facilitate a sale.

Marketing position. The salesperson should analyze and record the degree of cooperation he or she can expect to receive from the seller. Five elements are again rated:

The reason for and urgency of selling are two closely related factors. Dealing primarily with motivation, these areas forecast the seller's position in accepting offers for sale. For example, if the seller has been transferred across the country and must sell within 60 days, both ratings would probably be 20 percent.

Whether the sellers will help finance, as mentioned earlier, can be an important factor if the sellers are willing to accept a second mortgage, contract for deed, or a low down payment to facilitate a sale.

The seller's willingness to list at the competitive market value is an indication of his or her faith in the real estate salesperson. If the seller has set an unreasonable predetermined price and shows no signs of wavering from it, the listing salesperson should reflect such an attitude in this section.

Whether the sellers will pay for appraisal can be important if FHA commitments are needed to close the transaction. If FHA/VA loans are not a critical factor, the salesperson should simply work from an 80 percent marketing rating.

Market analysis. Essentially, the assets can represent any of the factors included in the buyer appeal section of the form. In addition, any amenities that the area or neighborhood itself might offer should be recorded here. Generally, though, an asset represents something unique about the property and its location. For example, even though the subject property has an attractive fireplace, it would not be considered an asset if many of the houses in the area have built-in fireplaces. If, however, it is the only house on the block with a back yard facing the park, then it possesses a unique feature that would be considered an asset. Even run-down properties should have at least one asset.

Needless to say, a property's drawbacks can dramatically reduce its market value. Certain constructional flaws, such as a bad floor plan, small rooms, low ceilings, or lack of a full bath or basement, cannot readily be corrected and may just have to be worked around. Minor drawbacks, however, such as poor maintenance, leaky plumbing, or cracked plaster, can be repaired. By listing such repairable drawbacks, the agent may be able to persuade the seller to repair them by demonstrating the negative effects they can have on the property's market value.

Area market conditions refer to anything that affects real estate activity in the area, such as financing conditions or how comparative properties are selling.

Recommended terms are those which the salesperson may feel are necessary to facilitate the sale, such as FHA/VA loans or a contract for deed.

Listing and selling prices. After all necessary information has been gathered and recorded, the salesperson and seller should mutually agree on a recommended listing price. This value must reflect all of the facts considered--assets, drawbacks, listing prices, selling prices, and so on. In determining the final sales price range, the salesperson and seller should, as a general rule, stay within five percent of the recommended listing price.

QUESTIONS

1. The market comparison approach depends on:

   I. the amount of return expected from a commercial property.
   II. prices of similar properties.

   a. I only
   b. II only
   c. both I and II
   d. neither I nor II

2. Which appraisal method is generally used by real estate brokers, rather than professional appraisers?

   a. cost approach
   b. income approach
   c. market comparison approach
   d. none of the above

3. Sources for a market data analysis include:

   I. FHA appraisals.
   II. brokerage listing records.

   a. I only
   b. II only
   c. both I and II
   d. neither I nor II

4. A property's marketing position is affected by:

   I. location.
   II. appeal.

   a. I only
   b. II only
   c. both I and II
   d. neither I nor II

5. Broker Alice uses five equally weighted elements, including urgency of selling, to determine marketing position. Her seller put his house on the market to see whether he could make a profit of at least 75 percent. Alice would rate urgency of selling at about:

   a. one percent.
   b. 18 percent.
   c. 40 percent.
   d. 95 percent.

19

Control of Land Use

ZONING--LAND-USE DEVELOPMENT

The Minnesota statutes include enabling acts, like those described in the text, that give townships, municipalities, counties, and regions authority to enact local zoning and subdivision ordinances and create programs for land-use development. In addition to enabling acts, the state **Municipal Housing and Redevelopment Act** was passed to aid in the clearance, replanning, reconstruction, and neighborhood rehabilitation of substandard areas. Depending on the locality, power to conduct such projects is vested in the municipal governing body or in a public corporation that is created as a housing and redevelopment authority.

Municipalities

The enabling acts give municipalities the necessary powers and uniform procedures to conduct municipal land-use planning. The law sets forth provisions for the structure and maintenance of **municipal planning agencies** that have the power to structure zoning and subdivision regulations within the municipality. Such regulations are subject to public hearings prior to their enactment and adoption by the governing bodies and judicial review afterwards.

Municipal zoning ordinances generally contain the requirements for each zoning district in the municipality and a map illustrating the geographical boundaries of these districts. In addition, such ordinances detail specific zoning regulations, primarily dealing with the following:

1. <u>use</u>--the uses for which land can legally function: single-family, commercial, and so forth;

2. <u>height</u>--the maximum height to which a building may be erected;

3. <u>area</u>--the amount of space that must be left open around structures, such as front, side and rear yards, as well as minimum lot areas, lot coverage, density, off-street parking, and loading requirements.

Determinations concerning zoning changes and subdivision approval are made by the municipal planning agency after its members confer with various city, county, school district, and local state agencies. Such reports are open for public discussion. Final recommendations are generally made to the municipal governing body, which makes all final zoning decisions. Final decisions are subject to judicial review in district court.

Generally, changes in a municipality's zoning regulatioins take the form of either an amendment, variance, or conditional use. A **zoning amendment** is a change of the zoning district boundaries to accommodate changing conditions in land use; a **variance** is an exception to the zoning ordinance granted to provide relief to a property owner because of undue hardship; a **conditional use** allows a property owner to use the land in a manner other than is allowed by the zoning ordinance if certain standards are met.

Counties

Any Minnesota county with a population of less than 300,000 is authorized by law to carry on county planning and zoning in much the same manner as municipalities. The county shoreland zoning may be more restrictive than the state zoning, and it must contain the minimum state requirements.

Regions

The Minnesota Regional Development Act of 1969 provides for the creation and structure of **regional development commissions**. These commissions may be formed by any combination of cities or counties that represent a majority of the population of a region petitioning the state planning officer to establish such a commission. The purpose of such commissions is to conduct regional planning activities beneficial to all participating areas. In addition, the commissions receive and distribute state and federal public words funds to the various participating areas.

Statewide Criteria and Standards of Shoreland Areas

Minnesota is the "land of 10,000 lakes." As such, preservation of the natural beauty and resort/tourist potential of these resources is of prime legislative concern. Minnesota law provides for various land-use restrictions, both physical and environmental, concerning shoreland development and construction. Shoreland areas are those that are 1,000 feet from the normal high watermark of a lake or 300 feet from a river or stream. The statute requires counties and municipalities to adopt ordinances regulating such activity. The State Department of Natural Resources has promulgated regulations both to guide and to force local governments into such regulatory activity. The guidelines include the following regulations and restrictions.

Size and setback requirements. Minnesota law regulates minimum lot size and setback requirements for structures located in shoreland areas. For these purposes, the regulations and model ordinance implementing the statute divide natural lakes into three separate classifications: **natural environment lakes, recreational development lakes,** and **general development lakes.** The classification of a particular water basin or water source may be determined from the county or municipal zoning official. The classification is made according to a number of established criteria, and the local government may challenge the classification.

The following chart illustrates exemplary minimum lot sizes, widths, and setbacks (distance from shorelines), as well as minimum septic tank setbacks allowed by law.

	Lot Size	Width	Structure Setbacks	Septic Tank Setbacks
Natural environment	80,000 sq. ft.	200'	200'	150'
Recreational development	40,000 sq. ft.	150'	100'	75'
General development	20,000 sq. ft.	100'	75'	50'

Effluent disposal restrictions. In addition to the minimum setback requirements just illustrated, septic tank, soil absorption, or similar waste disposal systems may not be used on lots adjacent to public waters under the following circumstances:

1. in low swampy ares, or areas subject to recurrent flooding;

2. in areas where the highest known ground water table is within four feet of the bottom of the proposed soil absorption system;

3. in areas where exposed bedrock lies within four feet of the proposed system or where subsurface conditions significantly restrict the effluent's percolation, or absorption, into the soil;

4. in areas where ground slope may allow effluent to seep onto the surface.

Minimum structure depths. According to Minnesota regulations, a building that borders a lake, pond, or flowage must be constructed so that its maximum depth (including basement) is at least three feet above the highest known water level. When water-level information is not available, the elevation of permanent terrestrial vegetation may be used instead. Exceptions to this regulation include structures such as boathouses, piers, and docks. In addition, when bordering streams or rivers, structures must be built at an elevation consistent with any applicable floodplain-management ordinances.

Proximity to roads and highways. Minnesota regulations stipulate that no shoreland structure may be built within 50 feet of any federal, state, or county trunk highway or within 30 feet of any town road, public street, or other unclassified thoroughfare.

Other state laws. In addition to these regulations, some other laws of the state are relevant. These include the Critical Areas Act, the Environmental Rights Act, the Environmental Quality Council Act, the Environmental Coordination Procedures Act, the Power Plant Siting Act, the Environmental Policy Act, the Wild, Scenic and Recreational Rivers Act, the Floodplain Management Act, and the Upper Mississippi River Conservation Ordinance.

114   MINNESOTA SUPPLEMENT for Modern Real Estate Practice

MINNESOTA ENVIRONMENTAL LEGISLATION

The Minnesota Pollution Control Agency has broad powers to establish standards and regulations regarding all manners of pollution--air, water, noise, and solid waste disposal. Violation of any such pollution standards is a misdemeanor, and each day of violation constitutes a separate offense. The agency, however, may grant variances from its regulations in cases of undue hardship. Such variances are subject to prior public hearings.

QUESTIONS

1. State laws vest zoning and land-use authority in:

    a. the state government.
    b. local governments.
    c. the Commissioner of Commerce.
    d. regional development commissions.

2. M. B. Ryan is having a second home built near the Minnosin River. It is a beautiful location, but unfortunately it often floods during the spring and fall months. According to Minnesota law:

    I. Ryan's home must have a foundation at least six feet deep.
    II. Ryan may not build a soil-absorption waste-disposal system on the property.

    a. I only
    b. II only
    c. both I and II
    d. neither I nor II

3. The authority to carry out state-funded projects provided for in the Municipal Housing and Redevelopment Act is based in:

    a. the individual municipalities.
    b. the individual counties.
    c. regional planning boards.
    d. the state government.

4. The Minnesota Pollution Control Agency:

    I. can establish regulations regarding noise pollution.
    II. may grant variances in cases of undue hardship.

    a. I only
    b. II only
    c. both I and II
    d. neither I nor II

5. Which of the following is generally not regulated by municipal zoning ordinances?

    a. the maximum height to which a building may be erected
    b. the amount of space that must be left open around structures
    c. the uses for which land can legally function
    d. the preferred racial or age composition of a municipality

6. The role of regional development commissions is to:

    I. conduct regional planning activities to benefit the participating areas.
    II. receive and distribute public works funds.

    a. I only   c. both I and II
    b. II only   d. neither I nor II

20

Subdividing and Property Development

MINNESOTA SUBDIVIDED LAND SALES PRACTICES ACT

Mass housing development, limited to the construction of single-family dwellings during the post-World War II years, greatly expanded in the 1950s. This expansion occurred as a result of population growth, new production techniques, and an increasing public interest in land use for future development, retirement, and recreation. As the industry grew, so did the number of fraudulent acts and practices perpetrated by unscrupulous dealers and developers against the unsuspecting public. The Minnesota Subdivided Land Sales Practices Act was adopted by the state legislature in 1973 (and substantially changed in 1984) in response to rising public concern. The act transcends the concept of mere disclosure and regulates every phase of large-scale property development within and outside the state.

The Subdivided Land Sales Practices Act is found in Minnesota Statutes, Chapter 83. In addition to it, the legislature has adopted a number of rules and regulations that elaborate on the basic law. The act is administered by the Commissioner of Commerce of the State Department of Commerce, Securities Division.

The summaries of the act and the rules and regulations presented in this chapter are intended to acquaint you with their general provisions. The act is reproduced verbatim in the back of this Supplement.

Scope of the Act (Section 83.40)

The act regulates subdivided land sales offers and dispositions (including sales, leases, options, assignments, licenses, and awards as prizes), whether or not either party to a transaction is present in Minnesota, when one of the following conditions applies:

1. the offer is originated in the state;

2. the offer is directed to and received by persons in the state;

3. the subdivided lands are located in the state.

The statute defines subdivided land as <u>any real estate, wherever located, improved or unimproved, that is divided or is proposed to be divided for the purpose of sale or lease of any timeshare interest, housing cooperative, condominium, or similar interest in real estate.</u>

Exemptions

Exempt from regulation under the act are mortgagee's liens not affiliated with the subdivider when attached to land pledged as collateral in a transaction negotiated with the purchaser. In other words, when a subdivider operating in Minnesota offers land to a prospective purchaser, and the purchaser seeks financing from a local lending institution, the mortgage lien the lender demands, to secure its interest in the property as collateral for the loan, is excluded from the provisions of the act.

In addition, the act does not attempt to regulate subdivided land ads published in bona fide newspapers or other publications of general, regular, and paid circulations that are not published in Minnesota or radio/television ads broadcast outside of the state. Examples of this would include ads published in such national newspapers as the Wall Street Journal and USA Today and broadcasts in Eau Claire, Wisconsin or Sioux Falls, South Dakota that are received in Minnesota. Such ads are not considered offers made in or specifically directed to the state.

The following are subdivided lands exempt from regulations:

1. any lands offered or sold by the United States Government, any state, or any political subdivision, or by any corporate instrumentality of one of these levels of government;

2. leases of apartments, stores, offices, or similar building space;

3. leases of rooms or space in hotels, motels, or similar space for a period of less than three years, including renewal options;

4. cemetery lots;

5. mortgages or deeds of trust securing evidence of indebtedness;

6. subdivided lands that are registered as securities;

7. offers or sales made by an owner other than the subdivider who is acting as a principal in a single transaction;

8. offers or sales of all subdivided land within a subdivision in a single transaction;

9. subdivided land consisting of not more than ten separate lots, units, parcels, or interests in the aggregate;

10. registered condominiums;

11. lands used primarily for agricultural purposes, providing that each parcel is at least ten acres in size.

Licensing (Section 83.25)

In addition to a Minnesota real estate license, a person must obtain a subdivided land license to offer or dispose of subdivided lands. Such licenses are obtained through the commissioner's office by submitting a verified application and paying a $10 fee.

The commissioner may also require an additional examination for this license. Licenses expire annually on June 30 and may be renewed, transferred, suspended, revoked, or denied in the same manner as real estate licenses, discussed in Chapter 14.

Subdivided Land Registration (Section 83.23)

Subdivided lands must be registered with the commissioner prior to their offering or disposition.

Application for registration (Section 83.23). The subdivider must file an application for registration with the commissioner. This includes meeting the following requirements for registration by notification:

1. The subdivision may consist of no more than one hundred separate lots, units, parcels, or interests.

2. At least 20 days before the offer, the subdivider must provide the following information to the commissioner:

    a. name and address of the subdivider and the form of business organization if the subdivider is not an individual;
    b. location and legal description of the subdivision and the total number of lots, parcels, units, or interests;
    c. a title opinion or certificate of title insurance or its equivalent acceptable to the commissioner;
    d. a copy of each instrument that will be delivered to a buyer to evidence his or her interest; a copy of each contract and other agreements a buyer will be required to sign; the range of selling prices, rates, or rentals; a list of monthly fees a buyer may be required to pay; and a copy of an approved plat map or its equivalent;
    e. a filing fee of $100;

3. The subdivider must be in compliance with the service of process provision of Section 83.39, which requires the subdivider to give irrevocable consent to the commissioner's appointment as the subdivider's attorney to receive service of any lawful process in civil proceedings against the subdivider.

A registration by notification is effective on the twentieth business day after the filing of the registration statement or last amendment, or at an earlier time determined by the commissioner.

Subdivided lands may also be registered by qualification, providing that all of the following requirements have been met:

1. An application for registration has been filed.

2. The commissioner has been furnished a proposed public offering statement.

3. A filing fee of $250 plus $1 per lot, unit, parcel, or interest included in the offering has been paid with the application.

4. The subdivider is in compliance with the service of process provisions.

5. The commissioner has been given the subdivider's current financial statement, audited by a certified public accountant. (If the subdivider's fiscal year is 90 days prior to the date of filing, an unaudited financial statement may be submitted.)

Certified financial statements are not required for subdivisions in which all improvements are complete and paid for by the subdivider, and for which clear title can be given to the purchaser at closing.

An application for registration by qualification becomes effective when the commissioner so orders.

Consolidated registration. If a subdivider wishes to offer additional subdivided lands for sale, their registration may be consolidated with the earlier registration if the lands are contiguous to those previously offered. An application for consolidation requires a $50 fee and, if the first registration is by qualification, the additional lots, units, parcels or interests require the payment of $1 each for the consolidation.

Notice of filing and registration (Section 83.29). Provided there are no grounds for denial, the commissioner will register the subdivided lands in a book called the Register of Subdivided Lands. The commissioner has the power to place any restrictions on a registration as may be necessary to carry out the provisions of the act. Each entry in the register lists the subdivided lands, the individual for whom the lands are registered, and any conditions, limitations, or restrictions to the registration.

Denial of registration (Section 83.29). The commissioner may deny any application for registration if, through inquiry and examination, he or she determines one of the following:

1. Any requirements of the act or its rules and regulations have not been met.

2. The proposed promotional plan or advertising is or tends to be fraudulent, deceptive, or misleading. If this is the case, the commissioner has 15 days to deny the application.

3. The land sales would constitute or tend to constitute fraud or deception of the purchasers.

4. The land sales would be unfair or inequitable to the purchasers.

5. The subdivider has violated any provision or rule of the act or order of the commissioner.

6. The subdivider is not in compliance with federal, state, or local environmental quality standards.

Minnesota regulations list and define 45 fraudulent, misleading, deceptive, unfair, and inequitable acts and practices. Performance of any of these acts constitutes grounds for denial, suspension, or revocation of a registration as well as denial, suspension, or revocation of the subdivider's license.

The commissioner may not deny any registration based solely on the proposed sale price of subdivided lands.

Every person denied registration may request a hearing to appeal. Such hearings are held within 30 days of the order of denial.

Public Offering Statement (Section 83.24)

Before any subdivided lands may be offered or disposed of, the subdivider must file a current public offering statement with and obtain the approval of the commissioner. Since no two parcels of land are exactly alike, what must be disclosed and the manner of disclosure will be somewhat different with every parcel of land. Regulation 1608 sets forth a sample public offering statement. In every case, it is the subdivider's obligation to include <u>all relevant and material information in the statement</u>.

Prior to disposing of any interest in subdivided lands, the subdivider must, at his or her own expense, give all prospective purchasers current public offering statements. The purchaser must be allowed a reasonable amount of time to examine the statement prior to the offer or disposition. The subdivider must obtain a signed receipt for the statement from the prospective purchaser and retain it on file for three years, subject to inspection by the commissioner.

The public offering statement must not be used for any promotional purpose prior to registration of the subdivided lands and must always be used in its entirety after registration. No one may advertise or represent that the commissioner has approved or recommended the subdivided lands or their sale. No portion of the statement may be italicized, underscored, or printed in larger, heavier, or different-colored type from the remainder of the text.

The public offering statement must <u>disclose fully</u> and <u>accurately</u> all unusual and material facts affecting the <u>subdivided lands</u>. Such facts include:

1. the name and principal address of the subdivider and its agents in Minnesota;

2. a general description of the subdivided lands, including the number of lots, parcels, units or interests being offered;

3. a statement of whether the subdivider has any rights or options to acquire an interest in adjacent properties and, if so, a description of the options, locations, and zoning status of the adjacent properties;

4. a statement of any assistance to be provided by the subdivider or its agents to the purchaser in the event of resale, and whether or not subdivider or agent will be in competition in the event of resale;

5. the material terms of any restrictions affecting the subdivided land and each unit or lot, including but not limited to encumbrances, easements, liens, and zoning; a statement of the subdivider's efforts to remove the restrictions; and a statement of existing taxes and existing and proposed special taxes or assessments that affect the subdivided land;

6. a statement of the use for which the property is being offered;

7. information on existing or proposed improvements and amenities and their completion dates;

8. additional information that may be required at the discretion of the commissioner to assure full and fair disclosure to prospective purchasers.

Advertising (Section 83.20 and Regulation 1600)

All subdivided land advertising must be filed with the commissioner prior to its use. Advertising, for purposes of the act, is defined as "any written or printed communication or any communication by telephone or transmitted on radio, television, electronic means or similar communications media published in connection with the offer or sale of subdivided lands or any communication made to induce prospective purchasers to attend an offer or sales presentation." Such communications can include:

1. newspapers or periodicals;

2. radio or television broadcasts;

3. written, printed, or photographic materials;

4. any photographs, drawings, or artist's representations of the property's physical conditions or facilities;

5. materials used to induce prospective purchasers to visit a subdivision, such as vacation certificates;

6. an entire promotional plan for subdivided land sales, including promotional displays, parties, dinners, and meetings;

7. the land sales contract;

8. other materials used in connection with subdivided land sales.

Advertising, however, does not include stockholder communications, documents circulated by a state or federal agency, or communications relating to people who have already purchased or have contracted to purchase the subdivider's lands (except when concerning the sale of additional property).

All claims or representations contained in the advertising must be accurate and provable. In addition, the following practices are prohibited:

1. employing any device, scheme, or artifice to defraud;

2. making any untrue statement of a material fact or failing to state a material fact that, by its omissions, would tend to make the statement misleading;

3. engaging in any act, practice, or course of business that operates or would operate as a fraud or deceit upon any person.

Regulation 1600 further sets forth a list of 30 fraudulent, deceptive, and misleading advertising practices that can result in the suspension or revocation of a subdivided land registration and/or a subdivider's license.

Sales Contracts (Section 83.28)

Every subdivided land sales contract must fully state the legal description of the lot, parcel, unit, or interest to be disposed of and contain a disclosure similar to the federal Truth-in-Lending Act. The contract is voidable at the discretion of the purchaser for a three-year period from the date of contract, if the land was not properly registered and/or the purchaser did not receive a current public offering statement. Each contract, agreement, or other evidence of indebtedness must expressly indicate that it is a document taken in connection with a subdivided land sale.

Rescission. Subdivided land purchasers have an unconditional right to rescind --that is, to break--any sales contract, agreement, or other evidence of indebtedness or revoke any offer within five days after delivery to the purchaser of a legible copy of the contract. Predating the document cannot affect or waive this right.

Each contract, agreement, or other evidence of indebtedness must contain one of the following notices, printed in type that is at least 4 points larger than the type used in the body of the document:

1. For land registered by notification: "Notice to Purchaser--You are entitled to rescind this agreement for any reason within five days from the date you actually received a legible copy of this document signed by all parties. The rescission must be in writing and mailed to the subdivider or his agent or the lender at the address stated in this document. Upon rescission you will receive a refund of all money paid." or;

2. For land registered by qualification: "Notice to Purchaser--You are entitled to rescind this agreement for any reason within five days from the date you actually received a legible copy of this document signed by all parties and a public offering statement. The rescission must be in writing and mailed to the subdivider or his agent or the lender at the address stated in this document. Upon rescission you will receive a refund of all money paid."

Each contract must provide enough blank space near the notice to allow the purchaser room to sign his or her name, acknowledging that the document has been read. No act of a purchaser can waive the right to rescind.

There is no prescribed form for the notice of rescission as long as it is in writing and expresses the purchaser's desire to void the agreement. If mailed, the notice takes effect when it is deposited in a mailbox, properly addressed and postage prepaid.

Blanket Encumbrances (Section 83.33)

When a subdivider acquires a blanket mortgage (see Chapter 15 in the text) to finance his or her purchase of lands for subdivision, he or she cannot subdivide and dispose of such lands until one or more of the following conditions are met:

1. All sums paid or advanced by the purchasers are placed in an escrow or similar depository account until one of the following occurs:

   a. The fee simple title contracted for is delivered to the purchaser with a complete release from financial encumbrances.
   b. One of the parties to the agreement defaults, and either the commissioner or a court of competent jurisdiction authorizes the disbursal of the funds.
   c. The funds are voluntarily returned to the purchaser.

2. The fee simple title is placed in trust under an agreement or trust acceptable to the commissioner. The title will be kept in trust until a proper release is obtained from each blanket encumbrance--including all taxes--and the title is delivered to the purchaser.

3. When the title is not delivered and a full release is not obtained from each blanket encumbrance, a surety bond is given to the commissioner. The bond, in an amount approved by the commissioner, provides for the return of monies paid or advanced by a purchaser toward any lot, parcel, or interest in the subdivision.

4. The blanket encumbrance contains a provision subordinating the subdivider's rights to those of the purchaser. The provision must further state that the subdivider is able to secure releases from the blanket encumbrance with respect to the property.

5. There must be an alternative plan that is acceptable to the commissioner.

Annual Report (Section 83.30)

Every subdivider must file an annual report with the commissioner within 120 days after the subdivider's fiscal year ends. Each report must be in a form prescribed by the commissioner and accompanied by a $50 fee. Failure to file a report will result in the cancellation of the subdivision's registration. In the event of such cancellation, the registration may be reinstated at a later date, following a filing of the report and payment of a $100 filing fee.

Changes Subsequent to Registration (Section 83.31)

Subdividers must within 30 days report any material changes in the information or documents included with an application for registration. An amendment fee of $25 must accompany such a report. In addition, all new advertising must be submitted to and approved by the commissioner prior to its use in Minnesota.

Inspection of Records (Section 83.32)

The subdivider must maintain all records pertaining to subdivided land sales or advertising. They are subject to inspection by the commissioner.

Other Operating Procedures

Regulations 1613, 1614, and 1615 pertain to numerous operating procedures, creation of an owner's association, general policies, recordable instruments, and apportionment of taxes. One should check these regulations thoroughly before preparing to engage in any business regarding subdivided lands.

Prohibited Acts (Section 83.33)

Anyone who engages in any unfair or deceptive act or practice concerning subdivided land offers and dispositions is subject to suspension or revocation of the subdivision registration or the subdivider's license. In addition, the use of any fraud, false pretense, false promise, or misrepresentation is prohibited under the act. These practices are prohibited whether or not any person has in fact been misled, deceived, or damaged.

Also prohibited are sales of options to purchase subdivided lands for more than 15 percent of the total purchase price of the parcel.

Investigation and Proceedings (Sections 83.34, 35, and 36)

The commissioner may conduct all necessary public and private investigations within or outside the state to determine if any person has violated or is about to violate any provision of the act. The commissioner or any person he or she designates may require or permit any person to file a written, sworn statement explaining the matter under investigation. In addition, the commissioner may subpoena witnesses, compel their attendance, take evidence, and require submission of all material relevant to the investigation. The commissioner may apply to district court for a contempt order against any person who fails to obey a subpoena or answer questions. The commissioner may also bring an action in district court to enjoin the subdivided land sales activities of a person under investigation.

When initiating a proceeding against a subdivider, the commissioner will schedule a hearing and notify the subdivider in writing. The notice will state the time, date, and place of the hearing, as well as the allegations of the charge raised. After giving notice and conducting a hearing, the commissioner may suspend or revoke a registration and may issue a cease and desist order to any subdivider or any other person if it is found that he or she has done or is about to do one of the following:

1. violated any provisions of the act or rules of the commissioner;

2. directly, or through an agent or employee, knowingly engaged in any false, deceptive, or misleading advertising, promotional, or sales methods to offer or dispose of subdivided lands;

3. made any material change in the advertising, plan of disposition, or development of subdivided lands after registration without first obtaining the commissioner's consent;

4. offered or disposed of any unregistered subdivided lands that are not exempt from the provisions of the act;

5. been convicted of a crime involving fraud, deception, false pretense, misrepresentation, false advertising, or dishonest dealing in real estate transactions after registering the subdivided lands (this applies to the subdivider as well as all officers, directors, partners, principals, or agents associated with him or her);

6. disposed of, concealed, or diverted any funds or assets of any person so as to defeat the rights of subdivision purchasers;

7. failed to faithfully perform any stipulation or agreement made with the commissioner to induce the commissioner to grant or reinstate any registration or permit any promotional plan or public offering statement;

8. made any misrepresentations or concealed material in an application for registration;

9. is permanently or temporarily enjoined by any court of competent jurisdiction from engaging in subdivided land sales;

10. failed to pay any filing or registration fee.

Penalties and Civil Remedies (Section 83.37)

Any person who knowingly authorizes, directs, or aids in the publication, distribution, or circulation of any promotional material containing a false statement or misrepresentation is considered guilty of a gross misdemeanor. In addition, any person not complying with or violating any other section of the act is considered guilty of a misdemeanor. An individual who violates the requirements for registration, the public offering statement, or sales contracts, or who engages in deceptive and dishonest practices, is subject to a fine of not more than $1,000 for each violation.

Any person who fails to pay any filing or inspection fees and continues to dispose of subdivided land may be liable in a civil action brought by the Minnesota attorney general on behalf of the commissioner. Penalty in such actions requires payment of triple the initial fees.

Aggrieved parties may file suit and recover damages incurred through a subdivided land purchase where fraud, false pretense, misrepresentation, false promises, or unfair and deceptive acts were employed, whether or not the purchaser has in fact been misled, deceived, or damaged. The aggrieved party may recover the consideration paid for the lot, parcel, unit, or interest in the subdivided lands, together with six percent annual interest, compounded from the date of purchase. He or she is also entitled to recover property taxes paid, attorney's fees, and other costs, less the amount of income received from the land. If the aggrieved person no longer owns the lot, he or she may still recover the amount that would normally be recoverable if he or she still owned the land, less the value of the land when sold and six percent annual interest on that amount, compounded from the day of disposition. All actions must be commenced within three years of the date that the aggrieved party discovered the unfair or deceptive act.

20/Subdividing and Property Development

QUESTIONS

1. Frank Hamburg suffered a huge financial loss connected with the purchase of subdivided land through what was later found to be a deceptive sales practice.

   I. The person who sold him the property can be subject to criminal charges if Hamburg decides to prosecute.
   II. Hamburg can still recover a portion of his losses, even if he already sold the property.

   a. I only
   b. II only
   c. both I and II
   d. neither I nor II

2. A developer must submit for approval all subdivided land sales advertising to the:

   I. Commissioner of Commerce.
   II. Real Estate Commission.

   a. I only
   b. II only
   c. both I and II
   d. neither I nor II

3. A public offering statement:

   I. must be given to each purchaser of subdivided lands.
   II. is almost identical with every parcel of land.

   a. I only
   b. II only
   c. both I and II
   d. neither I nor II

4. Richard Phelps bought a parcel of land without knowing that it was not registered with the state.

   I. His land sales contract is considered void.
   II. Phelps must negotiate a new contract with the seller after the property is registered.

   a. I only
   b. II only
   c. both I and II
   d. neither I nor II

5. Bernie Schwartz just became the proud owner of a parcel of subdivided land in sunny Florida. Although he just signed the sales contract this morning, he is now having second thoughts about the whole deal and might want to get out of the agreement. If Schwartz decides to rescind the land sales contract, how soon must he do so?

   a. within 24 hours
   b. within five days
   c. within one week
   d. He cannot rescind the contract--it is a legally binding agreement.

128   MINNESOTA SUPPLEMENT for Modern Real Estate Practice

6. Through an investigation by the commissioner, it was found that Subdivider Hank Harrison published in a local newspaper a subdivided land sales advertisement that contained many false, misleading, and deceptive statements. In doing this, Harrison has committed a:

   a. misdemeanor.
   b. gross misdemeanor.
   c. felony.
   d. violation of the Minnesota Statute of Frauds.

7. Which of the following subdivided land offers would not be under the jurisdiction of the Minnesota Subdivided Land Sales Practice Act?

   a. The Duluth Daily News carries the following ad in its classified section:

      Retire in style! Florida awaits!
      Construction sites from $2,400!
      Write--Box 12, Tallahassee, Fla.

   b. WMJ-TV in Minneapolis broadcasts the following spot announcement:

      Hi friends--Ed Platt here, telling you
      to call now! That's right--there's still
      plenty of land left in sunny Arizona!
      Lots and lots of it! So reserve your
      lots now. Call toll-free--800-363-7788.

   c. The following ad appears in the International Falls Tribune:

      Tired of the cold? C'mmmmmmmooooonnnnn
      down! Down to Minnesota, that is! New
      subdivision opening soon! Only 35 miles
      from downtown St. Paul. Write now--Box 55,
      St. Paul, Minnesota.

   d. USA Today publishes the following ad:

      Buy today--get rich tomorrow!
      No money down--build equity immediately!
      New subdivision in Hot Times, Nevada.
      Call toll-free--800-399-2929.

8. If a proposed subdivision consists of 101 lots, the subdivider must register by:

   I. notification.
   II. qualification.

   a. I only   c. both I and II
   b. II only   d. neither I nor II

21

Fair Housing Laws and Ethical Practices

The Minnesota Human Rights Act, Minnesota Statutes, Chapter 363, prescribes the practice of fair housing in this state. The act prohibits discrimination in several areas, including housing, employment, public services, and education. It is enforced by the state Department of Human Rights, headed by a commissioner who is appointed by the governor. The department receives charges of unfair discriminatory practices, conducts impartial investigations of the charges, determines whether or not discrimination has occurred, and attempts to eliminate the discriminatory practices through education, conference, conciliation, persuasion, and litigation.

The U.S. Department of Housing and Urban Development has ruled that the Minnesota Human Rights Act is "substantially equivalent" to the Federal Fair Housing Act. As explained in Chapter 21 of the text, complaints of discriminatory practices in Minnesota, including complaints filed with the U.S. Department of Housing and Urban Development, are investigated by state enforcement agencies.

DISCRIMINATORY PRACTICES

The law regarding fair housing is contained in Section 363.03, Subd. 2 of Minnesota Statutes. It addresses the practices of the following persons:

1. an owner, developer, lessee, sublessee, assignee, or managing agent of a real estate owner;

2. any real estate broker or salesperson;

3. any bank, mortgage company, insurance company or financial institution to which financing application is made;

4. any employees or agents of these persons or companies.

Thus, these provisions apply to all persons who engage in real estate practices, not just to real estate licensees.

The law prohibits discrimination on the basis of race, color, creed, religion, national origin, sex, marital status, status with regard to public assistance, disability, or familial status. It describes discriminatory practices as:

1. refusing to sell, rent, lease, negotiate with, or otherwise denying or withholding from any person or group of persons any real property;

2. discriminating against any person or group of persons in the terms, conditions, or privileges of the sale, rental, or lease of any real property or in the furnishing of facilities or services connected with such property;

3. being involved in any way with the creation, publication, or circulation of any printed material that expresses, directly or indirectly, any limitation, specification, or discrimination or attempts to make such discriminations (such printed material includes advertisements; signs; forms of purchase agreement, rental, or lease of real property; and records or inquiries in connection with prospective purchases, rentals, or leases);

4. evicting or prohibiting a tenant from renewing any lease because of familial status that commenced during a tenancy unless at least one year has elapsed since the familial status changed and the landlord has given the tenant at least six months' prior written notice of the intended action. Familial status refers to one or more minors residing with their parents or parent, guardian, or designee.

The familial status provisions of Minnesota law will not apply to adult-only rental buildings until all of the leases in effect on April 11, 1980, have expired. The provisions of the law also do not apply to a number of situations where an action or decision is based upon familial status. Minors may be prohibited from:

1. one building (defined as a structure housing five or more units) in a two-building complex or up to one-third of the buildings in complexes of three or more buildings. The owners must designate the exempt buildings and file the designation with the commissioner. After the designation has been filed, the owner may not withdraw it and so designate another building for a period of one year;

2. condominiums, except for conversion condominiums created after April 11, 1980 that were not created from an existing adults-only building;

3. buildings in which a majority of the units are occupied by at least one elderly person over 55 years of age or all of the units are available to elderly people only;

4. owner-occupied dwellings of one to four units;

5. up to one-third of the units in a building that is not part of a complex;

6. a building subject to a valid certificate filed with the commissioner and in which at least one-half of the units are occupied by at least one elderly person.

Note that in Minnesota prospective sellers or landlords may discriminate on the basis of age, pet ownership, or whether prospective buyers or tenants are smokers. A landlord may also evict noisy tenants.

Exemptions (Section 363.02, Subd. 2)

The provisions of the law do not apply to (a) the rental of rooms in a permanent residence operated by a nonprofit organization when the discrimination is by sex, and (b) the rental by an owner or occupier of a one-family accommodation in which he or she resides to another person if the discrimination is by sex, marital status, status with regard to public assistance, or disability.

Discrimination--Misrepresenting the Character of a Neighborhood

The law specifically prohibits any real estate licensee from representing that a change has, will, or may occur in the composition of the owners or occupants in a block, neighborhood, or area regarding their race, color, creed, religion, national origin, sex, marital status, status with respect to public assistance, or disability for the purpose of inducing real estate transactions. The licensee is prohibited from representing that such a change in the area will or may result in undesirable consequences, including, but not limited to, the lowering of property values, an increase in criminal or antisocial behavior, or a decline in the quality of schools or other public facilities. Such illegal practices are commonly referred to as blockbusting.

Financial Discrimination

Section 363.03, Subd. 2 also prohibits unfair discriminatory lending practices based on race, color, creed, religion, national origin, sex, marital status, status with regard to public assistance, or disability. The law considers it unfairly discriminatory for a person, bank, banking organization, mortgage company, insurance company, or other financial institution to:

1. discriminate in the granting, withholding, extending, modifying, or renewing of financial assistance; in the rates, terms, conditions, or privileges of any financial assistance; or in the extension of such services;

2. use any form of application or make any record or inquiry into applications for financial assistance for any person or group of persons that directly or indirectly expresses any limitations, specifications, or discriminations or any intent to make such limitations;

3. financially discriminate against any person or group of persons who desire to purchase, lease, acquire, construct, rehabilitate, repair, or maintain real property in a specific urban or rural area because of the social, economic, or environmental conditions of the area. (This is known as redlining).

ENFORCEMENT

As mentioned earlier, the Minnesota Human Rights Act is administered by the Department of Human Rights. Any person aggrieved by a violation of the law may file a charge with the Department of Human Rights. Complaints may be filed at the State Department of Human Rights, 240 Bremer Building, St. Paul, Minnesota 55101, (612) 296-5663.

A charge must be filed with the department within 300 days after the occurrence of the discriminatory act. The charge must contain the name and address of the person alleged to have committed the discriminatory act and must set forth the details of the action and any other information required.

When a charge is filed, an investigator conducts an impartial investigtion of the allegations. On the basis of the investigative findings and recommendations, the commissioner will determine whether or not discrimination has occurred. When the commissioner finds that there is evidence to support a charge of unfair discriminatory practice, the respondent is notified and requested to participate in a conciliation conference. If attempts to conciliate the matter are unsuccessful, the matter is forwarded to litigation, and a public hearing is scheduled. A respondent is required to answer the allegations of discriminatory practice at the hearing.

At any time after determining the existence of unfair discriminatory practices, the commissioner may file a petition in district court to restrain the defendant from such practices, pending an official hearing.

If the hearing panel or examiner finds that a respondent has committed an unfair discriminatory practice, the respondent will be ordered to cease and desist from the practice. Such an order is the final decision of the department and has the force and effect of law. In all cases, the examiner may order the defendant to pay compensatory damages (not including those for mental anguish and suffering) and attorney's fees to an aggrieved party who has suffered from discrimination. The panel or examiner may also order the defendant to pay punitive damages of up to $6,000. In addition, the panel or examiner may order the sale or lease of the housing accommodations or property to such an aggrieved party.

All decisions of the panel or examiner are subject to proper judicial review.

PROMOTION OF FAIR HOUSING

Victims of housing discrimination must be made aware of what discrimination is, what their rights are, and what remedies are available through local boards of Realtors' and municipal, state and federal laws. Several groups throughout Minnesota promote fair housing opportunity.

The U.S. Department of Housing and Urban Development has funded citizen groups to promote fair housing. The Community Housing Resource Boards, using a variety of promotional methods, increase community awareness for fair and equal housing opportunity. Community Housing Resource Boards exist in Minneapolis, Saint Paul, Mankato, Anoka, and Dakota counties.

21/Fair Housing Laws and Ethical Practices   133

Testing for housing discrimination and investigating the extent and kind of unfair practices are the primary objectives of the Minnesota Society for Open Communities. When a housing discrimination complaint is received by the Minnesota Society for Open Communities, and the case requires further investigation by testing, trained testers begin making inquiries as if they were seeking to rent or buy the property. If unfair practices arise, such as a black couple asked to pay larger amounts or offered different terms and conditions, discrimination is occurring. When discrimination is found, the appropriate federal, state, or municipal laws can be enforced for a remedy.

QUESTIONS

1. The owner of a residential apartment building may legally refuse to rent to:

   I. young single women.
   II. families with small children.

   a. I only   c. both I and II
   b. II only   d. neither I nor II

2. One of the tenants in Nancy Kupidloski's apartment building is very noisy and disturbs the other tenants. However, antidiscrimination laws will prohibit her from evicting the tenant:

   I. if the tenant is black.
   II. if the tenant is Hindu.

   a. I only   c. both I and II
   b. II only   d. neither I nor II

3. Because disability is a protected class under the Minnesota Human Rights Act, a landlord:

   I. cannot legally refuse a handicapped person housing on the basis of his or her disability.
   II. must make structural accommodations for disabled persons if so requested.

   a. I only   c. both I and II
   b. II only   d. neither I nor II

4. Danny Prince owns a 25-unit apartment building. Because he feels that welfare recipients are generally poor credit risks:

   I. he may legally refuse to rent to such persons.
   II. he may charge such persons a higher security deposit than is charged other tenants.

   a. I only   c. both I and II
   b. II only   d. neither I nor II

5. Decisions of the hearing panel or examiner concerning discrimination complaints:

   I. are final and have the effect of law.
   II. may not be appealed to higher courts.

   a. I only
   b. II only
   c. both I and II
   d. neither I nor II

6. Jack Twilley feels that he has been the victim of an unfair discriminatory practice committed by a local real estate broker. He must file a complaint against the broker within how many days of the alleged discrimination?

   a. 100
   b. 300
   c. 50
   d. 30

7. Which of the following people are exempt from regulation under the Minnesota Fair Housing Law?

   a. licensed brokers and salespersons
   b. private citizens
   c. secretaries and receptionists employed by real estate brokers
   d. none of the above--the laws apply to all persons

8. Which of the following situations is not in violation of the Minnesota Fair Housing Law?

   a. Property Manager Joe Kelley refuses to rent an apartment to an unmarried couple who live together and are otherwise qualified.
   b. The Locust Loan Company of St. Paul, as a general policy, avoids granting home-improvement loans to individuals in "changing neighborhoods."
   c. Real Estate Broker Harvey Hall purposely neglects to show a black family any property listing of homes in all-white neighborhoods.
   d. Agnes Taylor, a widow, is attempting to rent her spare bedroom but will only rent it to another woman.

9. Which of the following situations is an example of blockbusting?

   a. Peter Wolf has decided to sell his home because a Mexican family moved in on the next block. He is now urging his former neighbors to do the same.
   b. Insurance salesperson Ichabod McCloskey is spreading the word around a particular neighborhood that an increase in the number of Indian-Americans living in the area will raise auto and homeowner's insurance rates.
   c. Ivan Spinelli has six daughters. His friend Sam Shovel, a local real estate broker, has warned him repeatedly about the dangers of rape in a "changing neighborhood."
   d. Real estate salesperson Judy Dwyer has discovered that in a given neighborhood, she can almost double her listings if she tells homeowners that their property values are sure to decline in the coming years as the neighborhood becomes racially integrated.

23

Closing the Real Estate Transaction

THE CLOSING

In Minnesota, the majority of real estate transactions are closed in the office of either the title insurance company, the financial institution, or the broker. Normally, the broker presides at the closing, but either the buyers or the sellers may prefer an attorney to represent them and/or direct the closing. Although some brokers employ professional closers to conduct closings, every broker should understand the closing process and be able to prepare the closing statements.

Title Evidence

The seller must furnish the buyer with written title evidence prior to the closing--either an abstract of title or registered property abstract or certificate.

In addition, the seller should have the title evidence certified by a title insurance or abstract company to within 30 days of the date of closing. It must be updated to the day of closing by the title company or abstractor to ensure that the title conveyed is indeed clear, as described in Chapter 23 of the text. If the property is registered and the owner's certificate of title has been removed from the Torrens office, the certificate must be surrendered to the buyer at the time of closing in order for him or her to file the documents with the registrar of titles.

Documents Needed at the Closing

Some of the documents usually executed at the closing are:

1. The instrument of conveyance--usually a form of warranty deed (although in some instances a quitclaim deed may be used), signed by the seller. If a contract for deed is the instrument of conveyance, both buyer and seller must sign. Any deed or contract for deed must state the grantee's name and address and the address to which the real estate tax statements are to be sent.

2. A bill of sale--for all the items of personal property set forth in the purchase agreement, signed by the seller.

3. *An affidavit of liens and judgments*--signed by the seller, stating his or her occupation and military status and any liens, claims, or judgments against the property to be conveyed. In addition, the lender or title company may require an affidavit of liens and judgments from the buyer.

4. *A certificate of real estate value (CRV)*--which must be included with any deed or certificate for deed which is to be filed or recorded. A CRV must include the value of any personal property included in the sale price.

5. *Purchaser's affidavit of registered land*--must be included if the property is registered under the Torrens system.

6. *Mortgage note and deed*--to be executed by the buyer when the purchase is to be financed.

7. *Other documents*--used to cover special provisions in the purchase agreement, usually executed by the seller.

At the closing, the broker should review these documents with all parties to the transaction to ensure that names are spelled correctly, the legal description is correct, the signatures of the persons executing the documents are the same as the typewritten names, and that the documents are properly notarized. In addition, the broker must be sure that any recordable documents contain statements as to who prepared them.

Closing Procedures

At the time of the closing, the broker should remind the buyer to apply for homestead if he or she intends to occupy the property as a residence. The buyer should also be given any keys to the premises if the possession date is the same as the closing date.

If the buyer is assuming the seller's existing mortgage, he or she should be notified of the amount and due date of the next mortgage payment and should be provided with a statement of all current information regarding the mortgage. If possible, the buyer should receive any payment book or amortization schedule pertaining to the mortgage at the time of closing. *It is important that the buyer be aware of the terms of the assumed mortgage, particularly the maturity date.* Mortgage payments must be current at the time of assumption.

If the transaction involves a contract for deed, the broker should be prepared to advise both parties on the various aspects of this type of financing. This generally includes an explanation of the different clauses included in the document as well as a discussion regarding the salability of property under the contract. In addition, the broker should ensure that the information included in the contract--legal descriptions, rents, easements, and so forth is correct. The broker, however, should not attempt to give legal advice regarding the terms of the contract--this is the job of a practicing attorney.

If the municipality in which the property is located requires any inspection or compliance with building and/or occupancy codes, the seller should, at the time of closing, provide the buyer with a certificate of inspection or compliance. If any work has been done or improvements made on the property within 120 days of the closing, care must be taken to ensure that all suppliers of labor and materials have been paid. The seller should provide lien waivers obtained from the general contractor and all workers, materialmen, and architects.

If the property has insurable value and any form of financing is involved, the buyer must provide an insurance policy insuring any lender's interest in the property as well as the interest of the fee owner. Lenders usually require that a receipt from the insurance carrier and, in some cases, the policy be submitted prior to closing. These prove that the buyer has paid the first-year premiums and that a policy has actually been written.

The buyer's down payment (less any earnest money already deposited with the broker) should be in the form of a cashier's check, certified check, money order, or other type of certified funds. If the real estate to be conveyed is income property and the seller is to receive the rents for the day of the closing, the seller should pay all expenses for that day. Any rent security deposits held by the seller should be turned over to the buyer, together with any interest on the deposits as may be required by law.

THE CLOSING STATEMENT

The buyer and seller should both receive closing statements at the closing (see Regulation 1523). Unless otherwise provided for in the purchase agreement, the expenses for which each party is responsible are as follows:

Buyer's Expenses

The buyer's expenses are:

1. hazard insurance premiums;
2. title examination;
3. title insurance;
4. loan expenses (mortgage recording fees or registration taxes, credit reports, etc.);
5. recording fees for the title-conveying instruments.

Seller's Expenses

The seller's expenses are:

1. recording fees for any documents necessary to clear the title (quitclaim deeds, lien and judgment affidavits, etc.);
2. abstract continuation or registered property abstract;
3. preparation of closing documents;
4. broker's commission;
5. state deed tax;
6. discount or points on VA mortgages;
7. assessments (can be assumed);
8. pending assessment searches.

138   MINNESOTA SUPPLEMENT for Modern Real Estate Practice

Prorations

Generally, prorations for such items as interest, real estate taxes, and insurance premiums in Minnesota are as discussed in the text.

The broker should retain on file all copies of closing statements and related documents.

CLOSING PROBLEM

Complete the closing statement forms at the end of this chapter. Prepare one for the seller and one for the buyer according to the facts given in this description of a typical real estate transaction. All prorations should be made on the basis of the actual number of days in the month of closing. Remember to carry out all computations to three decimal places and round off only after you have arrived at the final figure for each computation.

Data Describing the Real Estate Transaction

Beverly Beauchamp, a salesperson for the Champlin Real Estate Brokerage, secured a six-month, exclusive-right-to-sell listing on December 13, 1984, from Maurice and Mabel Armbruster. The listing was for their home, located at 211 North Banana Avenue, Cherryvale, Minnesota, 50000 (Hennepin County). The house was built in 1953 of brick construction, and there is a detached one-car garage with a paved side drive on the property. The lot measures 60 feet by 150 feet, and the legal description is lot 27, block 8, Scenic Heights Addition to Cherryvale, Hennepin County, Minnesota. The Armbrusters own the property in fee and are including their carpeting and window shades in the total selling price of $45,000.

The First American Federal Savings and Loan of Cherryvale holds a first mortgage on the property. The mortgage will have an unpaid balance of $29,367.52 as of March 1. Interest on the loan is charged at the rate of 8 percent per year, with the final payment to be made within 13 years. The savings and loan has indicated that this mortgage may be assumed by a qualified buyer. Monthly payments of $287.87 are applied first to the interest, then to the balance of the principal.

The Armbrusters had taken out a three-year fire and hazard insurance policy on the property, which was effective January 1, 1983. They paid $561 for the coverage, and the new owners may assume the policy for the remainder of its term.

Real estate taxes payable in 1985 have not yet been paid (the first installment of $358 is due May 15, 1985). No special assessments are pending on the property. The agreed-upon broker's commission is seven percent of the gross sale price.

On January 21, 1985, the salesperson obtained a bona fide offer from Mark and Helen Time to purchase the real estate for $43,000. The offer was on the basis of the buyer's assumption of the balance of the existing mortgage, with the remainder in cash.

Possession was desired as of the date of closing--March 15, 1985. The offer was accompanied by a check for $1,000 in earnest money. The Armbrusters accepted the offer, and a contract was prepared on the basis of the Times' terms. The Armbrusters and the Times have agreed to prorate the real estate taxes due in 1985.

The expenses for closing this transaction also include the following:

1. Abstract extension--$125;

2. Title insurance policy--$150;

3. State deed tax--$1.10 per $500 or fraction thereof of the total selling price, less any lien remaining;

4. Recording fees--$1.00 per page; $5.00 minimum per document;

5. Mortgage assumption fee--the savings and loan charges 1/10 of 1% of the mortgage value.

CLOSING STATEMENT

Property Address _____
Seller _____
Buyer _____
Legal Description _____

	Date: _____		Debit		Credit	

Sale Price _____
Earnest Money _____

New Mortgage _____
New Contract or Second Mortgage _____
First Mortgage Paid/Assumed _____
    Principal $_____
    Interest from ____ to ____ $_____
    Penalty $_____
        Sub-Total $_____
    Less Reserves $_____
    Total $_____
Contract for Deed or Second Mortgage _____
    Principal $_____
    Interest from ____ to ____ $_____
    Less State Deed Tax $_____
    Total $_____
Abstract Extension _____ $_____
Title Insurance Premium _____
Judgment Searches _____
Recording Fees _____
    Mortgage $ _____ Affidavit $ _____ W.D. $ _____
    Q.C.D. $ _____ Satisfaction $ _____ C.D. $ _____
    Other $ _____
State Deed Tax _____
Mortgage Registration Tax _____
Special Assessments _____
    Levied $ _____ Pending $ _____
    Assessment Search _____
Taxes: Delinquent $ _____ Current $ _____
        Interest $ _____ Penalty $ _____
Placement Fee _____
Assumption Fee _____
Adjustments _____

    Rent _____ Gas/Fuel _____
    Water/Sewer _____ Electricity _____
Broker's Commission _____
Other _____
_____
_____
_____

    Sub-Totals _____
Balance of Down Payment _____

    TOTALS _____

23/Closing the Real Estate Transaction   141

CLOSING STATEMENT

Property Address _____
Seller _____
Buyer _____
Legal Description _____

	Date: _____	Debit	Credit
Sale Price _____			
Earnest Money _____			
New Mortgage _____			
New Contract or Second Mortgage _____			
First Mortgage Paid/Assumed _____			
Principal	$ _____		
Interest from ____ to ____	$ _____		
Penalty	$ _____		
Sub-Total	$ _____		
Less Reserves	$ _____		
Total	$ _____		
Contract for Deed or Second Mortgage _____			
Principal	$ _____		
Interest from ____ to ____	$ _____		
Less State Deed Tax	$ _____		
Total	$ _____		
Abstract Extension _____	$ _____		
Title Insurance Premium _____			
Judgment Searches _____			
Recording Fees _____			
Mortgage $ ____ Affidavit $ ____ W.D.	$ _____		
Q.C.D. $ ____ Satisfaction $ ____ C.D.	$ _____		
Other $ ____			
State Deed Tax _____			
Mortgage Registration Tax _____			
Special Assessments _____			
Levied $ ____ Pending $ ____			
Assessment Search _____			
Taxes: Delinquent $ ____ Current $ ____			
Interest $ ____ Penalty $ ____			
Placement Fee _____			
Assumption Fee _____			
Adjustments _____			
Rent ____ Gas/Fuel ____			
Water/Sewer ____ Electricity ____			
Broker's Commission _____			
Other _____			
Sub-Totals _____			
Balance of Down Payment _____			
TOTALS _____			

Solution to Closing Problem

Check all of your completed entries and computations against those listed and detailed below.

Purchase price. The purchase price is a debit to the buyers because they have promised to pay in cash or otherwise account for the agreed-upon price of the real estate. It is a credit to the sellers because they will be reimbursed for the selling price of the property.

Earnest money deposit. The buyers have agreed to pay a total of $1,000 in earnest money, which is held by the broker. This is a credit to the buyers because the amount is deducted from the total sales price of the house.

Assumed mortgage interest. The unpaid balance of the assumed mortgage on March 15 was the March 1 balance, and the prorated interest is based on that figure. Interest proration for March 1 to 15 is as follows:

$29,367.52 x 8% = $2,349.401 per year
$2,349.401 ÷ 12 = $195.783 per month
$195.783 ÷ 31 = $6.315 per day
$6.315 x 15 = $94.73 interest for March 1 to 15

Since the buyers agree to assume the sellers' remaining mortgage debt, the balance of the remaining principal is credited to them, as well as the interest that accrued on that principal while the sellers had possession of the property for part of the month of March. Since the sellers are relieved of their indebtedness for the remaining principal and interest for the part of March in which they were in possession of the property, both amounts are debited to them. In effect, the sellers are paying off their indebtedness with part of the property's purchase price.

Abstract extension. An abstracting company will prepare the abstract of title (since the property is not registered under the Torrens system), as agreed upon. This expense is debited to the sellers.

Title insurance premium. As agreed upon, the buyer pays for the title insurance as a means of verifying that the title conveyed is indeed clear, so this expense is debited to the buyer.

Recording fees. The buyers must record the warranty deed conveyed to them (W.D. on the statement), so this charge is debited to them.

Assumption fee. The savings and loan charges a 1/10 of 1% service charge for a buyer's assumption of an existing mortgage.

1/10 of 1% = .001
.001 x $29,367.52 = $29.37

Since it is the buyers who are assuming the loan, this expense is debited to them.

Fire and hazard insurance. Since the fire and hazard insurance was prepaid in a three-year policy to expire on December 31, 1985, the sellers are credited with the portion of the coverage remaining at the date of closing, and the buyers assuming the policy are debited the same amount.

> 3-year policy: $561.00
> 1 year: $561 ÷ 3 = $187 per year
> 9 months: $187 ÷ 12 = 15.583 per month
> $15.583 x 9 = $140.247
> 16 days: $15.583 ÷ 31 = .502 per day
> $.502 x 16 = $8.032
> $140.247 + $8.032 = $148.279, or $148.28

Broker's commission. The sellers must pay the broker's commission rate of 7% of the selling price of $43,000, as agreed upon. Since the sellers owe the broker this amount, it is a debit to the sellers.

State deed tax. The Minnesota state deed tax is $1.10 per $500 or fraction thereof of the total purchase price less the principal amount of the mortgage assumed by the buyers.

> $43,000 - $29,367.52 = $13,632.48 taxable purchase price
> $13,632.48 ÷ $500 = 27.264 = 28 (fraction thereof)
> 28 x $1.10 = $30.80

Since the transfer fee is always charged to the sellers, they are debited with this expense.

Taxes. Minnesota real estate taxes become a lien on real property on January 1. Taxes are due in two installments--May 15 and October 15. Since the sellers have not yet paid any property taxes during 1985, they, in fact, owe taxes for January, February, and 15 days of March. The tax would be computed as follows:

> 1 year: $716
> $716 ÷ 365 = $1.962 per day
>
> January: 31 days
> February: 28 days
> March: 15 days
>   74 days
>
> 74 x $1.962 = $145.19

Since the sellers haven't paid this portion of their taxes yet, the amount will be debited to them and credited to the buyers, who will eventually have to pay it.

Totaling the buyers' debit and credit columns. After adding all of the buyers' credits and debits, the debits should be greater than the credits. Subtracting the credits from the debits, the remainder is the amount owed by the buyers.

> Total buyers' debits $43,332.65
> Total buyers' credits   - 30,607.44
> Amount owed by buyers $12,725.21

Totaling the sellers' debit and credit columns. After adding all of the sellers' debits and credits, the credits should be greater than the debits. Subtracting the debits from the credits, the remainder is the balance due the seller.

>   Total sellers' credits $43,148.28
>   Total sellers' debits   - 32,773.24
>   Balance due sellers $10,375.04

After totaling all four columns at the bottom, the two columns in the buyers' statement should balance. Likewise, the two columns in the sellers' statement should balance.

Recapitulation of checks and expenses. This summary is a means of verifying the accuracy of the closing statement. All cash received by the broker in the transaction is totaled, and the cash disbursed by the broker is subtracted from that total. The resulting balance should be $.00, indicating that there is exactly enough cash to meet all requirements, with no funds left over.

>   Broker receives (from buyers' statement)--
>   Earnest money deposit $ 1,000.00
>   Balance due from buyers   12,725.21
> $13,725.21
>
>   Broker disburses--
>   Buyers' expenses:
>   Title insurance $ 150.00
>   Recording fees   5.00
>   Assumption fee   29.37
> $ 184.37
>
>   Sellers' expenses:
>   Broker's commission $ 3,010.00
>   Abstract extension   125.00
>   State deed tax   30.80
> $ 3,165.80
>
>   Total expenses:
>   Buyers' $ 184.37
>   Sellers'   3,165.80
> $ 3,350.17
>   Due to seller   10,375.04
> $13,725.21

BUYER'S CLOSING STATEMENT

Property Address: 211 North Banana Avenue, Cherryvale, Minnesota 50000
Sellers: Maurice and Mabel Armbruster
Buyers: Mark and Helen Time
Legal Description: Lot 27, block 8, Scenic Heights addition to Cherryvale, Hennepin County, Minnesota

Date: 3/15/84

Item	Debit	Credit
Sale Price $43,000	$43,000.00	
Earnest Money $1,000		$1,000.00
New Mortgage		
New Contract or Second Mortgage		
First Mortgage Paid/Assumed		29,462.25
Principal $29,367.52		
Interest from ___ to ___ $94.73		
Penalty $		
Sub-Total $		
Less Reserves $		
Total $29,462.25		
Contract for Deed or Second Mortgage		
Principal $		
Interest from ___ to ___ $		
Less State Deed Tax $		
Total $		
Abstract Extension $		
Title Insurance Premium $150	150.00	
Judgment Searches		
Recording Fees		
Mortgage $___ Affidavit $___ W.D. $3.00	3.00	
Q.C.D. $___ Satisfaction $___ C.D. $___		
Other $		
State Deed Tax		
Mortgage Registration Tax		
Special Assessments		
Levied $___ Pending $___		
Assessment Search		
Taxes: Delinquent $___ Current $ 2 mo. 15 days		148.19
Interest $___ Penalty $___		
Placement Fee		
Assumption Fee $29.37	29.37	
Adjustments FIRE & HAZARD INSURANCE, 9 mo. 16 days	148.28	
Rent ___ Gas/Fuel ___		
Water/Sewer ___ Electricity ___		
Broker's Commission		
Other		
Sub-Totals	43,330.65	30,610.44
Balance of Down Payment DUE TO SELLERS		12,720.21
TOTALS	43,330.65	43,330.65

SELLERS' CLOSING STATEMENT

Property Address   211 North Banana Avenue, Cherryvale, Minnesota 50000
Sellers   Maurice and Mabel Armbruster
Buyers   Mark and Helen Time
Legal Description   Lot 27, block 8, Scenic Heights addition to Cherryvale, Hennepin County, Minnesota

	Date: 3/15/84	Debit	Credit
Sale Price $43,000			$43,000.00
Earnest Money			
New Mortgage			
New Contract or Second Mortgage			
First Mortgage Paid/Assumed		$29,462.25	
Principal	$29,367.52		
Interest from ___ to ___	$ 94.73		
Penalty	$		
Sub-Total	$		
Less Reserves	$		
Total	$29,462.25		
Contract for Deed or Second Mortgage			
Principal	$		
Interest from ___ to ___	$		
Less State Deed Tax	$		
Total	$		
Abstract Extension $30.00	$	30.00	
Title Insurance Premium			
Judgment Searches			
Recording Fees			
Mortgage $___ Affidavit $___ W.D. $___			
Q.C.D. $___ Satisfaction $___ C.D. $___			
Other $___			
State Deed Tax $30.80		30.80	
Mortgage Registration Tax			
Special Assessments			
Levied $___ Pending $___			
Assessment Search			
Taxes: Delinquent $___ Current $ 2 mo. 15 days		148.19	
Interest $___ Penalty $___			
Placement Fee			
Assumption Fee			
Adjustments FIRE & HAZARD INSURANCE			148.28
Rent ___ Gas/Fuel ___			
Water/Sewer ___ Electricity ___			
Broker's Commission $3,010		3,010.00	
Other			
Sub-Totals		$32,681.24	$43,148.28
Balance of Down Payment DUE FROM BUYERS		10,467.04	
TOTALS		$43,148.28	$43,148.28

Real Estate Securities

As described in the text, blue sky law is a popular name for the act providing for the regulation and supervision of investments offered for sale to the public. Generally, before any security can be offered for sale in Minnesota, it must be registered with the Commissioner of Commerce as required by the Minnesota Securities Law. This is in addition to any requirements that may be imposed by the federal Securities and Exchange Commission (SEC), as discussed in the text.

SECURITIES DEFINED

The securities law (Chapter 80A, Minnesota Statutes) defines more than 20 different categories of securities. Stocks, bonds, and debentures are considered securities, as are less conventional forms of investment, the most important of which is the **investment contract**. This classification is used by the various regulatory agencies and courts to bring uncommon investment plans within the scope of the securities law. These investment opportunities frequently involve the real estate industry.

Generally, the courts have ruled that an investment opportunity will be considered an investment contract and, therefore, a security, if it involves the investment of money in a common enterprise with the expectation of profits or return on the investment, provided the profits are generated solely through the efforts of the promoter or third parties.

Under this definition, certain sales of real estate may be considered securities subject to regulation and registration under the securities law. Sales of contracts for deed, notes secured by mortgages, income properties, and condominiums may be securities if certain conditions are met. In each case, an attorney should be consulted to clarify the matter.

For example, if a seller offers a resort condominium for sale with a rental pool arrangement authorizing the pooling of rents in anticipation of paying a return to the owner, the sale of the unit may involve the sale of a security. In this instance, the buyer is involved in an investment of money (the purchase price of the unit) in a common enterprise (the seller's condo complex) for a return on the investment (rent) generated through actions of a third party (the seller), who finds tenants, collects rents, and manages the property on behalf of the buyer). If the buyer instead purchases the unit for strictly personal residential use or if he or she rents it out, collects rent, and manages it, no security would be involved.

SECURITIES REGISTRATION

In general, all securities not exempt from registration must be registered with the Minnesota Commissioner of Commerce prior to their sale. The securities law, however, provides for a number of exemptions to this rule. For real estate brokers and salespeople, two of the more significant registration exemptions contained in the Minnesota Securities Act are:

1. Five or fewer security interests are sold within a 12-month period. This exemption applies only if the securities are conveyed strictly for investment and not for resale, unless such securities are registered with the SEC.

2. Interests in a security are sold to 25 or fewer persons during a 12-month period. The seller, however, must file a "Statement of Issuer" form with the commissioner at least 10 days prior to such sales.

BROKER/DEALER LICENSING

Any person engaged in the business of buying or selling securities for others must be licensed under the securities law as a broker/dealer. In addition, persons representing broker/dealers must be registered as agents under the Minnesota law. As mentioned in Chapter 14, a licensed agent or broker/dealer who sells or offers to sell real estate-related registered securities need not be licensed as a real estate broker or salesperson. The broker/dealer-agent licensing structure is similar to that for broker-salespersons, discussed in Chapter 14, but it is far more complicated because of the application of federal law.

ANTIFRAUD PROVISIONS

The Minnesota law makes it illegal for any person involved in the offer, sale, or purchase of securities either directly or indirectly to:

1. employ any scheme, device, or artifice to defraud;

2. make an untrue statement or omit material facts concerning the security;

3. engage in any act, practice, or course of business that operates as a fraud or deceit against any person.

The antifraud provisions apply to all securities, regardless of whether or not they are exempt from registration under the law. Violation of these provisions exposes one to civil liability.

PENALTIES FOR VIOLATIONS

Willful violation of the Minnesota Securities Law is a felony, punishable by a fine of up to $5,000 and five years' imprisonment. In addition, violators are subject to administrative proceedings by the Commissioner of Commerce, who has the authority to issue a cease and desist order against the violators to prevent them from continuing their illegal activities.

In addition, persons selling securities in violation of the Minnesota Securities Law are subject to the civil penalties of an aggrieved party's damages plus court costs and attorney's fees.

QUESTIONS

1. Leo McGurk & Associates is selling the Chez Paul Restaurant to partners Tony Smoothe and Joe Neatobrava. It is agreed that while Smoothe and Neatobrava will own the venture and share equally in any profits or losses, McGurk & Associates will continue to operate the restaurant on their behalf. According to court rulings, this venture would probably be considered:

   I. an investment contract.
   II. a security.

   a. I only
   b. II only
   c. both I and II
   d. neither I nor II

2. Those who sell real estate on behalf of others for a living are called brokers and salespersons. Their counterparts in Minnesota securities sales are called:

   I. brokers.
   II. agents.

   a. I only
   b. II only
   c. both I and II
   d. neither I nor II

3. The antifraud provisions of the Minnesota Securities Law:

   a. apply to all securities.
   b. apply only to securities that must be registered with the Commissioner of Commerce.
   c. apply only to licensed persons selling securities.
   d. make it a gross misdemeanor to employ any scheme, artifice, or device to defraud in the offer, sale, or purchase of securities.

4. Sales of securities in Minnesota are subject to regulation and supervision by:

   a. the Minnesota Commissioner of Commerce.
   b. the federal Securities and Exchange Commission.
   c. both a and b
   d. none of the above

Real Estate Licensing Examination

Tests--you can't get away from them. A test is a measure of your ability to do something or your knowledge of a subject. The real estate licensing examination tests your knowledge of real estate principles and practices--knowledge you will need to participate in the real estate business as a broker or salesperson. Real estate licensing examinations vary in form and content throughout the United States. They utilize every form of question, from true-false and multiple-choice to essay questions and math problems. But whatever test form is used, each examination reflects the attitudes of the state's real estate licensing agency, stressing the areas of real estate knowledge that the members feel are important.

Can you locate and identify a parcel of real estate from the legal description given on the deed? Can you explain to your client how the difference between real estate and personal property affects the sale of a home? The Minnesota Commissioner of Commerce wants to determine the extent of your knowledge to find out whether you measure up to its standards. Modern Real Estate Practice and the Minnesota Supplement present a solid foundation of basic real estate principles and practices, as well as thorough coverage of principles and practices that are unique to Minnesota. This chapter is intended to help those applicants who are planning to take the Minnesota real estate licensing examination for either brokers or salespersons.

The Minnesota real estate licensing examination is prepared and administered by an independent testing service--the Educational Testing Service (ETS) of Princeton, New Jersey, under the supervision of the Minnesota Real Estate Commission. A number of states subscribe to the ETS program, which tests your reasoning process as well as your real estate knowledge. In each state, the program is adapted to local real estate laws and practices and the priorities of the state's licensing agency. All questions are multiple-choice, and the exams are machine-scored, so you will mark your answers on a special answer sheet.

The examinations for brokers and for salespersons are given in two parts. The first section on either examination is called the **Uniform Test** and consists of 80 general real estate questions. The second section, the **State Test**, consists of 40 questions on Minnesota laws and practices, including the Real Estate License Law and Rules and Regulations, the Subdivided Land Sales Practice Act, and the Human Rights Act--all discussed in this text.

TEST FORMAT

The Uniform Test in the salesperson examination covers the following topics:

1. Real estate contracts--13 percent

2. Financing--40 percent

3. Real estate ownership (deeds, title, condominiums, fair housing) --22 percent

4. Real estate brokerage (agency, property management, settlement procedures)--24 percent

5. Real estate valuation (appraisal, planning and zoning, legal descriptions)--17 percent

The Uniform Test in the broker examination covers the following topics:

1. Brokerage--35 percent

2. Contracts and legal aspects--27 percent

3. Finance and investment--23 percent

4. Pricing and valuation--15 percent

One form of multiple-choice question that appears throughout this text includes two statements that may or may not be true. You are asked to decide whether the true statement is the first one, the second one, both of them, or neither of them. For example, consider the following question:

29. The definition of real estate includes:

   I. mineral rights.
   II. improvements.

   a. I only   c. both I and II
   b. II only   d. neither I nor II

In answering this type of question, you must always consider both statements. If you read the question too quickly, you may see that statement I is indeed true and mark answer a without reading statement II. In this case, statement II is also true, so the correct answer is actually c. Answer a is incorrect. If you have answered the question correctly and filled in your answer sheet properly, the line for that answer will appear as follows:

```
      a    b    c    d
29. [ ]  [ ]  [■]  [ ]
```

These questions are valuable because you can be tested on two different principles in the same question. This form of multiple-choice question appears throughout the Minnesota licensing examination.

Mathematics

Math problems relating to real estate transactions generally make up a significant percentage of the Minnesota real estate licensing examination. The problems you will be asked to solve include the following calculations:

    area   profit
    commissions   prorations
    cost   rent
    interest   sales price
    percentage   value

As a real estate licensee, you will have to know how to make such calculations in order to advise your clients. Similar math problems have been included throughout this text. If you are having difficulty with such problems, you may want to secure a copy of Mastering Real Estate Mathematics, by Ventolo, Allaway, and Irby, published by Real Estate Education Company, 500 North Dearborn Street, Chicago, Illinois 60610. You will find an order form for this self-instructional text in the back of this book.

Problems in Comprehension and Application

While the Minnesota real estate licensing examination is designed to find out how much you know, it is also designed to find out how well you can think and apply your knowledge in appropriate situations. Many of these questions simply involve reading comprehension. Can you read a statement or form and answer questions based on what you've read? Others involve reading comprehension in combination with application. Can you read a selection or problem and answer questions based on what you have read and what you know about certain real estate principles?

Plat problem. The Questions section of Chapter 9 asks a series of questions based on information shown in a plat of the Honeysuckle Hills Subdivision. Most likely, there will be a similar exercise on the licensing examination. There are no tricks involved here. The information asked for in the questions is plainly printed on the plat. For example: Which lot has the most frontage on Wolf Road? The dimensions of all lots are given on the plat; just look at the lots that border on Wolf Road and determine the correct answer. In this case it is Lot 8. In similar questions you should determine the correct answer, find it among the choices given for that question, and mark the correct corresponding letter on your answer sheet.

Legal descriptions. Another problem you may be asked to solve on the licensing examination is locating a parcel of land on a diagram from a written legal description. The given diagram may show a large piece of land divided into smaller parcels, with all boundaries and natural landmarks marked. The parcel you must find would be indicated in a detailed metes and bounds description. If you read the description slowly, following the boundaries on the diagram, you will easily identify the correct parcel. Legal descriptions are covered in Chapter 9.

Instrument preparation and analysis. On the salesperson examination, you will find a section of questions involving a real estate transaction. You will be given a completed listing agreement and an agreement of sale indicating the details of this transaction, including a physical description of the property, financial information about the property and the seller, and the details of the actual sale. Then you will be asked to answer a series of questions based upon the information contained in the listing agreement and agreement of sale.

The key to answering this type of question, as with all the questions you will encounter in your studies or on the examination, is to read the question carefully and ask yourself: What is the examiner asking? What do I have to know in order to answer this question? Pinpointing the question this way makes it that much easier to identify the correct answer. With a general information question, you look at the choices and select the most nearly correct answer. With a property summary or other comprehension question, you now know what to look for when you refer back to the document. Once you have located the proper information in the property summary, you can choose the correct answer to the question.

Questions of this kind are included in the Questions section at the end of this chapter.

A similar section on the broker examination requires more knowledge and skill to complete than the one on the salesperson examination. You will be given a completed listing agreement and agreement of sale indicating the details of a real estate transaction. You also will be given a blank settlement statement worksheet. You will first fill out the settlement statement worksheet according to the information in the completed instruments; then you will turn in your listing and agreement of sale and answer a series of questions based upon your completed settlement statement. A copy of this worksheet is included at the end of this chapter.

Because of the uniform nature of the test, the information given for working the problem may differ somewhat from common Minnesota practice. In completing these instrument preparation problems on the examination, use all the information as it is given.

To use the worksheet most efficiently, you should follow these steps:

1. As you read through the information given for the problem (or the completed documents for the transaction) list the expenses included in the transaction in the first column of the worksheet.

2. Go through the list of expenses and consider those expenses related to the buyer; make any necessary proration computations and record each buyer-related expense as either a debit to the buyer (an amount the buyer owes) or a credit to the buyer (an amount the buyer has already paid or promises to pay in the form of a loan or note).

3. Next, go through the list of expenses and consider those expenses related to the seller; make necessary proration computations and record each seller-related expense as either a debit to the seller (an amount the seller owes) or a credit to the seller (the selling price of the property and any prorated expenses the seller has prepaid).

4. Total the buyer's debit and credit columns and subtract the lesser from the greater total to determine what amount the buyer must pay at the closing (if debits exceed credits) or what amount the buyer will be paid at the closing (if credits exceed debits).

5. Total the seller's debit and credit columns and subtract the lesser from the greater total to determine what amount the seller will pay at the closing (if debits exceed credits) or what amount the seller will be paid at the closing (if credits exceed debits).

Remember, since the results of the computations recorded on the worksheet are used to answer your exam questions, the settlement statement worksheet must be filled in accurately and clearly enough to be referred to easily.

Documents

The listing agreement, sales contract, and settlement statement worksheet that appear on the following pages are very similar to those you will encounter on the Minnesota real estate examination. They have already been filled in, based upon the model transaction set forth in Chapter 23 of the Supplement. Look over the documents and answer the questions that appear on pages 159 through 161.

REAL ESTATE LISTING CONTRACT (EXCLUSIVE RIGHT TO SELL)

SALES PRICE **$45,000**	TYPE HOME **Colonial**	TOTAL BEDROOMS **2**	TOTAL BATHS **1**
ADDRESS **211 N. Banana Ave.**		JURISDICTION OF **Hennepin County**	
AMT OF LOAN TO BE ASSUMED $ **30,228.93**	AS OF WHAT DATE **12/13/83**	TAXES & INS INCLUDED	YEARS TO GO **8**	AMOUNT PAYABLE MONTHLY $ **287.87** to **8** % LOAN	TYPE **Dir. red.**
MORTGAGE COMPANY **First American S & L of Cherryvale**		2nd MORTGAGE	
OWNER'S NAME **Maurice & Mabel Armbruster**		PHONES (HOME) **311-2704**	(BUSINESS) **601-2101**
TENANT'S NAME		PHONES (HOME)	(BUSINESS)
POSSESSION **90 days**	DATE LISTED **12/13/83**	EXCLUSIVE FOR **6 months**	DATE OF EXPIRATION **6/12/84**
LISTING BROKER **Champlin Real Estate**		PHONE	KEY AVAILABLE AT
LISTING SALESMAN **Beverly Beauchamp**		HOME PHONE	HOW TO BE SHOWN

ENTRANCE FOYER ☒   CENTER HALL ☐   AGE ___   AIR CONDITIONING ☐   TYPE KITCHEN CABINETS ___
LIVING ROOM SIZE **12 x 12**   FIREPLACE ☐   ROOFING ___   TOOL HOUSE ☐   TYPE COUNTER TOPS ___
DINING ROOM SIZE ___   GARAGE SIZE **1 car detached**   PATIO ☐   EAT-IN SIZE KITCHEN ☐
BEDROOM TOTAL ___ DOWN ___ UP **2**   SIDE DRIVE ☐   CIRCULAR DRIVE ☐   TYPE STOVE ☐
BATHS TOTAL ___ DOWN ___ UP ___   PORCH ☐ SIDE ☒ REAR ☐   SCREENED ☐   BUILT-IN OVEN & RANGE ☐
DEN SIZE ___   FIREPLACE ☐   FENCED YARD ___   OUTDOOR GRILL ☐   SEPARATE STOVE INCLUDED ☐
FAMILY ROOM SIZE ___   FIREPLACE ☐   STORM WINDOWS ☒   STORM DOORS ☒   REFRIGERATOR INCLUDED ☐
RECREATION ROOM SIZE ___   FIREPLACE ☐   CURBS & GUTTERS ☐   SIDEWALKS ☐   DISHWASHER INCLUDED ☐
BASEMENT SIZE ___   STORM SEWERS ☒   ALLEY ☐   DISPOSAL INCLUDED ☐
NONE ☐ 1/4 ☐ 1/3 ☒ 1/2 ☐ 3/4 ☐ FULL ☐   WATER SUPPLY ___   DOUBLE SINK ☐ SINGLE SINK ☐
UTILITY ROOM ___   SEWER ☒   SEPTIC ☐   STAINLESS STEEL ☐ PORCELAIN ☐
TYPE HOT WATER SYSTEM **Electric**   TYPE GAS NATURAL ☒   BOTTLED ☐   WASHER INCLUDED ☐ DRYER INCLUDED ☐
TYPE HEAT ___   WHY SELLING **New home purchased**   LAND ASSESSMENT $ ___
EST FUEL COST ___   IMPROVEMENTS $ ___
ATTIC ☒ **Partial floor**   PROPERTY DESCRIPTION ___   TOTAL ASSESSMENT $ ___
PULL DOWN STAIRWAY ☐   REGULAR STAIRWAY ☐   TRAP DOOR ☐   TAX RATE ___
NAME OF BUILDER ___   LOT SIZE ___   TOTAL ANNUAL TAXES $ **716.00**
SQUARE FOOTAGE **1,200**   LOT NO ___ BLOCK ___ SECTION ___
EXTERIOR OF HOUSE **Brick**

NAME OF SCHOOLS   ELEMENTARY **Silverman Grammar**   JR HIGH ___
HIGH **Gorzelany Vocational**   PAROCHIAL **St. Rick's**
PUBLIC TRANSPORTATION **Bus/3 blocks north**
NEAREST SHOPPING AREA **1 mile east**
REMARKS **w/w carpeting included in entrance & living room. All shades included**

DEFINITIONS

This Contract involves the property located at **211 N. Banana Ave.** (property)

"I" means: **Maurice and Mabel Armbuster**

"You" means: **Champlin Real Estate** (the real estate broker)

LISTING

I give you the exclusive right to sell the property for the price of $ **45,000.00** I will require the following terms **Conventional, FHA, V.A and Assumption**. This contract starts **Dec. 13,** 19**83** and ends at 11:59 p.m. on **June 12** 19**84**.

In exchange, you agree to list the property and try to sell it. You may place a "For Sale" sign and a lock box with keys on the property.

I understand you are a member of the Multiple Listing Service (MLS) and you will give information to MLS concerning the property. I will keep you notified of new information important to the sale of the property. If you sell the property, you may notify MLS and members of the Greater Minneapolis Area Board of REALTORS of the price and terms of the sale.

MY DUTIES

I will cooperate with you in selling the property. I will promptly tell you about all inquiries I receive about the property. I agree to provide and pay for any inspections and reports if required by the city or state. I agree to provide homeowners association documents if required. I will give the buyer an updated abstract of title, or owner's duplicate certificate of title and registered property abstract, or title insurance to the property. I have the full legal right to sell the property. I will sign all closing documents (including a warranty deed or contract for a Buyer full and unquestioned ownership of the property.

NOTICE: THE COMMISSION RATE FOR THE SALE, LEASE, RENTAL OR MANAGEMENT OF REAL PROPERTY SHALL BE DETERMINED BETWEEN EACH INDIVIDUAL REAL ESTATE BROKER AND ITS CLIENT.

YOUR COMMISSION

I will pay you as your commission **7** % of the selling price if I sell or agree to sell the property before this contract ends. In addition, if before this contract ends you present a Buyer who is willing and able to buy the property at the price and terms required in this contract, but I refuse to sell, I will still pay you the same commission. I agree to pay your commission whether you, I, or another agent or broker sells the property. I agree to pay your commission in full upon the happening of any of the following events: (1) The closing of the sale, (2) My refusal to close the sale, or (3) My refusal to sell at the price and terms required in this contract.

If within **180** days after the end of this contract, I sell or agree to sell the property to anyone who:
(1) During this contract made inquiry of me about the property and I did not tell you about the inquiry; or
(2) During this contract made an affirmative showing of interest in the property or was physically shown the property by you and whose name is on a written list you give me within 72 hours after the end of this contract, then

I will still pay you your commission on the selling price, even if I sell the property without your assistance.

I understand that I do not have to pay your commission if I sign another valid listing contract after the expiration of this Contract, under which I am obligated to pay a commission to another licensed real estate broker.

NOTICES ABOUT MY REAL ESTATE

As of this date I have not received notices from any municipality, government agency or homeowners association about the property that I have not told you about, and I agree to promptly tell you of any notices of that type that I receive.

ACCEPTED BY: **Champlin Real Estate**
Real Estate Company
By **Charles Champlin**
Agent
Date signed **December 13,** 19**83**

ACCEPTED BY: *Maurice Armbuster* Owner
Mabel Armbuster Owner
Address **211 N Banana Ave**
Phone **698-5566**
Date signed **12/13** 19**83**

REAL ESTATE SALES CONTRACT (OFFER TO PURCHASE)

This AGREEMENT made as of __January 21__, 19__84__,

among __Mark & Helen Time__ (herein called "Purchaser"),

and __Maurice & Mabel Armbruster__ (herein called "Seller"),

and __Champlin Real Estate__ (herein called "Broker"), provides that Purchaser agrees to buy through Broker as agent for Seller, and Seller agrees to sell the following described real estate, and all improvements thereon, located in the jurisdiction of __Hennepin County, Minnesota__,

(all herein called "the property"): __lot 27, block 8, Scenic Heights Addition to Cherryvale__, and more commonly known as __211 Banana Avenue, Cherryvale, Minnesota, 50000__ (street address).

1. The purchase price of the property is __Fourty-three thousand__ Dollars ($__43,000__), and such purchase price shall be paid as follows: __$1,000 down with contract, Assume existing mortgage balance remainder at closing__

2. Purchaser has made a deposit of __one thousand__ Dollars ($__1,000__) with Broker, receipt of which is hereby acknowledged, and such deposit shall be held by Broker in escrow until the date of settlement and then applied to the purchase price, or returned to Purchaser if the title to the property is not marketable.

3. Seller agrees to convey the property to Purchaser by Deed with the usual covenants of title and free and clear from all monetary encumbrances, tenancies, liens (for taxes or otherwise), except as may be otherwise provided above, but subject to applicable restrictive covenants of record. Seller further agrees to deliver possession of the property to Purchaser on the date of settlement and to pay the expense of preparing the deed of conveyance.

4. Settlement shall be made at __First American Savings & Loan of Cherryvale__ on or before __March 15__, 19__84__, or as soon thereafter as title can be examined and necessary documents prepared, with allowance of a reasonable time for Seller to correct any defects reported by the title examiner.

5. All taxes, interest, rent, and impound escrow deposits, if any, shall be prorated as of the date of settlement.

6. All risk of loss or damage to the property by fire, windstorm, casualty, or other cause is assumed by Seller until the date of settlement.

7. Purchaser and Seller agree that Broker was the sole procuring cause of this Contract of Purchase, and Seller agrees to pay Broker for services rendered a cash fee of __7__ per cent of the purchase price. If either Purchaser or Seller defaults under such Contract, such defaulting party shall be liable for the cash fee of Broker and any expenses incurred by the non-defaulting party in connection with this transaction.

Subject to: __wall-to-wall carpeting and shades included in purchase__

8. Purchaser represents that an inspection satisfactory to Purchaser has been made of the property, and Purchaser agrees to accept the property in its present condition except as may be otherwise provided in the description of the property above.

9. This Contract of Purchase constitutes the entire agreement among the parties and may not be modified or changed except by written instrument executed by all of the parties, including Broker.

10. This Contract of Purchase shall be construed, interpreted, and applied according to the law of the jurisdiction of _____ and shall be binding upon and shall inure to the benefit of the heirs, personal representatives, successors, and assigns of the parties.

All parties to this agreement acknowledge receipt of a certified copy.

WITNESS the following signatures:

Maurice Armbruster Seller   _Mark Time_ Purchaser
Mabel Armbruster Seller   _Helen Time_ Purchaser
Champlin Real Estate Broker

Deposit Rec'd $ __1,000__

Personal Check   Cash
(Cashier's Check)   Company Check

Sales Agent:

SETTLEMENT STATEMENT WORKSHEET

Property: 211 North Banana Avenue, Cherryvale, Minnesota 50000
Seller: Maurice & Mabel Armbruster
Buyer: Mark & Helen Tima
Settlement Date: 3/15/84

	BUYER'S STATEMENT DEBIT	BUYER'S STATEMENT CREDIT	SELLER'S STATEMENT DEBIT	SELLER'S STATEMENT CREDIT
Purchase Price	$43,000.00			$43,000.00
Earnest Money		$1,000.00		
Mortgage Principal		29,367.52	$29,367.52	
Mortgage Interest		94.73	94.73	
Title Insurance	150.00			
Abstract			30.00	
Recording Fees	3.00			
State Deed Tax			30.80	
Real Estate Tax		148.19	148.19	
Assumption Fee	29.37			
Fire & Hazard Insurance	148.28			148.28
Broker's Commission			3,010.00	
Total Debits & Credits	43,330.65	30,610.44	32,681.24	43,148.28
To Sellers at Closing		12,720.21		
From Buyers at Closing			10,467.04	
	$43,330.65	$43,330.65	$43,148.28	$43,148.28

QUESTIONS

INSTRUCTIONS: Answer the following questions according to the information contained in the agreement for the sale of real estate (sales contract) on page 157 and the listing agreement on page 156.

1. As of the date of the listing, the owners' mortgage loan:

    I. has an unpaid balance of $30,228.93.
    II. requires monthly payments of $287.87.

    a. I only
    b. II only
    c. both I and II
    d. neither I nor II

2. Among the extras included in the sale of the house is(are):

    I. a range.
    II. an air conditioner.

    a. I only
    b. II only
    c. both I and II
    d. neither I nor II

3. The floor plan of the house includes:

    I. a one-third basement downstairs.
    II. three bedrooms upstairs.

    a. I only
    b. II only
    c. both I and II
    d. neither I nor II

4. This house:

    I. was built in 1950.
    II. is a two-story colonial of brick construction.

    a. I only
    b. II only
    c. both I and II
    d. neither I nor II

5. The basement of this house includes:

    I. a laundry room.
    II. an unfinished recreation room.

    a. I only
    b. II only
    c. both I and II
    d. neither I nor II

6. The listing agreement:

   I. grants the broker an exclusive right to sell.
   II. is valid for a period of 90 days.

   a. I only
   b. II only
   c. both I and II
   d. neither I nor II

7. Financial arrangements for this sale include:

   I. the assumption of an existing mortgage by the Times.
   II. an installment contract.

   a. I only
   b. II only
   c. both I and II
   d. neither I nor II

8. According to the agreement of sale, at the closing of this transaction:

   I. the Times will deliver the balance of the purchase price, which will be approximately $10,375.
   II. the Armbrusters will execute and deliver a special warranty deed.

   a. I only
   b. II only
   c. both I and II
   d. neither I nor II

9. Champlin Real Estate will receive a commission on this sale of:

   I. 9 percent of the sale price.
   II. $3,010.00.

   a. I only
   b. II only
   c. both I and II
   d. neither I nor II

10. Maurice and Mabel Armbruster are selling their home for the price of:

    a. $25.500.
    b. $39,975.
    c. $43,000.
    d. $45,000.

Answer the following questions based on your completed settlement worksheet for the closing problem that is included in this chapter.

11. The sellers' expenses in this transaction include the:

    I. title insurance policy.
    II. abstract extension.

    a. I only
    b. II only
    c. both I and II
    d. neither I nor II

12. At the closing the sellers will receive:

    I. $6,150 from the broker.
    II. $10,375.04 from the buyers.

        a. I only   c. both I and II
        b. II only   d. neither I nor II

13. The broker's commission is:

    I. seven percent of the purchase price.
    II. a debit to the sellers.

        a. I only   c. both I and II
        b. II only   d. neither I nor II

14. The total amount due from the buyers at the closing is:

        a. $14,165.97.   c. $12,725.21.
        b. $13,841.91.   d. $10,375.04.

15. The unpaid balance of the assumed mortgage at the closing is:

        a. $29,367.52.   c. $43,000.00.
        b. $32,773.24.   d. $94.73.

16. At the closing the sellers will receive:

        a. $12,725.21.   c. $32,773.24.
        b. $30,607.44.   d. $10,375.04.

17. The buyers' total expenses come to:

        a. $43,332.65.   c. $32,773.24.
        b. $30,607.44.   d. $43,148.28.

Appendix A:

Real Estate License Law and Rules and Regulations

82.17 [DEFINITIONS.]

Subdivision 1. For the purposes of this chapter the terms defined in this section have the meanings given to them.

Subd. 2. "Person" means a natural person, firm, partnership, corporation or association, and the officers, directors, employees and agents thereof.

Subd. 3. "Commissioner" means the commissioner of securities and real estate or his designee.

Subd. 4. "Real estate broker" or "broker" means any person who:

(a) for another and for commission, fee or other valuable consideration or with the intention or expectation of receiving the same directly or indirectly lists, sells, exchanges, buys or rents, manages, or offers or attempts to negotiate a sale, option, exchange, purchase or rental of an interest or estate in real estate, or advertises or holds himself, herself, or itself out as engaged in these activities;

(b) for another and for commission, fee or other valuable consideration or with the intention or expectation of receiving the same directly or indirectly negotiates or offers or attempts to negotiate a loan, secured or to be secured by a mortgage or other encumbrance on real estate;

(c) for another and for commission, fee or other valuable consideration or with the intention or expectation of receiving the same directly or indirectly lists, sells, exchanges, buys, rents, manages, offers or attempts to negotiate a sale, option, exchange, purchase or rental of any business opportunity or business, or its goodwill, inventory, or fixtures, or any interest therein;

(d) for another and for commission, fee or other valuable consideration or with the intention or expectation of receiving the same directly or indirectly offers, sells or attempts to negotiate the sale of property that is subject to the registration requirements of chapter 83, concerning subdivided land;

(e) engages in the business of charging an advance fee or contracting for collection of a fee in connection with any contract whereby he or she undertakes to promote the sale of real estate through its listing in a publication issued primarily for this purpose;

(f) engages wholly or in part in the business of selling real estate to the extent that a pattern of real estate sales is established, whether or not the real estate is owned by the person. A person shall be presumed to be engaged in the business of selling real estate if the person engages as principal in five or more transactions during any 12-month period, unless the person is represented by a licensed real estate broker or salesperson.

Subd. 5. "Real estate salesperson" means one who acts on behalf of a real estate broker in performing any act authorized by this chapter to be performed by the broker.

Subd. 6. "Trust account" means, for purposes of this chapter, a demand deposit or checking account maintained for the purpose of segregating trust funds from other funds. A trust account shall not be an interest bearing account except by agreement of the parties and subject to rules of the commissioner, and shall not allow the financial institution a right of set off against moneys owed it by the licensee.

Subd. 7. "Trust funds" means funds received by a broker or salesperson in a fiduciary capacity as a part of a real estate or business opportunity transaction, pending the consummation or termination of a transaction, and includes all down payments, earnest money deposits, rents for clients, tax and insurance escrow payments, damage deposits, and any funds received on behalf of any person.

Subd. 8. For purposes of sections 82.17 to 82.34, real estate shall also include, a manufactured home, when such manufactured home is affixed to land. Manufactured home means any factory built structure or structures equipped with the necessary service connections and made so as to be readily movable as a unit or units and designed to be used as a dwelling unit or units.

Subd. 9. "Public member" means a person who is not, or never was, a real estate broker or real estate salesperson or the spouse of such person, or a person who has no, or never has had a material financial interest in acting as a real estate broker or real estate salesperson or a directly related activity

82.18 [EXCEPTIONS.]

Unless a person is licensed or otherwise required to be licensed under this chapter, the term real estate broker does not include:

Appendix A: Real Estate License Law and Rules and Regulations

(a) a licensed practicing attorney acting solely as an incident to the practice of law if the attorney complies in all respects with the trust account provisions of this chapter;

(b) a receiver, trustee, administrator, guardian, executor, or other person appointed by or acting under the judgment or order of any court;

(c) any person owning and operating a cemetery and selling lots therein solely for use as burial plots;

(d) any custodian, janitor, or employee of the owner or manager of a residential building who leases residential units in the building;

(e) any bank, trust company, savings and loan association, industrial loan and thrift company, regulated lender under chapter 56, public utility, or land mortgage or farm loan association organized under the laws of this state or the United States, when engaged in the transaction of business within the scope of its corporate powers as provided by law;

(f) public officers while performing their official duties;

(g) employees of persons enumerated in clauses (b), (e) and (f), when engaged in the specific performance of their duties;

(h) any person who acts as an auctioneer bonded in conformity with section 330.02, when that person is engaged in the specific performance of his or her duties as an auctioneer;

(i) any person who acquires real estate for the purpose of engaging in and does engage in, or who is engaged in the business of constructing residential, commercial or industrial buildings for the purpose of resale if no more than 25 such transactions occur in any 12-month period and the person complies with section 82.24;

(j) any person who offers to sell or sells an interest or estate in real estate which is a security registered pursuant to chapter 80A, when acting solely as an incident to the sale of these securities;

(k) any person who offers to sell or sells a business opportunity which is a franchise registered pursuant to chapter 80C, when acting solely to sell the franchise;

(l) any person who contracts with or solicits on behalf of a provider a contract with a resident or prospective resident to provide continuing care in a facility, pursuant to the Continuing Care Facility Disclosure and Rehabilitation Act (chapter 80D), when acting solely as incident to the contract;

(m) any broker-dealer or agent of a broker-dealer when participating in a transaction in which all or part of a business opportunity or business, including any interest therein, is conveyed or acquired pursuant to an asset purchase, merger, exchange of securities or other business combination, if the agent or broker-dealer is licensed pursuant to chapter 80A.

82.19 [PROHIBITIONS.]

Subdivision 1. No person shall act as a real estate broker or salesperson unless he is licensed as herein provided.

Subd. 2. No person shall advertise or represent himself to be a real estate broker or salesperson unless licensed as herein provided.

Subd. 3. No real estate broker or salesperson shall offer,

definition of real estate broker, to obtain the special license.

Subd. 2. [QUALIFICATION OF APPLICANTS.] Every applicant for a real estate broker or real estate salesperson license shall be at least 18 years of age at the time of making application for said license.

Subd. 3. [APPLICATION FOR LICENSE; CONTENTS.] (a) Every applicant for a license as a real estate broker or real estate salesperson shall make his application in writing upon forms prepared and furnished by the commissioner. Each application shall be signed and sworn to by the applicant and shall be accompanied by the license fee required by this chapter;

(b) Each application for a real estate broker license and real estate salesperson license shall contain such information as required by the commissioner consistent with the administration of the provisions and purposes of this chapter;

(c) Each application for a real estate salesperson license shall give the applicant's name, age, residence address and the name and place of business of the real estate broker on whose behalf said salesperson is to be acting;

(d) The commissioner may require such further information as he deems appropriate to administer the provisions and further the purposes of this chapter.

Subd. 4. [CORPORATE AND PARTNERSHIP LICENSES.] (a) A corporation applying for a license shall have at least one officer individually licensed to act as broker for the corporation. The corporation broker's license shall extend no authority to act as broker to any person other than the

pay or give, and no person shall accept, any compensation or other thing of value from any real estate broker or salesperson by way of commission-splitting, rebate, finder's fees or otherwise, in connection with any real estate or business opportunity transaction; provided this subdivision does not apply to transactions (1) between a licensed real estate broker or salesperson and the person by whom he is engaged to purchase or sell real estate or business opportunity, (2) among persons licensed as provided herein, and (3) between a licensed real estate broker or salesperson and persons from other jurisdictions similarly licensed in that jurisdiction.

Subd. 4. No real estate broker or salesperson shall engage or authorize any person, except one licensed as provided herein, to act as a real estate broker or salesperson on his behalf.

82.20 [LICENSING REQUIREMENTS.]

Subdivision 1. [GENERALLY.] (a) The commissioner shall issue a license as a real estate broker or real estate salesperson to any person who qualifies for such license under the terms of this chapter;

(b) The commissioner is authorized to establish by rule a special license for real estate brokers and real estate salespersons engaged solely in the rental or management of an interest or estate in real estate, to prescribe qualifications for the license, and to issue the license consistent with the terms of this chapter. This clause shall not be construed to require those owners or managers or their agents or employees who are excluded by section 82.18, clause (d) from the

Appendix A: Real Estate License Law and Rules and Regulations   167

corporate entity. Each officer who intends to act as a broker shall obtain a license;

(b) A partnership applying for a license shall have at least one partner individually licensed to act as broker for the partnership. Each partner who intends to act as a broker shall obtain a license;

(c) Applications for a license made by a corporation shall be verified by the president and secretary. Applications made by a partnership shall be verified by at least two partners;

(d) Any partner or officer who ceases to act as broker for a partnership or corporation shall notify the commissioner upon said termination. The individual licenses of all salespersons acting on behalf of a corporation or partnership, are automatically ineffective upon the revocation or suspension of the license of the partnership or corporation. The commissioner may suspend or revoke the license of an officer or partner without suspending or revoking the license of the corporation or partnership;

(e) The application of all officers of a corporation or partners in a partnership who intend to act as a broker on behalf of a corporation or partnership shall accompany the initial license application of the corporation or partnership. Officers or partners intending to act as brokers subsequent to the licensing of the corporation or partnership shall procure an individual real estate broker's license prior to acting in the capacity of a broker. No license as a real estate salesperson shall be issued to any officer of a corporation or member of a partnership to which a license was issued as a broker;

(f) The corporation or partnership applicant shall make available upon request, such records and data required by the commissioner for enforcement of this chapter.

Subd. 5. [RESPONSIBILITY.] Each broker shall be responsible for the acts of any and all of his sales people while acting on his behalf as his agents. Each officer of a corporation or partner in a partnership licensed as a broker shall have the same responsibility under this chapter as a corporate or partnership broker with regard to the acts of the salespersons acting on behalf of the corporation or partnership.

Subd. 6. [ISSUANCE OF LICENSE; SALESPERSON.] A salesperson must be licensed to act on behalf of a licensed broker and may not be licensed to act on behalf of more than one broker in this state during the same period of time. The license of each real estate salesperson shall be mailed to and remain in the possession of the licensed broker with whom he is or is to be associated until canceled or until such licensee leaves such broker.

Subd. 7. [EFFECTIVE DATE OF LICENSE.] Every license issued pursuant to this chapter shall expire on the June 30 next following the issuance of said license.

Subd. 8. [RENEWALS.] (a) Persons whose applications have been properly and timely filed who have not received notice of denial of renewal are deemed to have been approved for renewal and may continue to transact business either as a real estate broker or salesperson whether or not the renewed license has been received on or before July 1. Application for renewal of a license shall be deemed to have been timely filed if received by the commissioner on or before June 15 in each year. Applications for renewal shall be deemed properly filed if made upon forms duly executed and sworn to, accompanied by fees prescribed by this chapter and contain any information which the commissioner may require. An application mailed shall be deemed proper and timely received if addressed to the commissioner and postmarked prior to 12:01 A.M. on June 14;

(b) Persons who have failed to make a timely application for renewal of a license and who have not received the renewal license as of July 1, shall be unlicensed until such time as the license has been issued by the commissioner and is received.

Subd. 9. [TERMINATIONS; TRANSFERS.] (a) Except as provided in paragraph (b), when a salesperson terminates his activity on behalf of a broker, the salesperson's license shall be ineffective. Within ten days of the termination the broker shall notify the commissioner in writing, and shall return to the commissioner the license of the salesperson. The salesperson may apply for transfer of the license to another broker at any time during the remainder of the license period, on forms provided by the commissioner. If the application for transfer qualifies, the commissioner shall grant the application. Upon receipt of a transfer application and payment of the transfer fee, the commissioner may issue a 45 day temporary license. If an application for transfer is not made within the license period, the commissioner shall require that an application for a new license be filed.

(b) When a salesperson terminates his activity on behalf of a broker in order to begin association immediately with another broker, the commissioner shall permit the automatic transfer of the salesperson's license. The transfer shall be effective either upon the mailing of the required fee and the executed documents by certified mail or upon personal delivery of the fee and documents to the commissioner's office. The commissioner may adopt rules and prescribe forms as necessary to implement this paragraph.

Subd. 10. [EFFECT OF SUSPENSION OR REVOCATION.] The license of a salesperson is not effective during any period for which the license of the broker on whose behalf he is acting is suspended or revoked. The salesperson may apply for transfer to some other licensed broker by complying with subdivision 9.

Subd. 11. [NOTICE.] Notice in writing shall be given to the commissioner by each licensee of any change in personal name, trade name, address or business location not later than ten days after such change. The commissioner shall issue a new license if required for the unexpired period.

Subd. 12. [NONRESIDENTS.] A nonresident of Minnesota may be licensed as a real estate broker or real estate salesperson upon compliance with all provisions of this chapter.

Subd. 13. [LIMITED BROKER'S LICENSE.] The commissioner shall have the authority to issue a limited real estate broker's license authorizing the licensee to engage in transactions as principal only. Such license shall be issued only after receipt of the application described in subdivision 3 and payment of the fee prescribed by section 82.21, subdivision 1. No salesperson may be licensed to act on behalf of an individual holding a limited broker's license. An officer of a corporation or a partner of a partnership licensed as a limited broker may act on behalf of that corporation or partnership without being subject to the licensing requirements.

Subd. 14. [LICENSES; EXTENDING DURATION.] Notwithstanding the provisions of subdivisions 7 and 8, the commissioner may institute a system by rule pursuant to chapter 14 to provide three year licenses from the date of issuance for any license prescribed by this section.

82.21 [FEES.]

Subdivision 1. [AMOUNTS.] The following fees shall be paid to the commissioner:

(a) A fee of $50 for each initial individual broker's license, and a fee of $25 for each annual renewal thereof;
(b) A fee of $25 for each initial salesperson's license, and a fee of $10 for each annual renewal thereof;
(c) A fee of $50 for each initial corporate or partnership license, and a fee of $25 for each annual renewal thereof;
(d) A fee not to exceed $40 per year for payment to the education, research and recovery fund in accordance with section 82.34;
(e) A fee of $10 for each transfer.

Subd. 2. [FORFEITURE.] All fees shall be retained by the commissioner and shall be nonreturnable, except that an overpayment of any fee shall be the subject of a refund upon proper application.

Subd. 3. [DEPOSIT OF FEES.] Unless otherwise provided by this chapter, all fees collected under this chapter shall be deposited in the state treasury.

82.22 [EXAMINATIONS.]

Subdivision 1. [GENERALLY.] Each applicant for a license must pass an examination conducted by the commissioner. The examinations shall be of sufficient scope to establish the competency of the applicant to act as a real estate broker or as a real estate salesperson.

Subd. 2. [BROKER'S EXAMINATION.] (a) The examination for a real estate broker's license shall be more exacting than that for a real estate salesperson, and shall require a higher degree of knowledge of the fundamentals of real estate practice and law.

(b) Every application for a broker's examination shall be accompanied by proof that the applicant has had a minimum of two years of actual experience as a licensed real estate salesperson in this or in another state having comparable requirements or is, in the opinion of the commissioner, otherwise or similarly qualified by reason of education or practical experience. An applicant for a limited broker's license pursuant to section 82.20, subdivision 13, shall not be required to have a minimum of two years of actual experience as a real estate person in order to obtain a limited broker's license to act as principal only.

Subd. 3. [RE-EXAMINATIONS.] An examination may be required

before the renewal of any license which has been suspended, or before the issuance of a license to any person whose license has been ineffective for a period of one year, except no re-examination shall be required of any individual who has failed to cause renewal of an existing license because of the absence from the state while on active duty with the armed services of the United States of America.

Subd. 4. [EXAMINATION FREQUENCY.] The commissioner shall hold examinations at such times and places as he may determine, except that said examinations will be held at least every 45 days.

Subd. 5. [PERIOD FOR APPLICATION.] An applicant who obtains an acceptable score on a salesperson's examination must file an application for the license within one year of the date of successful completion of the examination or a second examination must be taken to qualify for the license.

Subd. 6. [INSTRUCTION; NEW LICENSES.] (a) Every salesperson, licensed after July 1, 1973 and before July 1, 1976 shall, within two years of the date his license was first granted be required to successfully complete a course of study in the real estate field consisting of not less than 60 hours of instruction, approved by the commissioner. Upon appropriate showing of hardship by the licensee, or for persons licensed pursuant to section 82.20, subdivision 1, clause (b), the commissioner may waive or modify the requirements of this subdivision. Every salesperson licensed after July 1, 1976 and before July 1, 1978 shall, within three years of the date his license was first issued, be required to successfully complete a course of study in the real estate field consisting of not less than 90 hours of instruction, approved by the commissioner.

(b) After July 1, 1978, and before January 1, 1984, every applicant for a salesperson's license shall be required to successfully complete a course of study in the real estate field consisting of 30 hours of instruction approved by the commissioner before taking the examination specified in subdivision 1. Every salesperson licensed after July 1, 1978, and before January 1, 1984, shall, within one year of the date his license was first issued, be required to successfully complete a course of study in the real estate field consisting of 60 hours of instruction approved by the commissioner.

(c) After December 31, 1983, every applicant for a salesperson's license shall be required to successfully complete a course of study in the real estate field consisting of 30 hours of instruction approved by the commissioner before taking the examination specified in subdivision 1. After December 31, 1983, every applicant for a salesperson's license shall be required to successfully complete an additional course of study in the real estate field consisting of 30 hours of instruction approved by the commissioner before filing an application for the license. Every salesperson licensed after December 31, 1983, shall, within one year of the date his license was first issued, be required to successfully complete a course of study in the real estate field consisting of 30 hours of instruction approved by the commissioner.

(d) The commissioner may approve courses of study in the real estate field offered in educational institutions of higher learning in this state or courses of study in the real estate field developed by and offered under the auspices of the national association of realtors, its affiliates, or private real estate schools licensed by the state department of education. The commissioner may by rule prescribe the curriculum and qualification of those employed as instructors.

Subd. 7. [INSTRUCTION; LICENSEES SUBSEQUENT TO JULY 1, 1969.] Every salesperson licensed prior to July 1, 1973, but subsequent to July 1, 1969, within two years of the date his license was first granted, shall be required to successfully complete a course of study in the real estate field consisting of not less than 30 hours of instruction, approved by the commissioner. Upon the failure of a licensee covered by this subdivision to complete the required 30 hours of instruction, the licensee must pass a second examination more difficult in degree than the one required for granting of his salesman's license.

Subd. 8. [DURATION.] No renewal of a salesperson's license shall be effective beyond a date two years after the granting of such salesperson's license unless the salesperson has furnished evidence of compliance with either subdivisions 6 or 7. The commissioner shall cancel the license of any salesperson who fails to comply with subdivisions 6 or 7.

Subd. 9. [APPLICATION.] Subdivisions 6 to 8 shall not apply to salespersons licensed in Minnesota prior to July 1, 1969.

Subd. 10. [RENEWAL; EXAMINATION.] Except as provided in subdivisions 3 and 7, no examination shall be required for the renewal of any license, provided, however, any licensee having been licensed as a broker or salesperson in the state of Minnesota and who shall fail to renew the license for a period of one year shall be required by the commissioner to again take an examination.

Subd. 11. [EXAMINATION ELIGIBILITY; REVOCATION.] No applicant shall be eligible to take any examination if his license as a real estate broker or salesperson has been revoked in this or any other state within two years of the date of the application.

Subd. 12. [RECIPROCITY.] The requirements of this section may be waived for individuals of other jurisdictions, provided: (1) a written reciprocal licensing agreement is in effect between the commissioner and the licensing officials of that jurisdiction, (2) the individual is licensed in that jurisdiction, and (3) the licensing requirements of that jurisdiction are substantially similar to the provisions of this chapter.

Subd. 13. [CONTINUING EDUCATION.] (a) After July 1, 1978, all real estate salespersons not subject to or who have completed the educational requirements contained in subdivision 6 and all real estate brokers shall be required to successfully complete 45 hours of real estate education, either as a student or a lecturer, in courses of study approved by the commissioner,

172 MINNESOTA SUPPLEMENT for Modern Real Estate Practice

within three years after their annual renewal date.

(b) For the purposes of administration, the commissioner shall classify by lot, the real estate brokers and salespersons subject to (a) above, in three classifications of substantially equal size. The first class shall complete 15 hours of approved real estate study between July 1, 1978 and June 30, 1979 inclusive. The second class shall complete 30 hours of approved real estate study between the dates of July 1, 1978 and June 30, 1980 inclusive. The third class shall complete 45 hours of approved real estate study between the dates of July 1, 1978 and June 30, 1981. After the first period, each class shall complete the prescribed educational requirements during successive three year periods.

(c) The commissioner shall adopt rules defining the standards for course and instructor approval, and may adopt rules for the proper administration of this subdivision.

(d) Any program approved by Minnesota Continuing Legal Education shall be approved by the commissioner of securities and real estate for continuing education for real estate brokers if the program or any part thereof relates to real estate.

82.23 [BROKER'S RECORDS.]

Subdivision 1. [RETENTION.] A licensed real estate broker shall retain for three years copies of all listings, deposit receipts, purchase money contracts, cancelled checks, trust account records, and such other documents as may reasonably be related to carrying on a real estate brokerage business. The retention period shall run from the date of the closing of the transaction, or from the date of the listing if the transaction is not consummated.

Subd. 2. [DELIVERY.] Each real estate broker or real estate salesperson shall furnish parties to a transaction a true and accurate copy of any document pertaining to their interests as the commissioner through appropriate rules may require.

Subd. 3. [EXAMINATION OF RECORDS.] The commissioner may make examinations within or without this state of each broker's records at such reasonable time and in such scope as is necessary to enforce the provisions of this chapter.

82.24 [TRUST ACCOUNT REQUIREMENTS.]

Subdivision 1. [GENERALLY.] All trust funds received by a broker or his salespersons shall be deposited forthwith upon receipt in a trust account, maintained by the broker for such purpose in a bank designated by the broker, except as such moneys may be paid to one of the parties pursuant to express written agreement between the parties to a transaction. The depository bank shall be a Minnesota bank or trust company or any foreign bank and shall authorize the commissioner to examine its records of such deposits upon demand by the commissioner.

Subd. 2. [LICENSEE ACTING AS PRINCIPAL.] Any licensed real estate broker or salesperson acting in the capacity of principal in the sale of interests in real estate owned by him shall deposit in a Minnesota bank or trust company, or any foreign bank which authorizes the commissioner to examine its records of such deposits, in a trust account, those parts of all payments received on contracts which are necessary to meet any amounts concurrently due and payable on any existing mortgages, contracts for deed or other conveyancing instruments, and reserve for taxes and insurance or any other encumbrance on such receipts. Such deposits shall be maintained until disbursement is made under the terms of the encumbrance pertaining thereto and proper accounting on such property made to the parties entitled thereto.

Subd. 3. [NONDEPOSITABLE ITEMS.] Any instrument or equity or thing of value received by a broker or salesperson in lieu of cash as earnest money or down payment in a real estate transaction shall be held by an authorized escrow agent, whose authority is evidenced by a written agreement executed by the offeror and the escrow agent.

Subd. 4. [COMINGLING FUNDS.] A broker or salesperson shall deposit only trust funds in a trust account and shall not comingle personal funds or other funds in a trust account, except that a broker or salesperson may deposit and maintain a sum not to exceed $100 in a trust account from his personal funds, which sum shall be specifically identified and used to pay service charges relating to the trust account.

Subd. 5. [TRUST ACCOUNT RECORDS.] Each broker shall maintain and retain records of all trust funds and trust accounts. The commissioner may prescribe information to be included in the records by appropriate rules and regulations.

Subd. 6. [NOTICE OF TRUST ACCOUNT STATUS.] The names of the banks and the trust account numbers used by a broker shall be provided to the commissioner at the time of application for the broker's license. The broker shall immediately report to the commissioner any change of trust account status including changes in banks, account numbers, or additional accounts in the same or other banks. A broker shall not close an existing trust account without giving ten days written notice to the commissioner.

Subd. 7. [INTEREST BEARING ACCOUNTS.] Notwithstanding the provisions of sections 82.17 to 82.31, a real estate broker may establish and maintain interest bearing accounts for the purpose of receiving deposits in accordance with the provisions of section 504.20.

82.25 [INVESTIGATION AND SUBPOENAS.]

Subdivision 1. When it appears by reasonable evidence that any provision of this chapter or any rule or order hereunder has been violated or is about to be violated, the commissioner may make necessary public or private investigations within or outside this state to aid in the enforcement of this chapter. The commissioner may also make necessary investigation incident to the promulgation of rules hereunder.

Subd. 2. The commissioner may require or permit any person to file a statement in writing, under oath or otherwise as the commissioner determines, as to all the facts and circumstances concerning the matter to be investigated.

Subd. 3. For the purpose of any investigation hearing or proceeding under this chapter, the commissioner or any person designated by him may administer oaths or affirmations, and may subpoena witnesses, compel their attendance, take evidence, and compel the production of documents or other tangible items which the commissioner deems relevant or material to the inquiry.

Subd. 4. Upon failure to obey a subpoena or to answer questions propounded by the investigating officer and upon reasonable notice to all persons affected thereby, the commissioner may apply to the district court for an order for contempt.

82.26 [LEGAL ACTIONS; INJUNCTIONS.]

Whenever it appears to the commissioner that any person has engaged or is about to engage in any act or practice constituting a violation of this chapter or any rule or order hereunder, he may bring an action in the name of the state in the district court of the appropriate county to enjoin the acts or practices and to enforce compliance with this chapter or any rule or order hereunder, or he may refer the matter to the attorney general. Upon a proper showing, a permanent or temporary injunction, restraining order, or other appropriate relief shall be granted.

82.27 [DENIAL, SUSPENSION AND REVOCATION OF LICENSES.]

Subdivision 1. The commissioner may by order deny, suspend or revoke any license or may censure a licensee if he finds (1) that the order is in the public interest, and (2) that the applicant or licensee or, in the case of a broker, any officer, director, partner, employee or agent or any person occupying a similar status or performing similar functions, or any person directly or indirectly controlling the broker or controlled by the broker:

(a) Has filed an application for a license which is incomplete in any material respect or contains any statement which, in light of the circumstances under which it is made, is false or misleading with respect to any material fact;

(b) Has engaged in a fraudulent, deceptive or dishonest practice;

(c) Is permanently or temporarily enjoined by any court of competent jurisdiction from engaging in or continuing any conduct or practice involving any aspect of the real estate business;

(d) Has failed to reasonably supervise his brokers or salesperson so as to cause injury or harm to the public; or

(e) Has violated or failed to comply with any provision of this chapter or any rule or order under this chapter.

Subd. 2. The commissioner may promulgate rules and regulations further specifying and defining those actions and omissions which constitute fraudulent, deceptive or dishonest practices, and establishing standards of conduct for real estate brokers and salespersons.

Subd. 3. The commissioner shall issue an order requiring a licensee or applicant for a license to show cause why the license should not be revoked or suspended, or the licensee censured, or the application denied. The order shall be calculated to give reasonable notice of the time and place for hearing thereon, and shall state the reasons for the entry of the order. The commissioner may by order summarily suspend a license pending final determination of any order to show cause.

if a license is suspended pending final determination of an order to show cause, a hearing on the merits shall be held within 30 days of the issuance of the order of suspension. All hearings shall be conducted in accordance with the provisions of chapter 14. After the hearing, the commissioner shall enter an order making such disposition of the matter as the facts require. If the licensee or applicant fails to appear at a hearing of which he has been duly notified, such person shall be deemed in default, and the proceeding may be determined against him upon consideration of the order to show cause, the allegations of which may be deemed to be true.

Subd. 4. The commissioner may delegate to a hearing examiner his authority to conduct a hearing. The examiner shall make proposed findings of fact and submit them to the commissioner. The examiner shall have the same power as the commissioner to compel the attendance of witnesses, to examine them under oath, to require the production of books, papers and other evidence, and to issue subpoenas and cause the same to be served and executed in any part of the state.

Subd. 5. Orders of the commissioner shall be subject to judicial review pursuant to chapter 14.

Subd. 6. The commissioner may promulgate rules of procedure concerning all hearings and other proceedings conducted pursuant to this chapter.

82.28 [RULE MAKING POWERS.]

The commissioner may promulgate such rules and regulations as are reasonably necessary to carry out and make effective the provisions and purposes of this chapter.

82.29 [PUBLICATION OF INFORMATION.]

The commissioner may publish by newspaper, newsletter or otherwise information to assist in the administration of sections 82.17 to 82.34, or to educate and protect the public regarding fraudulent, deceptive or dishonest practices. The commissioner may also publish materials for the benefit of license applicants.

82.30 [ADVISORY TASK FORCE.]

Subdivision 1. The commissioner of real estate and securities shall appoint a real estate advisory task force. The task force shall include real estate brokers with at least five years experience as licensed real estate brokers in Minnesota and public members. The task force may advise the commissioner on all matters relating to education of licensees, prelicensing requirements, and other policy matters relating to the administration of sections 82.17 to 82.34. The task force shall expire and the terms, compensation, and removal of members shall be as provided in section 15.059. No member of the real estate advisory task force may establish, own, operate, invest in a course designed to fulfill any requirement of Minnesota law pertaining to licenses for real estate salespersons or brokers.

82.31 [NONRESIDENT SERVICE OF PROCESS.]

Subdivision 1. Every nonresident, before being licensed as a real estate broker or real estate salesman, shall appoint the commissioner and his successor or successors in office as true and lawful attorney, upon whom may be served all legal process in any action or proceedings against such person, or in which such person may be a party, in relation to or involving any transaction covered by this chapter or any rule or order hereunder, which appointment shall be irrevocable. Service upon such attorney shall be as valid and binding as if due and personal service had been made upon such person. Any such appointment shall be effective upon the issuance of the license in connection with which the appointment was filed.

Subd. 2. The commission of any act which constitutes a violation of this chapter or rule or order hereunder by any nonresident person who has not theretofore appointed the commissioner his attorney in compliance with subdivision 1 shall be conclusively deemed an irrevocable appointment by such person of the commissioner and his successor or successors in any action or proceedings against him or in which he may be a party in relation to or involving such violation; and such violation shall be a signification of his agreement that all such legal process which is so served shall be as valid and binding upon him as if due and personal service thereof had been made upon him.

Subd. 3. Service of process under this section may be made by filing a copy of the process with the commissioner or his representative, but is not effective unless:

(a) The plaintiff, who may be the commissioner in an action or proceeding instituted by him, sends notice of the service and a copy of the process by certified mail to the defendant or respondent at his address as shown by the records at the office of the commissioner in the case of service made on the commissioner as attorney pursuant to appointment in compliance with subdivision 1, and at his last known address in the case of service on the commissioner as attorney pursuant to appointment by virtue of subdivision 2; and

(b) The plaintiff's affidavit of compliance with this subdivision is filed in the action or proceeding on or before the return day of the process, if any, or within such further time as the court or hearing examiner allows.

82.32 [PENALTY.]

Any person who violates any provision of this chapter, or any rule or order of the commissioner, shall be guilty of a gross misdemeanor.

82.33 [CIVIL ACTIONS.]

Subdivision 1. No person shall bring or maintain any action in the courts of this state for the collection of compensation for the performance of any of the acts for which a license is required under this chapter without alleging and proving that he was a duly licensed real estate broker or salesperson at the time the alleged cause of action arose.

Subd. 2. No person not required by this chapter to be licensed shall bring or maintain any action in the courts for any commission, fee or other compensation with respect to the sale, lease or other disposition or conveyance of real property, or with respect to the negotiation or attempt to negotiate any sale, lease or other disposition or conveyance of real property unless such property was first listed in writing for sale, lease

Appendix A: Real Estate License Law and Rules and Regulations 177

2800.0100 DEFINITIONS.

Subpart 1. **Scope.** For the purposes of parts 2800.0100 to 2800.1700, 2800.1800 to 2800.2100, 2800.3100 to 2800.7100, 2800.7200, 2800.7300, 2800.7400, 2800.7500, 2800.7600 to 2800.8700, and 2800.9905, the terms defined in this part have the meanings given them.

Subp. 2. **Commissioner.** "Commissioner" means the commissioner of commerce.

Subp. 3. **Licensee.** "Licensee" means a person duly licensed under Minnesota Statutes, chapter 82.

Subp. 4. **Loan broker.** "Loan broker" means a licensed real estate broker or salesperson who, for another and for a commission, fee, or other valuable consideration or with the intention or expectation of receiving the same, directly or indirectly negotiates or offers or attempts to negotiate a loan secured or to be secured by a mortgage or other encumbrance on real estate, or represents himself or herself or otherwise holds himself or herself out as a licensed real estate broker or salesperson, either in connection with any transaction in which he or she directly or indirectly negotiates or offers or attempts to negotiate a loan, or in connection with the conduct of his or her ordinary business activities as a loan broker.

"Loan broker" does not include a licensed real estate broker or salesperson who, in the course of representing a purchaser or seller of real estate, incidentally assists the purchaser or seller in obtaining financing for the real property in question if the licensee does not receive a separate commission, fee, or other valuable consideration for this service.

Subp. 5. **Overpayment.** "Overpayment" means any payment of moneys in excess of a statutory fee or for a license for which a person does not qualify.

Subp. 6. **Override clause.** "Override clause" means a provision in a listing agreement or similar instrument allowing the broker to receive a commission when, after the listing agreement has expired, the property is sold to persons with whom a broker or salesperson had negotiated or exhibited the property prior to the expiration of the listing agreement.

Subp. 7. **Person.** "Person" means a natural person, firm, institution, partnership, corporation, or association.

Subp. 8. **Primary broker.** "Primary broker" means the broker on whose behalf salespersons are licensed to act pursuant to Minnesota Statutes, section 82.20, subdivision 6. In the case of a corporation licensed as a broker, "primary broker" means each officer of the corporation who is individually licensed to act as a broker for the corporation. In the case of a partnership, "primary broker" means each partner licensed to act as a broker for the partnership.

Subp. 9. **Property.** "Property" means real property or other property within the scope of Minnesota Statutes, chapter 82, unless the context clearly indicates otherwise.

Subp. 10. **Protective list.** "Protective list" means the written list of names and addresses of prospective purchasers with whom a licensee has negotiated the sale or rental of the property or to whom a licensee has exhibited the property prior to the expiration of the listing agreement. For the purposes of this subpart, "property" means the property that is the subject of the listing agreement in question.

Subp. 11. **Real estate broker; broker.** "Real estate broker" or "broker" as set forth in Minnesota Statutes, section 82.17, subdivision 4, clause (b) shall not apply to the originating, making, processing, selling, or servicing of a loan in connection with his or her ordinary business activities by a mortgagee, lender, or servicer approved or certified by the secretary of housing and urban development, or approved or certified by the administrator of veterans affairs, or approved or certified by the administrator of the farmers home administration, or approved or certified by the federal home loan mortgage corporation, or approved or certified by the federal national mortgage association.

Subp. 12. **Rental service.** "Rental service" means a person who gathers and catalogs information concerning apartments or other units of real estate available for rent, and who, for a fee, provides information intended to meet the individual needs of specifically identified lessors or prospective lessees. This term shall not apply to newspapers or other periodicals with a general circulation or individual listing contracts between an owner or lessor of property and a licensee.

Subp. 13. **School.** "School" means a person offering or providing real estate education.

MS s 82.28

2800.0200 SCOPE OF APPLICATION.

Prior rules exclusively govern all suits, actions, prosecutions, or proceedings that are pending or may be initiated on the basis of facts or circumstances occurring before the effective date of these rules. Judicial review of all administrative orders issued prior to the effective date of these rules as to which review proceedings have not been instituted by the effective date of these rules is governed by prior rules.

MS s 82.28

2800.0300 COMPUTATION OF TIME.

Subpart 1. **Days.** Where the performance or doing of any act, duty, matter, payment, or thing is ordered or directed, and the period of time or duration for the performance or doing thereof is prescribed and fixed by law, rule or order, such time, except as otherwise provided in subpart 2, shall be computed so as to exclude the first and include the last day of any such prescribed or fixed period or duration of time. When the last day of such period falls on Sunday or on any day made a legal holiday, by the laws of this state or of the United States, such day shall be omitted from the computation.

Subp. 2. **Months.** When the lapse of a number of months before or after a certain day is required by law, rule or order, such number of months shall be computed by counting the months from such day, excluding the calendar month in which such day occurs, and including the day of the month in the last month so counted having the same numerical order as the day of the month from which the computation is made, unless there be not so many days in the last month so counted, in which case the period so computed shall expire with the last day of the months so counted.

MS s 82.28

EXAMINATION AND LICENSING

2800.1100 PAYMENT OF FEES.

Subpart 1. Cash not accepted. All fees shall be paid by check, draft, or other negotiable or nonnegotiable instrument or

Appendix A: Real Estate License Law and Rules and Regulations

order of withdrawal that is drawn against funds held by a financial institution. Cash will not be accepted.

Subp. 2. Overpayment of fees. An overpayment of a fee paid pursuant to Minnesota Statutes, chapter 82 shall be refunded within a reasonable time after a letter requesting the refund is received by the commissioner and signed by the person making the overpayment.

Refunds shall not be given for other than overpayment of fees. A request for a refund of an overpayment must be received by the commissioner within six months of the date of deposit or it will be forfeited.

MS s 82.28

2800.1200 PASSING GRADE FOR EXAMINATION.

A passing grade for a salesperson's and broker's examination shall be a score of 75 percent or higher on the uniform portion and a score of 75 percent or higher on the state portion of the examination.

The commissioner shall not accept the scores of a person who has cheated on an examination. Cheating on a real estate examination shall be grounds for denying an application for a broker's or salesperson's license.

MS s 82.28

2800.1300 LICENSE.

Subpart 1. Application for broker's license. After successful completion of the real estate broker's examination, an individual shall have one year from the date of the examination to apply for a broker's license, unless the individual is a salesperson who remains continuously active in the real estate field as a licensee. Failure to apply for the broker's license or to remain continuously active in the real estate field will necessitate a reexamination.

An individual who holds a broker's license in his or her own name or for or on behalf of a corporation or partnership shall be issued an additional broker's license only upon demonstrating that the additional license is necessary in order to serve a legitimate business purpose; that he or she will be capable of supervising all salespersons over whom he or she will have supervisory responsibility or, in the alternative, that he or she will have no supervisory responsibilities under the additional license; and that he or she has a substantial ownership interest in each corporation or partnership for or on whose behalf he or she holds or will hold a broker's license.

The requirement of a substantial ownership interest shall not apply where the broker seeking the additional license or licenses is an officer of a corporation for or on whose behalf he or she already holds a license and he or she is applying for the additional license or licenses for or on behalf of an affiliated corporation or corporations of which he or she is also an officer. For the purpose of this part, "affiliated corporation" means a corporation which is directly or indirectly controlled by the same persons as the corporation for or on whose behalf he or she is already licensed to act.

For the purposes of this part, a legitimate business purpose includes engaging in a different and specialized area of real estate or maintaining an existing business name.

Subp. 2. Cancellation of salesperson's or broker's license. A salesperson's or broker's license that has been cancelled for failure of a licensee to complete postlicensing education requirements must be returned to the commissioner by the licensee's broker within ten days of receipt of notice of cancellation. The license shall be reinstated without reexamination by completing the required instruction, filing an application, and paying the fee for a salesperson's or broker's license within one year of the cancellation date.

Subp. 3. Waivers. The commissioner may waive the real estate licensing experience requirement for the broker's examination.

A. An applicant for a waiver shall provide evidence of:

(1) successful completion of a minimum of 90 quarter credits or 270 classroom hours of real estate-related studies;

(2) a minimum of five consecutive years of practical experience in real estate-related areas; or

(3) successful completion of 30 credits or 90 classroom hours and three consecutive years of practical experience in real estate-related areas.

B. A request for a waiver shall be submitted to the commissioner in writing and be accompanied by documents necessary to evidence qualification as set forth in item A.

C. The waiver will lapse if the applicant fails to successfully complete the broker's examination within one year from the date of the granting of the waiver.

MS s 82.28

2800.1400 TEMPORARY BROKER'S PERMIT.

In the event of death or incapacity of a broker, the commissioner may issue a 45-day temporary permit to an individual who has had a minimum of two years actual experience as a licensed real estate salesperson and who is otherwise reasonably qualified to act as a broker. Upon application prior to its expiration, the 45-day temporary permit shall be renewed once by the commissioner if the applicant demonstrates that he or she has made a good faith effort to obtain a broker's license within the preceding 45 days and an extension of time will not harm the public interest.

Only those salespersons licensed to the deceased or incapacitated broker at the time of death or incapacity may conduct business for or on behalf of the person to whom the temporary broker's license was issued.

MS s 82.28

2800.1500 COMPLIANCE WITH UNCLAIMED PROPERTY ACT.

Upon the initial application for a real estate broker's license and upon each annual application for renewal, the applicant or broker shall be required to inform the commissioner that he has complied with the requirements set forth in Minnesota Statutes, chapter 345 relating to unclaimed property.

MS s 82.28

2800.1600 NOTICE TO THE COMMISSIONER.

Subpart 1. Mandatory. Licensees shall notify the

commissioner of the facts in subparts 2 to 5.

Subp. 2. **Change of application information.** The commissioner shall be notified in writing of a change of information contained in the license application on file with the commissioner within ten days of the change.

Subp. 3. **Civil judgment.** The commissioner shall be notified in writing within ten days of a final adverse decision or order of a court, whether or not the decision or order is appealed, regarding any proceeding in which the licensee was named as a defendant, and which alleged fraud, if the final adverse decision relates to the allegations of fraud, misrepresentation, or the conversion of funds.

Subp. 4. **Disciplinary action.** The commissioner shall be notified in writing within ten days of the suspension or revocation of a licensee's real estate or other occupational license issued by this state or another jurisdiction.

Subp. 5. **Criminal offense.** The commissioner shall be notified in writing within ten days if a licensee is charged with, adjudged guilty of, or enters a plea of guilty or nolo contendere to a charge of any felony, or of any gross misdemeanor alleging fraud, misrepresentation, conversion of funds or a similar violation of any real estate licensing law.

MS s 82.28

2800.1700 AUTOMATIC TRANSFER OF SALESPERSON'S LICENSE.

Subpart 1. **Scope.** A salesperson may utilize the automatic license transfer provisions of Laws of Minnesota 1982, chapter 478, section 1, subdivision 9, clause (b) if the salesperson commences his or her association with the broker to whom he or she is transferring, as evidenced by the dates of the signatures of both brokers on the form in part 2800.9955, within five days after terminating his or her association with the broker from whom he or she is transferring, provided the salesperson's educational requirements are not past due.

A salesperson may not utilize the automatic license transfer provisions of Laws of Minnesota 1982, chapter 478, section 1, subdivision 9, clause (b) if he or she has failed to notify the commissioner within ten days of any change of information contained in his or her license application on file with the commissioner or of a civil judgment, disciplinary action, or criminal offense, which notice is required pursuant to part 2800.1600.

Subp. 2. **Procedure.** An application for automatic transfer shall be made only on the form in part 2800.9955. The transfer is ineffective if the form is not completed in its entirety.

The form in part 2800.9955 shall be accompanied by a $10 transfer fee, and the license renewal fee, if applicable, plus an additional $10 if the salesperson holds a subdivided land license. Cash will not be accepted. If the licensee holds a subdivided land license it must be transferred at the same time as the salesperson's license. In order for the transfer of the subdivided land license to be effective the broker to whom the salesperson is transferring must also hold a subdivided land license.

The signature on the form in part 2800.9955 of the broker from whom the salesperson is transferring must predate the signature of the broker to whom the salesperson is transferring. The salesperson is unlicensed for the period of time between the times and dates of both signatures. The broker from whom the salesperson is transferring shall sign and date

the transfer application upon the request of the salesperson and shall destroy the salesperson's license immediately.

Subp. 3. **Effective date.** Effective date:

A. The transfer is effective when the broker to whom the salesperson is transferring signs and dates the transfer application form in part 2800.9955, provided the commissioner receives the form and fee within 72 hours after the date and time of the new broker's signature, either by certified mail or personal delivery to the commissioner's office. In the event of a delay in mail delivery, an application postmarked within 24 hours of the date of the signature of the new broker shall be deemed timely received.

B. The transfer is ineffective if the fee is paid by means of a check, draft, or other negotiable or nonnegotiable instrument or order of withdrawal drawn on an account with insufficient funds.

C. The salesperson shall retain the certified mail return receipt, if the transfer application is delivered to the commissioner by mail, retain a photocopy of the executed transfer application, and provide a photocopy of the executed transfer application to the broker from whom he or she is transferring.

MS s 82.20 subd 9

2800.1750 REAL ESTATE SALESPERSON AUTOMATIC TRANSFER.

The real estate salesperson automatic transfer shall be in the form set forth in part 2800.9955.

MS s 82.20 subd 9

2800.1751 INDIVIDUAL APPOINTMENT OF ATTORNEY FOR SERVICE OF PROCESS.

STATE OF MINNESOTA
DEPARTMENT OF COMMERCE
CENTRAL LICENSING SECTION -- REAL ESTATE
5th Floor, Metro Square Bldg.
(Seventh and Robert Streets)
St. Paul, Minnesota 55101

INDIVIDUAL APPOINTMENT OF ATTORNEY FOR SERVICE OF PROCESS

KNOW ALL PERSONS BY THESE PRESENTS:

That in compliance with the Laws of the State of Minnesota, a non-resident, does hereby appoint the Commissioner of Securities of the State of Minnesota, his/her successor or successors as his/her true and lawful attorney upon whom may be served all legal process in any action or proceeding in which he/she may be a party and which relates to or involves any transaction covered by Chapter 82, Minnesota Statutes, and does hereby expressly consent and agree that service upon such attorney shall be as valid and binding as if due and personal service had been made upon him/her and that such appointment shall be irrevocable.

IN WITNESS WHEREOF, I have hereunto set my hand this _____ day of _____, 19____.

Appendix A: Real Estate License Law and Rules and Regulations 181

2800.2100 COURSE COMPLETION CERTIFICATES FOR SALESPERSON'S LICENSE.

Applicants for a salesperson's license shall submit to the commissioner, along with their application for licensure, a copy of the course completion certificate in part 2800.9910 for course I, and for courses II and III if completed prior to being licensed.

Students are responsible for maintaining copies of course completion certificates.

MS s 82.22 subd 13; 82.28

2800.2150 COURSE COMPLETION CERTIFICATE.

The real estate education course completion certificate shall be in the form in part 2800.9910.

MS s 82.28

2800.2175 COURSE II AND III RECORD OF COMPLETION.

The real estate education courses II and III record of completion shall be in the form in part 2800.9930.

MS s 82.28

BROKER PRACTICE

2800.3100 TRUST FUNDS.

Subpart 1. **Listing broker.** Unless otherwise agreed upon in writing by the parties to a transaction, the broker with whom trust funds are to be deposited in satisfaction of Minnesota Statutes, section 82.24, subdivision 1 shall be the listing broker.

Subp. 2. **Maintenance.** Trust funds shall be maintained in a trust account until disbursement is made in accordance with the terms of the applicable agreements and proper accounting is made to the parties entitled to an accounting.

Disbursement shall be made within a reasonable time following the consummation or termination of a transaction if the applicable agreements are silent as to the time of disbursement.

Subp. 3. **Consent to place in special account.** Trust funds may be placed by the broker in a special account, which may be an interest-bearing account or certificate of deposit if the buyer and the seller consent in writing to the special account and to the disposition of the trust funds, including any interest thereon.

Subp. 4. **Licensee as principal.** Funds which would constitute trust funds if received by a licensee acting as an agent must, if received by a licensee acting as principal, be placed in a trust account unless a written agreement signed by all parties to the transaction specifies a different disposition of the funds. The written agreement shall state that the funds would otherwise be placed in a real estate trust account.

MS s 82.28

2800.3200 TRUST ACCOUNT RECORDS.

STATE OF _____)
) SS.
COUNTY OF _____)

On this _____ day of _____, 19___, personally appeared before me, a notary public in and for said County and State, _____, to me known to be the person described in and who executed the foregoing instrument and who, being by me first sworn, acknowledged that he/she executed the same as his/her free act and deed.

_____
Notary Public

(NOTARIAL SEAL) My Commission expires:_____ County_____

MS s 82.28

2800.1800 WITHDRAWAL OF LICENSE OR APPLICATION.

A licensee or license applicant may at any time file with the commissioner a request to withdraw from the status of licensee or to withdraw a pending license application. Withdrawal from the status of licensee or withdrawal of a license application becomes effective 30 days after receipt of a request to withdraw or within a shorter period the commissioner determines unless a revocation, suspension, or denial proceeding is pending when the request to withdraw is filed or a proceeding to revoke, suspend, deny, or to impose conditions upon the withdrawal is instituted within 30 days after the request to withdraw is filed. If a proceeding is pending or instituted, withdrawal becomes effective at the time and upon the conditions the commissioner by order determines. If no proceeding is pending or instituted and withdrawal automatically becomes effective, the commissioner may institute a revocation or suspension proceeding within one year after withdrawal became effective and enter a revocation or suspension order as of the last date on which the license was in effect.

MS s 82.28

2800.1900 FAILURE TO RENEW LICENSE.

If a license lapses or becomes ineffective due to the licensee's failure to file a timely renewal application or otherwise, the commissioner may institute a revocation or suspension proceeding within one year after the license was last effective and enter a revocation or suspension order as of the last date on which the license was in effect.

MS s 82.28

2800.2000 REVOCATIONS.

If the commissioner finds that any licensee or applicant is no longer in existence or has ceased to do business as a broker or salesperson or is subject to an adjudication of mental incompetence or to the control of a committee, conservator, or guardian, or cannot be located after reasonable search, the commissioner may by order revoke the license or deny the application.

MS s 82.28

Trust account records:

A. Every broker shall keep a record of all trust funds received, including notes, savings certificates, uncashed or uncollected checks, or other similar instruments. Said records shall set forth:

(1) date funds received;

(2) from whom received;

(3) amount received;

(4) with respect to funds deposited in a trust account the date of said deposit;

(5) with respect to funds previously deposited in a trust account, the check number or date of related disbursements; and

(6) a monthly balance of the trust account.

Each broker shall maintain a formal trust cash receipts journal and a formal cash disbursement journal, or similar records, in accordance with generally accepted accounting principles. All records and funds shall be subject to inspection by the commissioner or his agent at any time.

B. Each broker shall keep a separate record for each beneficiary or transaction, accounting for all funds therein which have been deposited in the brokers trust bank account. These records shall set forth information sufficient to identify the transaction and the parties thereto. At a minimum, each such record shall set forth:

(1) the date funds are deposited;

(2) the amount deposited;

(3) the date of each related disbursement;

(4) the check number of each related disbursement;

(5) the amount of each related disbursement; and

(6) a description of each disbursement.

C. A check received from the potential buyer shall be deposited into the listing broker's trust account not later than the next business day after delivery of the check to the broker except that the check may be held by the listing broker until acceptance or rejection of the offer if:

(1) the check by its terms is not negotiable by the broker or if the potential buyer has given written instructions that the check shall not be deposited nor cashed until acceptance or shall be immediately returned if the offer is rejected; and

(2) the potential seller is informed that the check is being so held before or at the time the offer is presented to him for acceptance.

If the offer is accepted, the check shall be deposited in a neutral escrow depository or the trust fund account of the listing broker not later than the next business day following acceptance of the offer unless said broker has received written authorization from all parties to the transaction to continue to hold the check. If the offer is rejected, the check shall be returned to the potential buyer not later than the next business day after rejection.

MS s 82.24 subd 5

2800.3300 NONDEPOSITABLE ITEMS.

In the event earnest money or other down payments are received by the broker or salesman in the form of a nondepositable item such as a note, bond, stock certificate, treasury bill or any other item of value taken in lieu of cash, a receipt shall be issued to the buyer for the value thereof and such items shall be deposited immediately with an authorized escrow agent.

In the event the broker acts as the escrow agent, he shall obtain written authority from the buyer and seller to hold such items in escrow. In all cases the parties shall be advised of the details relative to the nondepositable item, including the nature of the item, the amount, and in whose custody such item is being held. The fact that such an item is being held by the broker shall be duly recorded in the brokers trust account records.

MS s 82.28

2800.3400 LOAN BROKERS; STANDARDS OF CONDUCT.

Subpart 1. Compliance. Loan brokers shall comply with the requirements of subparts 2 to 7.

Subp. 2. Contract provisions. A loan broker shall enter into a written contract with each customer and shall provide a copy of the written contract to each customer at or before the time of receipt of any fee or valuable consideration paid for loan brokerage services. The written contract shall:

A. identify the escrow account into which the fees or consideration will be deposited;

B. set forth the circumstances under which the loan broker will be entitled to disbursement from the escrow account;

C. set forth the circumstances under which the customer will be entitled to a refund of all or part of the fee;

D. specifically describe the services to be provided by the loan broker and the dates by which the services will be performed;

E. state the maximum rate of interest to be charged on any loan obtained;

F. contain a statement which notifies the customer of his or her rights to cancel the contract pursuant to subpart 3;

G. disclose, with respect to the 12-month period ending ten business days prior to the date of the contract in question, the percentage of the loan broker's customers for whom loans have actually been funded as a result of the loan broker's services (this disclosure need not be made for any period prior to the effective date of this rule); and

H. disclose the cancellation rights and procedures set forth in subpart 3.

Subp. 3. Cancellation. Any customer of a loan broker who pays a fee prior to the time a loan is actually funded shall have an unconditional right to rescind the contract for loan brokerage services at any time until midnight of the third business day after the day on which the contract is signed. Cancellation is evidenced by the customer giving written notice of cancellation to the loan broker at the address stated in the

Appendix A: Real Estate License Law and Rules and Regulations   183

contract. Notice of cancellation, if given by mail, is effective upon deposit in a mailbox properly addressed to the loan broker with postage prepaid. Notice of cancellation need not take a particular form and is sufficient if it indicates by any form of written expression the intention of the customer not to be bound by the contract. No act of a customer of a loan broker shall be effective to waive the right to rescind as provided in this subpart.

Subp. 4. Escrow account. The loan broker shall deposit in an escrow account within 48 hours all fees received prior to the time a loan is actually funded. The escrow account shall be in a bank located within the state of Minnesota and shall be controlled by an unaffiliated accountant, lawyer, or bank officer or employee.

Subp. 5. Records. The loan broker shall maintain a separate record of all fees received for services performed or to be performed as a loan broker. Each record shall set forth the date funds are received; the person from whom the funds are received; the amount received; the date of deposit in the escrow account; the account number; the date the funds are disbursed and the check number of the disbursement; and a description of each disbursement and the justification for the disbursement.

Subp. 6. Monthly statement. The loan broker shall provide to each customer at least monthly a detailed written accounting of all disbursements of the customer's funds from the trust account.

Subp. 7. Disclosure of lenders. The loan broker shall provide to each customer at the expiration of the contract a list of the lenders or loan sources to whom loan applications were submitted on behalf of the customer.

MS s 82.27 subd 2

2800.3500 PENALTY FOR NONCOMPLIANCE WITH STANDARDS OF CONDUCT.

The methods, acts, or practices set forth in parts 2800.1600 and 2800.3600 to 2800.4400 are standards of conduct governing the activities of real estate brokers and salespersons under Minnesota Statutes, chapter 82. Failure to comply with these standards shall constitute grounds for license denial, suspension, or revocation, or for censure of the licensee.

MS s 82.27 subd 2

2800.3600 RESPONSIBILITIES OF BROKERS.

Subpart 1. Supervision of personnel. Brokers shall adequately supervise the activities of their salespersons and employees. Supervision includes the on-going monitoring of listing agreements, purchase agreements, other real estate-related documents which are prepared or drafted by the broker's salespersons or employees or which are otherwise received by the broker's office, and the review of all trust account books and records. If an individual broker maintains more than one place of business, each place of business shall be under the broker's direction and supervision. If a partnership or corporate broker maintains more than one place of business, each place of business shall be under the direction and supervision of an individual broker licensed to act on behalf of the partnership or corporation.

The primary broker shall maintain records specifying the name of each broker responsible for the direction and supervision of each place of business. If an individual broker, who may be the primary broker, is responsible for supervising more than one place of business, the primary broker shall, upon written request of the commissioner, file a written statement specifying the procedures which have been established to assure that all salespersons and employees are adequately supervised. Designation of another broker to supervise a place of business does not relieve the primary broker of the ultimate responsibility for the actions of licensees.

Subp. 2. Preparation and safekeeping of documents. Brokers shall be responsible for the preparation, custody, safety, and accuracy of all real estate contracts, documents and records, even though another person may be assigned these duties by the broker.

Subp. 3. Documentation and resolution of complaints. Brokers shall investigate and attempt to resolve complaints made regarding the practices of any individual licensed to them and shall maintain, with respect to each individual licensed to any them, a complaint file containing all material relating to any complaints received in writing for a period of three years.

Subp. 4. Disclosure of listed property information. No broker shall allow any unlicensed person to disclose any information regarding a listed property except to state the address of the property and whether it is available for sale or lease.

MS s 82.27 subd 2

2800.3700 DISCLOSURE OF LICENSEE AS AGENT OF BROKER.

A salesperson shall only conduct business under the licensed name of and on behalf of the broker to whom he or she is licensed. An individual broker shall only conduct business under his or her licensed name. A broker licensed to a corporation or partnership shall only conduct business under the licensed corporate or partnership name. A licensee shall affirmatively disclose prior to the negotiation or consummation of any transaction the licensed name of the broker under whom he or she is authorized to conduct business in accordance with this part.

MS s 82.28

2800.3800 LISTING AGREEMENTS.

Subpart 1. Requirement. Licensees shall obtain a signed listing agreement, or other written authorization, from the owner of real property or from another person authorized to offer the property for sale or lease prior to advertising to the general public that the real property is available for sale or lease.

For the purposes of this part "advertising" shall include placing a sign on the owner's property which indicates that the property is being offered for sale or lease.

Subp. 2. Contents. All listing agreements shall be in writing and shall include:

A. a definite expiration date;

B. a description of the real property involved;

C. the list price and any terms required by the seller;

D. the amount of any compensation or commission or the basis for computing the commission;

E. a clear statement explaining the events or

conditions that will entitle a broker to a commission;

F. information regarding an override clause, if applicable, including a statement to the effect that the override clause will not be effective unless the licensee supplies the seller with a protective list within 72 hours after the expiration of the listing agreement; and

G. The following notice in not less than ten point boldface type immediately preceding any provision of the listing agreement relating to compensation of the licensee:

"NOTICE: THE COMMISSION RATE FOR THE SALE, LEASE, RENTAL, OR MANAGEMENT OF REAL PROPERTY SHALL BE DETERMINED BETWEEN EACH INDIVIDUAL BROKER AND ITS CLIENT."

Subp. 3. Prohibited provisions. Licensees shall not include in a listing agreement a holdover clause, automatic extension, or any similar provision, or an override clause in which the length of which is more than six months after the expiration of the listing agreement.

Subp. 4. Override clauses. Licensees shall not seek to enforce an override clause unless a protective list has been furnished to the seller within 72 hours after the expiration of the listing agreement.

Subp. 5. Protective lists. A broker or salesperson has the burden of demonstrating that each person on the protective list has, during the period of the listing agreement, either made an affirmative showing of interest in the property by responding to an advertisement or by contacting the broker or salesperson involved or has been physically shown the property by the broker or salesperson. For the purpose of this part the mere mailing or other distribution by a licensee of literature setting forth information about the property in question does not, of itself, constitute an affirmative showing of interest in the property on the part of a subsequent purchaser.

The protective list shall contain the following notice in boldface type:

"IF YOU RELIST WITH ANOTHER BROKER WITHIN THE OVERRIDE PERIOD AND THEN SELL YOUR PROPERTY TO ANYONE WHOSE NAME APPEARS ON THIS LIST, YOU COULD BE LIABLE FOR FULL COMMISSIONS TO BOTH BROKERS. IF THIS NOTICE IS NOT FULLY UNDERSTOOD, SEEK COMPETENT ADVICE."

The protective list need not contain this notice if the written listing agreement specifically states that after its expiration the seller will not be obligated to pay the licensee a fee or commission if the seller has executed another valid listing agreement pursuant to which the seller is obligated to pay a fee or commission to another licensee for the sale, lease, or exchange of the real property in question.

MS s 82.28

2800.3900 GUARANTEED SALE PROGRAMS.

If a broker advertises or offers a guaranteed sale program, or other program whereby the broker undertakes to purchase real property in the event he or she is unable to effectuate a sale to a third party within a specified period of time, a written disclosure that sets forth clearly and completely the general terms and conditions under which the broker agrees to purchase the property and the disposition of any profit at the time of resale by the broker must be provided to the seller prior to the execution of a listing agreement.

MS s 82.28

2800.4000 DISCLOSURE REQUIREMENTS.

Subpart 1. Advertising. Each licensee shall identify himself or herself as either a broker or an agent in any advertising for the purchase, sale, lease, exchange, mortgaging, transfer, or other disposition of real property, whether the advertising pertains to his or her own property or the property of others.

Subp. 2. Financial interests of licensee. Prior to the negotiation or consummation of any transaction, a licensee shall affirmatively disclose to the owner of real property that the licensee is acting, if the licensee directly, or indirectly through a third party, purchases for himself or herself or acquires, or intends to acquire, any interest in, or any option to purchase, the owner's property.

Subp. 3. Material facts. Licensees shall disclose to any prospective purchaser all material facts pertaining to the property, of which the licensee is aware, which could adversely and significantly affect an ordinary purchaser's use or enjoyment of the property, or any intended use of the property of which the licensee is aware.

Subp. 4. Nonperformance of any party. If a licensee is put on notice by any party to a real estate transaction that the party will not perform in accordance with the terms of a purchase agreement or other similar written agreement to convey real estate, the licensee shall immediately disclose the fact of that party's intent not to perform to the other party or parties to the transaction. Whenever reasonably possible the licensee shall inform the party who will not perform of the licensee's obligation to disclose this fact to the other party or parties to the transaction prior to making the disclosure. The obligation required by this part shall not apply to notice of a party's inability to keep or fulfill any contingency to which the real estate transaction has been made subject.

MS s 82.28

2800.4100 PROHIBITION ON GUARANTEEING FUTURE PROFITS.

Licensees shall not, with respect to the sale or lease of real property, guarantee or affirmatively encourage another person to guarantee future profits or earnings that may result from the purchase or lease of the real property in question unless the guarantee and the assumptions upon which it is based are fully disclosed and contained in the contract, purchase agreement, or other instrument of sale or lease.

MS s 82.28

2800.4200 NEGOTIATIONS.

Subpart 1. Written offers. All written offers to purchase or lease shall be promptly submitted in writing to the seller or lessor.

Subp. 2. Nondisclosure of terms of offer. A licensee shall not disclose the terms of an offer to another prospective buyer or the buyer's agent prior to the presentation of the offer to the seller.

Subp. 3. Closing costs. Licensees shall disclose to a buyer or a seller at or before the time an offer is written or presented that the buyer or seller may be required to pay certain closing costs, which may effectively reduce the proceeds from the sale or increase the cash outlay at closing.

Subp. 4. **Required documents.** Licensees shall furnish to the parties to the transaction at the time the documents are signed or become available a true and accurate copy of listing agreements, earnest money receipts, purchase agreements, contracts for deed, option agreements, closing statements, truth-in-housing forms, energy audits, and any other record, instrument, or document that is material to the transaction and that is in the licensee's possession.

Subp. 5. **Closing statement.** The listing broker or his or her designee shall deliver to the seller at the time of closing a complete and detailed closing statement setting forth all of the receipts and disbursements handled by the broker for the seller. The listing broker shall also deliver to the buyer at the time of closing a complete and detailed statement setting forth the disposition of all moneys received in the transaction from the buyer.

Subp. 6. **Exclusive agency agreements.** A licensee shall not negotiate the sale, exchange, lease, or listing of any real property directly with the owner or lessor knowing that the owner or lessor has executed a written contract granting exclusive agency in connection with the property to another real estate broker. The licensee shall inquire of the owner or lessor whether such a contract exists.

Subp. 7. **Prohibition against interference with contractual relationships of others.** Licensees shall not induce any party to a contract of sale or lease, option, or exclusive listing agreement, to breach the contract, option, or agreement.

Subp. 8. **Prohibition against discouraging use of attorney.** Licensees shall not discourage prospective parties to a real estate transaction from seeking the services of an attorney.

MS s 82.28

2800.4300 COMPENSATION.

Subpart 1. **Licensee to receive only from broker.** A licensee shall not accept a commission or other valuable consideration for the performance of any acts requiring a real estate license from any person except the real estate broker to whom he is licensed or to whom he was licensed at the time of the transaction.

Subp. 2. **Undisclosed compensation.** A licensee shall not accept, give, or charge any undisclosed commission or realize any direct or indirect remuneration that inures to the benefit of the licensee on an expenditure made for a principal.

Subp. 3. **Limitation on broker when transaction not completed.** When the owner fails or is unable to consummate a real estate transaction, through no fault of the purchaser, the listing broker may not claim any portion of any trust funds deposited with the broker by the purchaser, absent a separate agreement with the purchaser.

MS s 82.28

2800.4400 ACCESS TO GOVERNING STATUTES AND RULES.

Every real estate office and branch office shall have a current copy of Minnesota Statutes, chapters 82 and 83 and the rules adopted thereunder, available for the use of licensees.

MS s 82.28

2800.4500 RENTAL SERVICES.

Subpart 1. **License.** A rental service shall obtain a real estate broker's license prior to engaging in business or holding itself out as being engaged in business. No person shall act as a real estate salesperson on behalf of a rental service without first obtaining a real estate salesperson's license on behalf of the rental service.

Subp. 2. **Dissemination of unit information.** A rental service shall not provide information regarding a rental unit without the express authority of the owner of the unit.

Subp. 3. **Availability of unit.** A rental service shall not represent a unit as currently available unless its availability has been verified within 72 hours preceding the representation.

Subp. 4. **Advertising.** A rental service shall not advertise in a manner that is misleading with regard to fees charged, services provided, the availability of rental units, or rental terms or conditions.

MS s 82.28

2800.4600 FRAUDULENT, DECEPTIVE, AND DISHONEST PRACTICES.

Subpart 1. **Prohibitions.** For the purposes of Minnesota Statutes, section 82.27, subdivision 1, clause (b), the following acts and practices constitute fraudulent, deceptive, or dishonest practices:

A. act on behalf of more than one party to a transaction without the knowledge and consent of all parties;

B. act in the dual capacity of licensee and undisclosed principal in any transaction;

C. receive funds while acting as principal which funds would constitute trust funds if received by a licensee acting as an agent, unless the funds are placed in a trust account. Funds need not be placed in a trust account if a written agreement signed by all parties to the transaction specifies a different disposition of the funds, in accordance with part 2800.3100, subpart 4;

D. violate any state or federal law concerning discrimination intended to protect the rights of purchasers or renters of real estate;

E. make a material misstatement in an application for a license or in any information furnished to the commissioner;

F. procure or attempt to procure a real estate license for himself or herself or any person by fraud, misrepresentation, or deceit;

G. represent membership in any real-estate related organization in which the licensee is not a member;

H. advertise in any manner that is misleading or inaccurate with respect to properties, terms, values, policies, or services conducted by the licensee;

I. make any material misrepresentation or permit or allow another to make any material misrepresentation;

J. make any false or misleading statements, or permit or allow another to make any false or misleading statements, of a character likely to influence, persuade, or induce the consummation of a transaction contemplated by Minnesota Statutes, chapter 82;

K. fail within a reasonable time to account for or to

remit any money coming into the licensee's possession which belongs to another;

L. commingle with his or her own money or property trust funds or any other money or property of another held by the licensee;

M. demand from a seller a commission to which the licensee is not entitled, knowing that he or she is not entitled thereto;

N. pay or give money or goods of value to an unlicensed person for any assistance or information relating to the procurement by a licensee of a listing of a property or of a prospective buyer of a property (this item does not apply to money or goods paid or given to the parties to the transaction);

O. fail to maintain a trust account at all times, as provided by law;

P. engage, with respect to the offer, sale, or rental of real estate, in an anticompetitive activity.

Subp. 2. Determining violation. A licensee shall be deemed to have violated this part if he has been found to have violated the Minnesota Antitrust Law of 1971, Minnesota Statutes, sections 325D.49 to 325D.66 by a final decision or order of a court of competent jurisdiction.

Subp. 3. Commissioner's authority. Nothing in this part limits the authority of the commissioner to take actions against a licensee for fraudulent, deceptive, or dishonest practices not specifically described in this part.

MS s 82.27 subd 2

INITIAL REAL ESTATE EDUCATION

2800.5100 NINETY-HOUR INITIAL EDUCATION.

An approved 90-hour course of initial education shall consist of three 30-classroom-hour courses to be designated as course I, course II, and course III. Pursuant to Minnesota Statutes, section 82.22, subdivision 6, each applicant for a salesperson's license or salesperson is required to complete all courses successfully. Courses I, II, and III must be taken in sequence and may not be taken concurrently.

MS s 82.28

2800.5200 SALESPERSON'S EXAMINATION.

Applicants must successfully complete the salesperson's examination within one year after the successful completion of course I. After this date, credit for course I will expire and successful completion of the first 30-hour course must be repeated before taking the salesperson's examination.

An exception will be made for students pursuing a full-time course of study in either a two-year or four-year real estate education program. The burden of demonstrating full-time status is on the student. Applicants must successfully complete the salesperson's examination within one year after the successful completion of the two-year or four-year course of study.

MS s 82.28

2800.5300 APPLICATION FOR SALESPERSON'S LICENSE.

Applicants must apply for a salesperson's license within one year after successful completion of the licensing examination. Applicants who fail to apply for a license within the one-year period must retake course I and successfully complete the examination.

MS s 82.28

2800.5400 POSTLICENSING EDUCATION COURSE.

Courses II and III must be completed within one year after obtaining a salesperson's license.

MS s 82.28

2800.5500 ALTERNATIVE MEANS OF COMPLETING INITIAL EDUCATION.

Applicants may elect to complete course II and course III prior to examination or licensure and shall receive credit for those courses successfully completed if the applicant is otherwise in compliance with the time limitations set forth in parts 2800.5200 and 2800.5300.

MS s 82.28

2800.5600 LIMITATIONS ON COURSE SUBSTITUTIONS.

No course may be substituted for course I. Written requests for substitutions for courses II and III shall be granted if the request is submitted no later than six months prior to the date upon which that education is due to be completed, if:

A. the salesperson is engaged exclusively in a specialized field, such as property management, and the course proposed to be substituted for course II or III provides the student with at least 30 hours of instruction in that field; or

B. the salesperson demonstrates successful completion of a course in another jurisdiction that is substantially similar to course II or III.

MS s 82.28

2800.5700 LIMITATION ON USE TOWARD CONTINUING EDUCATION COURSES.

Courses I and II may not be taken for credit toward a licensee's continuing education requirements.

Any course III may be taken for credit toward a licensee's continuing education requirements if the licensee has not previously received credit for that course or a substantially similar course.

MS s 82.28

2800.5800 TEXTBOOKS REQUIRED.

Courses I, II, and III shall require the use of a textbook. The textbook shall cover substantially the subject matter of the course. The textbook shall be current and may be disallowed by the commissioner upon demonstration that it contains material errors.

MS s 82.28

Appendix A: Real Estate License Law and Rules and Regulations 187

2800.5900 COMPLETION OF INITIAL EDUCATION.

Successful completion of courses I, II and III includes full-time classroom attendance throughout the course, completion of required assignments or reading materials if applicable, and passage of an examination designed by the school that is sufficiently comprehensive to measure the student's knowledge of all aspects of the course.

MS s 82.28

2800.6000 COURSE I HOURS.

Course I shall incorporate the following number of hours for each of the following topics, for a total of 30 hours:

A. introduction to real estate, one hour;

B. real estate licensing law (Minnesota Statutes chapters 82 and 83), four hours;

C. law of agency, four hours;

D. law of contracts, five hours;

E. real estate financing, six hours;

F. types and classifications of property, three hours;

G. examination of title, one hour; and

H. title closing, six hours.

MS s 82.28

2800.6100 COURSE I CURRICULUM.

The course I curriculum shall be based on the following outline:

I. Introduction to real estate
   A. Overview of course I
      1. Course goals
      2. Attendance
      3. Examination policy
      4. Course and instructor evaluation
   B. Scope of industry
   C. Areas of specialization
   D. Industry terminology
   E. Professional standards and ethics
   F. Broker-salesperson relationship

II. Real estate license law, (Minnesota Statutes, chapter 82), Subdivided Land Sales Practices Act (Minnesota Statutes, chapter 83) and securities act (Minnesota Statutes, chapter 80A)
   A. Real estate license law
      1. Purpose of law and rules
      2. Administration of law
      3. Substantive provisions of law
         a. Trust accounts
         b. Prohibition of fraudulent, deceptive or dishonest practices
         c. Standards of conduct
         d. Federal and state antidiscrimination laws
         e. Licensing requirements
         f. Education requirements
         g. Real estate education, research and recovery fund
   B. Subdivided land sales practices act
      1. Scope of law
      2. Registration and public disclosure provisions
      3. Licensing requirements
   C. Securities act; potential applicability to real estate

III. Law of agency
   A. Agent and agency
      1. Broker-principal relationship
      2. Termination of relationships
      3. Dual agency
      4. Cooperative broker
   B. Duties of broker and agent
      1. Accountability
      2. Fiduciary responsibility to seller
      3. Full disclosure
   C. Listing contract
      1. Types
      2. Essential elements of a listing agreement
      3. Multiple listing
      4. Commissions earned
   D. Responsibilities to buyer

IV. Contracts
   A. Definition
      1. Types
      2. Essentials

3. Breach; remedies
B. Purchase agreements
   1. Examination and analysis
C. Other types of contracts
   1. Contract for deed
   2. Options
D. Cancellation of contract
E. Property description
   1. Lot and block number
   2. Metes and bounds
   3. Government survey
   4. Datum planes
   5. Measurement and mathematics

V. Real estate financing
A. Note as evidence of indebtedness
B. Sources of mortgage funds
   1. Lenders
   2. Secondary mortgage market
   3. Owner financing
C. Mortgage
   1. Legal elements
   2. Theories
      a. Lien
      b. Title
   3. Mortgage clauses
      a. Covenants
         1. Indebtedness
         2. Insurance
         3. Removal
         4. Taxes
         5. Acceleration clause
         6. Warranty of title
      b. Special clauses
         1. Attorney's fees
         2. Receiver
         3. Sale in one parcel
         4. Trust
         5. Prepayment penalties
         6. Subordination
         7. Due-on-sale clause
         8. Condemnation clause
         9. Defeasance clause
         10. Good repair
D. Types of mortgages
   1. FHA
   2. VA
   3. Conventional/insured conventional, types currently available
   4. Other
   5. Points
E. Mortgage assumption and nonalienation
F. Contract for deed financing
G. Foreclosure (default)
   1. Mortgage
   2. Contract for deed
H. Buyer qualifications
   1. Credit information
   2. Standards for approval
I. Usury law

VI. Types of property
A. Classification
   1. Real property
   2. Personal property
   3. Fixtures
B. Title
   1. Private grant
   2. Public grant
   3. Political relations
      a. Eminent domain
      b. Escheat
   4. Public policy
      a. Adverse possession
      b. Prescription

Appendix A: Real Estate License Law and Rules and Regulations

      c. License
- C. Estates and interests in land
  1. Estates
  2. Fee simple
  3. Life estate (waste)
  4. Remainders and reversions
  5. Other
- D. Concurrent ownership
  1. Joint tenancy
  2. Tenancy in common
  3. Other
- E. Easements

VII. Examination of title
- A. History
- B. Examination of abstract
- C. Title insurance
  1. Owners
  2. Purchasers
  3. Mortgage
- D. Title registration (Torrens)

VIII. Title closing
- A. Review of topics I-VII
- B. Closing checklist
- C. Methods of closing
  1. Closing through escrow
  2. Other
- D. Delivery of deed
- E. Responsibilities of buyer and seller
  1. Taxes and liens
  2. Reduction certificate (assumption statement)
  3. Insurance
  4. Leases
  5. Bill of sale
  6. Title search
  7. Survey
  8. Leases
  9. Certificate of occupancy
  10. Violations (ordinances)
  11. Apportionments
- F. Adjournment of closing (settlement)
- G. Real estate settlement procedures act
  1. Lender requirements
  2. Truth-in-lending (regulation Z)
  3. Settlement (closing)
- H. Broker's responsibilities

MS s 82.28

2800.6200 COURSE II HOURS.

Course II shall incorporate the following number of hours for each of the following topics, for a total of 30 hours:

- A. deeds, three hours;
- B. search and examination of title, one hour;
- C. residential appraisal, six hours;
- D. residential construction, two hours;
- E. land development and use, three hours;
- F. condominiums, cooperatives, planned unit developments, and manufactured housing, three hours;
- G. taxation, four hours;
- H. investment and appraisal, four hours;
- I. real property management, two hours; and
- J. leases and leasing, two hours.

MS s 82.28

2800.6300 COURSE II CURRICULUM.

The course II curriculum shall be based on the following outline:

I. Deeds
- A. Parts of a deed
  1. Parties
  2. Consideration
  3. Words of conveyance
  4. Property description
  5. Appurtenances
  6. Habendum (estate)
  7. Execution and acknowledgement

       8. Seal
    B. Delivery
    C. Recording
    D. Types of deeds
       1. Quitclaim
       2. Warranty deed and covenants
       3. Special warranty deed
       4. Other
    E. Covenants running with the land
    F. Validity
II. Search and examination of title
    A. Object of search
       1. Chain of title
       2. Recording acts
    B. Grantor-grantee system of indexing
       1. Running the chain of title
       2. Grantors
       3. Mortgages
       4. Lis pendens
       5. Judgments
       6. Liens
       7. Taxes
       8. Probate court
       9. Special assessments
    C. Lot and block indexing
III. Residential appraisal
    A. Values
       1. Economic concepts
       2. Value and price
       3. Cost
       4. Elements of value
          a. Physical
          b. Economic
          c. Social
          d. Legal
       5. Characteristics of value
          a. Utility
          b. Scarcity, demand
          c. Transferability
       6. Principles of value
          a. Substitution
          b. Conformity
          c. Anticipation
    B. Fundamental considerations
       1. Population trends
       2. Neighborhood characteristics
       3. Building description
       4. Site evaluation
       5. Market value
    C. Highest and best use
       1. Factors of production
       2. Diminishing returns
       3. Over and under improvement
    D. Approaches to value
       1. Cost
       2. Market
       3. Income
    E. Appraisal report
IV. Residential construction
    A. Government regulations
    B. Architectural styles
    C. Plans and specifications
       1. Foundations
       2. Exterior
       3. Interior
    D. Disclosure
V. Land development and use
    A. Public land use control
       1. City planning
          a. Enabling acts
          b. Planning commissions
          c. Capital improvements

            d. Master planning
            e. Future scope of planning
        2. Zoning
            a. Purpose
            b. Form of ordinances
            c. Exclusionary zoning
            d. Board of appeals
            e. Nonconforming use
            f. Variance
            g. Green acres law
        3. Building codes
        4. Environmental impact statements
        5. Subdivision regulations
    B. Prepurchase
        1. Analysis of market
        2. Site selection
        3. Land costs
        4. Drainage, soil tests, topography
        5. Utilities
        6. Road costs
        7. Transportation, schools, shopping
        8. Covenants
        9. Government
        10. Financing
            a. Purchase, option or escrow
            b. Rolling option
    C. Planning
        1. Subdivision
        2. Planned urban development
        3. Filing the plat
        4. Consumerism and environmental protection
        5. Subdivided land sales practices act
        6. State and local land use regulations
    D. Urban development and revitalization
VI. Condominiums, cooperatives, planned unit developments and manufactured housing
    A. Cluster housing
        1. History
        2. Economics
            a. Land use efficiency
            b. Amenities
    B. Condominiums
        1. Rights and obligations
            a. Declaration
                (1) Bylaws
                (2) Rules and regulations
                (3) Assessments and collections
                (4) Homeowners' associations
            b. Map
            c. Conveyance
            d. Management agreement
                (1) Duties
                (2) Enforcement of rules
                (3) Collection of fees and dues
        2. Financing
        3. Time share ownership
        4. Minnesota Condominium Act
        5. Conversions
            a. Physical changes
            b. Feasibility
            c. Tenant rights
            d. Moratoriums
    C. Cooperatives
        1. Cooperator (individual shareholder)
        2. Refinancing methods
        3. Owner's association
        4. Tax treatment (the 80 percent rule)
        5. Other forms
    D. Planned unit developments
        1. Planned land uses
        2. Organization
    E. Manufactured housing
        1. Definition

2. Considerations
    a. Site
    b. Value
    c. Safety
3. Financing

VII. Taxation
A. Real property taxes
    1. Tax assessment levies
        a. City
        b. County
        c. School district
    2. Obtaining tax information
    3. Appraisal and classification
    4. Homestead status
B. Residential property
    1. Basis
    2. Adjustment of basis
    3. Installment plan sales
    4. Tax deferral on sale and repurchase
    5. Tax implications of residential ownership
C. Income producing property
    1. Long term capital gain and loss
    2. Offsetting gains and losses
    3. Classification
D. Depreciation on real property
E. Residential rehabilitation expense

VIII. Investment and appraisal
A. Risks
    1. Purchasing power
    2. Market
    3. Interest rates
    4. Earning power
    5. Liquidity
B. Leverage
C. Cash and tax flow
D. Investment analysis
    1. Effective gross income
    2. Margin
    3. Return on investment
E. Real estate syndication
    1. General partners
    2. Limited partners
    3. Regulation
    4. Risks and rewards
F. Real estate investment trusts
G. Appraisal of investment property
    1. Net operating income
        a. Converting net income to value
        b. Rate of return (discount rate)
    2. Estimate of value

IX. Real property management
A. Background
    1. Development of management
    2. Scope of management
        a. Residential
        b. Commercial
        c. Industrial
        d. Agricultural
    3. Professional management
    4. Types of owners
B. Management plan
    1. Objectives
    2. Regional analysis
    3. Neighborhood analysis
    4. Property analysis
        a. Physical
        b. Fiscal
        c. Operational
    5. Market analysis
        a. Costs and profit
        b. Comparable
        c. Escalation base

Appendix A: Real Estate License Law and Rules and Regulations 193

```
        6. Analysis of alternatives
        7. Conclusions and recommendations
     C. Government and real estate management
        1. Local government
           a. Rent control
           b. Handicapped requirements
           c. Fire code requirements
           d. Miscellaneous ordinances
        2. State government
           a. Landlord-tenant laws
           b. Nondiscrimination
           c. Extension of tenants' rights
        3. Federal government
           a. Nondiscrimination
           b. HUD subsidies
           c. Regulated housing
        4. Housing programs
     D. Management operations
        1. Marketing
        2. Tenant underwriting
        3. Tenant administration
        4. Physical plant maintenance
           a. Preventative maintenance
           b. Energy management
        5. Operational record keeping
           a. Physical records
           b. Tenant files
           c. Budget
           d. Fiscal
  X. Leases and leasing
     A. Statute of frauds
     B. Elements of a contract (review)
     C. Types of tenancies
        1. Estate for years
        2. Tenancy from year to year
        3. Tenancy at will
        4. Tenancy at sufferance
        5. Holdover tenants
     D. Types of leases
        1. Gross
        2. Net
        3. Percentage
        4. Land
        5. Farm
     E. Form of lease
        1. Common covenants
        2. Residential leases
        3. Responsibilities of lessor
        4. Responsibilities of lessee
        5. Termination
           a. Expiration
           b. Automatic renewal
           c. Breach of conditions
           d. Abandonment
           e. Eviction
        6. Minnesota landlord-tenant act

                                        MS s 82.28

2800.6400 COURSE III HOURS.

    Course III shall be a 30-hour course consisting of one of
the following:

    A. real estate appraisal, 30 hours;
    B. closing procedures, 30 hours;
    C. farm and ranch brokerage, 30 hours;
    D. real estate finance, 30 hours;
    E. real estate investment, 30 hours;
    F. real estate law, 30 hours;
    G. real estate management, 30 hours;
    H. real estate mathematics, 30 hours;
    I. business brokerage, 30 hours; or
    J. a combination course of no more than three of the
subjects set forth in items A to I, 30 hours.

                                        MS s 82.28
```

2800.6500 COURSE III CURRICULUM.

Subpart 1. Real estate appraisal. The real estate appraisal course shall be based on the following outline:

Real estate appraisal

I. Nature, importance and purposes of appraisals
II. Nature, importance and characteristics of property and value
III. Principles controlling real estate value
IV. The appraisal process
V. Economic and neighborhood analysis
VI. Considerations and fundamentals of site evaluation
VII. Construction methods and materials
VIII. Architectural styles and utility
IX. Cost approach: estimating costs and accrued depreciation
X. Analysis
XI. Market data approach
XII. Income approach: income and expense analysis, capitalization theory and techniques
XIII. Reconciliation and final value estimate
XIV. Writing the report
XV. Course examination

Subp. 2. Closing procedures. The closing procedures course shall be based on the following outline:

Closing procedures

I. Overview of closing: persons present, protocol, timeliness
II. Review of purchase agreement, supplements, addenda
III. Compilation of data needed to prepare a closing file
IV. Legal documents
V. Abstracts, title procedures
VI. Review of settlement costs: buyer, seller
VII. Closing statement: prorations and other math
VIII. Review of sample cases
IX. Follow-up procedures
X. Course examination

Subp. 3. Farm and ranch. The farm and ranch brokerage course shall be based on the following outline:

Farm and ranch brokerage

I. Responsibilities of broker to seller and buyer
II. Selling options
III. Sources of financing
IV. Factors in selecting a farm or ranch
V. Advantages and disadvantages of irrigation systems
VI. Determination of farm and ranch value
VII. Considerations in the constructing of purchase agreements
VIII. Course examination

Subp. 4. Real estate finance. The real estate finance course shall be based on the following outline:

Real estate finance

I. Introduction to the mortgage market
II. Sources of mortgage money
III. Real estate investment trusts and syndication
IV. Mortgage banking
V. Financing residential properties
VI. Financing income producing properties
VII. Construction and land development loans
VIII. Special techniques used in financing real estate
IX. Junior mortgages
X. Land contracts
XI. Financing long term leases
XII. Course examination

Subp. 5. Real estate investment. The real estate investment course shall be based on the following outline:

Real estate investment

I. Real estate investments
II. Discounted cash flow analysis
III. Measuring investment returns
IV. Estimation of real estate cash flows
V. Real estate financing
VI. The tax process
VII. Acquisitions and operations
VIII. Dispositions and exchanges
IX. After tax investment analysis
X. Speculative land investment
XI. Multiple exchanges
XII. Course examination

Appendix A: Real Estate License Law and Rules and Regulations   195

Subp. 6. **Real estate law.** The real estate law course shall be based on the following outline:

Real estate law

I. The process of real estate law
II. Real estate brokerage
III. Contract for the sale of real estate
IV. Property conveyance
V. Title insurance and closing
VI. Property ownership and taxes
VII. Estates in land and landlord/tenant relationships
VIII. Cooperatives, condominiums and planned unit developments
IX. Real estate lending and land use regulations
X. Course examination

Subp. 7. **Real estate management.** The real estate management course shall be based on the following outline:

Real estate management

I. Overview and economics of real estate management
II. Government involvement
III. The management plan
IV. Owner relations and record keeping
V. Marketing and leasing
VI. Property operations
   A. Tenant administration
   B. Physical plant maintenance
   C. Staffing and employee relations
VII. Residential management
   A. Rental housing
   B. Condominiums and cooperatives
VIII. Commercial management
   A. Office building and special purpose properties
   B. Shopping centers and retail properties
IX. The management office
X. Creative property management
XI. Course examination

Subp. 8. **Real estate mathematics.** The real estate mathematics course shall be based on the following outline:

Real estate mathematics

I. Functions
   A. Percentages, fractions, decimals, equivalencies, functions
   B. Basic geometric rules
   C. Ratio, proportion, scale
   D. Basic algebraic operations
II. Areas of application to real estate
   A. Broker trust accounts
   B. Sales and listings
   C. Valuation and spatial problems
   D. Finance
   E. Income and investment property
   F. Closing
III. Course examination

Subp. 9. **Business brokerage.** The business brokerage course shall be based on the following outline:

Business brokerage

I. Business financial statements
II. Financial statement ratio analysis
III. Cash flow, rate of return, and breakeven analysis
IV. Competitive market analysis
V. Valuation of the business
VI. Developing the business plan
VII. Qualifying the buyer
VIII. Terms of the purchase agreement
IX. Financing the business opportunity
X. Evaluation of business risk
XI. Course examination

Subp. 10. **Combination course.** A combination course shall consist of no more than three of the preceding nine subparts and shall devote at least ten hours to each subject. A school that proposes to offer a combination course III shall submit to the commissioner, as part of the application for approval, an outline setting forth the subjects to be addressed and the number of hours proposed to be devoted to each topic.

MS s 82.28

2800.6600 COURSE III OBJECTIVES.

Subpart 1. **Real estate appraisal.** Upon completion of the real estate appraisal course, a student should be able to explain the nature, importance and characteristics of the factors affecting property value; perform an economic and neighborhood analysis; discuss and apply the cost, market and income approaches to value; estimate the value of one to four unit residential properties; and prepare a written report of the appraisal.

Subp. 2. **Closing procedures.** Upon completion of the closing procedures course, a student should be able to develop a checklist of activities and documents needed to carry out a closing; coordinate the compilation of information and documents from all parties to a closing; interpret all information on a purchase agreement; compute prorations and other calculations required for a closing; complete acceptable legal formats for all documents serving to transfer title; prepare an accurate closing statement; and develop a closing file system.

Subp. 3. **Farm and ranch brokerage.** Upon completion of the farm and ranch brokerage course, a student should be able to utilize the management assistance available to brokers, buyers, and sellers of farm real estate; determine the value of farm or ranch real estate; understand the components that make up farm and ranch real estate; identify and describe methods of financing farm and ranch property; and understand the considerations in the preparation of a purchase agreement for the sale of farm or ranch property.

Subp. 4. **Real estate finance.** Upon completion of the real estate finance course, a student should be able to identify and describe methods of financing real property; explain the role of financial institutions in financing the purchase or sale of real estate; utilize compound interest or "time value of money" concepts to facilitate investment and financing decisions; apply these methods to solve client financing problems; and discuss the practices and procedures of loan application, analysis, closings and foreclosure.

Subp. 5. **Real estate investment.** Upon completion of the real estate investment course, a student should be able to understand and describe investment tax considerations such as depreciation, capital gains, installment sales and exchanges; utilize the mathematics of real estate investment; perform feasibility studies including market analysis; perform property analysis; and apply techniques of investment analysis to specific types of real estate.

Subp. 6. **Real estate law.** Upon completion of the real estate law course, a student should be able to understand the process of real estate law, its historical origins, and the legal responsibilities placed upon real estate salespersons and brokers; prepare and understand the basic contracts of property conveyance; explain the major legal aspects of property taxes, and leasing agreements; recognize and apply the specific requirements in planned unit developments, condominium, and cooperative housing transactions; and understand the requirements of real estate lending and land use rules.

Subp. 7. **Real estate management.** Upon completion of the real estate management course, a student should be able to explain and discuss the scope, nature, and importance of property management; outline the essentials of a management plan; and understand the significant differences between residential, commercial, industrial, and retail property management.

Subp. 8. **Real estate mathematics.** Upon completion of the real estate mathematics course, a student should be able to identify required mathematical procedures to be used in real estate transactions; perform required mathematical functions with a high level of accuracy; isolate and explain the steps of each calculation; and explain mathematical procedures to clients as needed.

Subp. 9. **Business brokerage.** Upon completion of the business brokerage course, a student should be able to evaluate business financial statements, qualify potential buyers, review relevant markets including competition, develop a business plan, value the firm's assets and goodwill, negotiate the terms of a purchase agreement, and explain terms of financing, valuation, and business risk to a potential buyer.

MS s 82.28

CONTINUING EDUCATION COURSES

2800.6800 CONTINUING EDUCATION.

Subpart 1. **Content.** Continuing education shall consist of approved courses that impart substantive and procedural knowledge in the real estate field.

Subp. 2. **Attendance.** Courses must be attended in their entirety in order for a licensee to obtain credit. No credit will be given for partial attendance at a course.

Subp. 3. **Credit approved.** Courses will be approved only in hour segments. No fractional hours will be approved, nor will applicants be given credit for any period of less than a whole hour.

Subp. 4. **Examinations.** Course examinations will not be required for continuing education courses unless they are required by the school or the licensee elects to take course III for continuing education credit.

Subp. 5. **Textbooks.** Textbooks are not required to be used for continuing education courses. In instances in which textbooks are not used, students are to be provided with a syllabus containing, at a minimum, the course title; the times and dates of the course offering; the names and addresses or telephone numbers of the course coordinator and instructor; and a detailed outline of the subject materials to be covered.

Subp. 6. **Credit earned.** Upon completion of approved courses, students shall earn one hour of continuing education credit for each hour of attendance and approved instructors shall earn three hours of continuing education credit for each hour of instruction. Credit may not be earned if the licensee has previously obtained credit for the same course as either a student or instructor.

Subp. 7. **Disapproved courses.** Approval will not be granted for courses designed to prepare students for passing any licensing examinations; in mechanical office or business skills, including typing, speed-reading, use of calculators, or other machines or equipment; in sales promotion, including meetings held in conjunction with the general business of the licensee's broker; or in motivation, salesmanship, psychology, or time management.

Subp. 8. **Continuing education credit for course III.** Licensees may attend or teach course III for continuing education credit. Credit will be given for course III for less than the entire course III only for combination courses offered pursuant to part 2800.6400, subpart 10. Credit will be given only for attendance at segments of the combination course III which completely cover a subject. An examination will be required only if the licensee takes the entire combination course or if the school requires a separate examination for each subject covered.

Subp. 9. **Burden of proof.** The burden of demonstrating that courses impart substantive and procedural knowledge in the real estate field is upon the person seeking approval or credit.

MS s 82.22 subd 13; 82.28

Appendix A: Real Estate License Law and Rules and Regulations 197

GENERAL COURSE AND CONTINUING EDUCATION REQUIREMENTS

2800.7100 GENERAL REAL ESTATE EDUCATION REQUIREMENTS.

Parts 2800.7200 to 2800.8750 constitute general requirements applicable to all real estate education courses.

MS s 82.22 subd 13; 82.28

2800.7150 APPLICATION FOR COURSE APPROVAL FOR COURSES I, II, AND III.

The real estate education application for course approval for courses I, II, and III shall be in the form in part 2800.9920.

MS s 82.28

2800.7175 APPLICATION FOR COURSE APPROVAL FOR CONTINUING EDUCATION.

The real estate education application for course approval for continuing education shall be in the form in part 2800.9935.

MS s 82.22 subd 13

2800.7200 COURSE APPROVAL.

Subpart 1. **Advance approval.** Courses must be approved by the commissioner in advance and will be approved or disapproved on the basis of their compliance with the provisions of Minnesota Statutes, section 82.22 and the rules adopted thereunder.

No advance approval is required for continuing education offerings if the licensee demonstrates attendance at an offering that was in substantial compliance with Minnesota Statutes, chapter 82 and the rules adopted thereunder.

Approval will not include time spent on breaks, meals, or other unrelated activities.

Subp. 2. **Permitted course offerings.** Courses complying with Minnesota Statutes, chapter 82 and the rules adopted thereunder may be offered or sponsored by schools.

Coordinators must immediately notify the commissioner of any material change in an application for approval or in the exhibits attached to it.

Subp. 3. **Limitation on advertising.** Courses may not be advertised prior to approval.

Subp. 4. **Applications.** Applications for course approval will be accepted on forms prescribed by the commissioner no later than 30 days prior to the course offering and shall include the following:

A. the course title;

B. the date, time, and place of the course offering;

C. the name, address, and telephone number of the sponsoring entity;

D. the name, address, and telephone number of the course coordinator;

E. the name, address, and telephone number of the instructor;

F. the name, edition, and date of publication of the text to be used, if applicable;

G. a detailed outline of the course offering, or a statement of compliance with the prescribed outlines for course I, II, or III; and

H. compliance with the service of process provisions of Minnesota Statutes, section 82.31, if applicable.

Subp. 5. **Application forms.** The form in part 2800.9920 shall be used for courses I, II, and III and the form in part 2800.9935 shall be used for continuing education courses.

Subp. 6. **Subsequent offerings of courses.** Approval shall be granted for subsequent offerings of identical continuing education courses without requiring a new application if a notice of subsequent offerings, as in part 2800.9945, is filed with the commissioner at least 30 days in advance of the date the course is to be held.

Subsequent offerings of identical courses I, II, and III do not require the approval of or notice to the commissioner.

MS s 82.22 subd 13; 82.28

2800.7250 NOTICE OF SUBSEQUENT OFFERINGS OF CONTINUING EDUCATION COURSES.

The real estate education notice of subsequent offerings of continuing education courses shall be in the form in part 2800.9945.

MS s 82.22 subd 13

2800.7300 COURSES OPEN TO ALL.

All course offerings shall be open to any interested individuals. Discounts of tuition shall not be given because of affiliation with any particular brokerage or franchise.

MS s 82.22 subd 13; 82.28

2800.7400 COURSE COORDINATOR.

Subpart 1. **Mandatory.** Each course of study shall have one coordinator, approved by the commissioner, who is responsible for supervising the program and assuring compliance with Minnesota Statutes, chapter 82 and the rules adopted thereunder. Schools may engage an additional approved coordinator in order to assist the coordinator or to act as a substitute for the coordinator in the event of an emergency or illness.

Subp. 2. **Qualifications.** The commissioner shall approve as a coordinator a person meeting one or more of the following criteria: a minimum of the previous five years as an active real estate broker; at least three years of full-time experience in the administration of an education program during the five-year period immediately preceding the date of application; or a degree in education plus two years real estate experience.

Subp. 3. **Form for coordinator approval.** Application for approval must be submitted on the form in part 2800.9915.

Subp. 4. **Responsibilities.** A coordinator shall be

responsible for:

A. assuring compliance with all laws and rules pertaining to real estate education;

B. assuring that students are provided with current and accurate information relating to the laws and rules governing their real estate activity;

C. supervising and evaluating courses and instructors. Supervision shall include assuring, especially when a course will be taught by more than one instructor, that all areas of the curriculum are addressed without redundancy and that continuity is present throughout the entire course;

D. furnishing the commissioner, upon request, with copies of evaluations of instructors or courses;

E. investigating complaints related to course offerings and instructors;

F. maintaining records relating to course offerings, instructors, and student attendance for a period of three years from the date on which the course was completed; these records shall be made available to the commissioner upon request (in the event that a school should cease operation for any reason, the coordinator shall be responsible for maintaining the records or providing a custodian for the records acceptable to the commissioner. Under no circumstances will the commissioner act as custodian of the records. In order to be acceptable to the commissioner, custodians must agree to make copies of acknowledgements available to students at a reasonable fee);

G. assuring that the coordinator is available to instructors and students throughout course offerings and providing the name of the coordinator and a telephone number at which the coordinator can be reached;

H. attending workshops or instructional programs as reasonably required by the commissioner;

I. reporting on the form in part 2800.9930 the attendance of licensed students in courses II and III to the commissioner within 14 days of their completion of the course; and

J. providing students with course completion certificates as in part 2800.9910, for courses I, II, and III, and continuing education courses.

MS s 82.22 subd 13; 82.28

2800.7450 APPLICATION FOR COORDINATOR APPROVAL.

The real estate education application for coordinator approval shall be in the form in part 2800.9915.

MS s 82.28

2800.7500 INSTRUCTORS.

Subpart 1. **Requirement.** Each course of study shall have an instructor who is qualified by education, training, or experience to insure competent instruction.

Subp. 2. **Qualifications.** The following provisions relate to the approval and qualification of instructors:

A. Applicants shall submit requests for instructor approval on the form in part 2800.9925 for courses I, II, and III and the form in part 2800.9940 for continuing education courses. Requests must be submitted at least 30 days prior to instruction in an approved course.

B. Applicants for courses I, II, and III shall be approved if they achieve a rating of 70 points or higher based upon the scale in part 2800.9905.

C. The same instructor may teach all three courses. Instructors may engage a nonapproved or guest instructor to teach up to ten hours of specialized coursework covered in course I, II, or III. Approved instructors remain responsible for complying with the provisions of subpart 3.

D. Continuing education instructors must have:

(1) a degree in any area plus two years practical experience in the subject area being taught;

(2) five years practical experience in the subject area being taught;

(3) a college or graduate degree in the subject area being taught; or

(4) have held a broker's license for three years or have three years practical experience in the subject area being taught. These individuals shall also have completed at least 60 hours of approved continuing education in the subject area being taught.

Subp. 3. **Responsibilities.** Approved instructors shall be responsible for the following:

A. compliance with all laws and rules relating to real estate education;

B. providing students with current and accurate information;

C. maintaining an atmosphere conducive to learning in the classroom;

D. assuring and certifying attendance of students enrolled in courses;

E. providing assistance to students and responding to questions relating to course materials; and

F. attending such workshops or instructional programs as are reasonably required by the commissioner.

MS s 82.22 subd 13; 82.28

2800.7550 APPLICATION FOR INSTRUCTOR APPROVAL FOR COURSES I, II, III.

The real estate education application for instructor approval for courses I, II, and III shall be in the form in part 2800.9925.

MS s 82.28

2800.7575 APPLICATION FOR INSTRUCTOR APPROVAL FOR CONTINUING EDUCATION.

The real estate education application for instructor approval for continuing education shall be in the form in part 2800.9940.

Appendix A: Real Estate License Law and Rules and Regulations   199

MS s 82.22 subd 13

2800.7600 PROHIBITED PRACTICES FOR COORDINATORS AND INSTRUCTORS.

Subpart 1. **Prohibitions.** In connection with an approved course, coordinators and instructors shall not:

A. recommend or promote the services or practices of any particular real estate brokerage, franchise, coordinator, instructor, or school;

B. encourage or recruit individuals to engage the services of, or become associated with, any particular real estate brokerage or franchise;

C. use materials, clothing, or other evidences of affiliation with any particular real estate brokerage or franchise;

D. require students to participate in other programs or services offered by the school, coordinator, or instructor;

E. take a Minnesota real estate licensing examination without the prior approval of the commissioner;

F. attempt, either directly or indirectly, to discover questions or answers on a real estate licensing examination; or

G. disseminate to any other person specific questions, problems, or information known or believed to be included in licensing examinations.

Subp. 2. **Notification of misconduct.** Coordinators and instructors shall notify the commissioner within ten days of a felony conviction or of disciplinary action taken against a real estate or other occupational license held by the coordinator or instructor.

Subp. 3. **Change in information in application.** Coordinators and instructors shall notify the commissioner within ten days of any change in the information set forth in the application for approval on file with the commissioner.

MS s 82.22 subd 13; 82.28

2800.7700 EXTENSIONS.

Upon appropriate showing of a bona fide financial or medical hardship, the commissioner may extend the time period during which postlicensing or continuing education instruction must be successfully completed. Loss of income resulting from cancellation of a license is not a bona fide hardship. Requests for extensions must be submitted in writing no later than 45 days prior to the date of license cancellation and shall include an explanation and verification of the hardship, and a verification of enrollment in an approved course of study and the dates during which the course will be held.

MS s 82.22 subd 13; 82.28

2800.7800 WAIVERS.

Required real estate education shall not be waived for any licensee or applicant for a license.

MS s 82.22 subd 13; 82.28

2800.7900 FEES.

Fees for approved courses and related materials shall be reasonable and clearly identified to students. In the event that a course is cancelled for any reason, all fees shall be returned promptly. In the event that a course is postponed for any reason, students shall be given the choice of attending the course at a later date or of having their fees refunded in full. If a student is unable to attend a course or cancels his or her registration in a course, school policies regarding refunds shall govern.

MS s 82.22 subd 13; 82.28

2800.8000 FACILITIES.

Each course of study shall be conducted in a classroom or other facility that is adequate to implement the offering. Approved courses shall not be held on the premises of a real estate brokerage, franchise, or an affiliate thereof.

MS s 82.22 subd 13; 82.28

2800.8100 CONFLICT OF INTEREST.

A course will not be approved if it is offered by a person who derives substantial income from the real estate brokerage business.

MS s 82.22 subd 13; 82.28

2800.8200 SUPPLEMENTARY MATERIALS.

An adequate supply of supplementary materials to be used or distributed in connection with an approved course must be available in order to ensure that each student receives all of the necessary materials. Outlines and any other materials that are reproduced shall be of readable quality.

MS s 82.22 subd 13; 82.28

2800.8300 ADVERTISING COURSES.

Subpart 1. **True.** Advertising must be truthful and not deceptive or misleading.

Subp. 2. **Approval statement.** No advertisement, pamphlet, circular, or other similar materials pertaining to an approved offering may be circulated or distributed in this state unless the following statement is prominently displayed on the cover of it:

For initial education courses, "This course has been approved by the commissioner of commerce pursuant to Minnesota Statutes, section 82.22, subdivision 6 for initial education courses;" or

For continuing education courses, "This course has been approved by the commissioner of commerce pursuant to Minnesota Statutes, section 82.22, subdivision 13, relating to continuing real estate education."

The preceding language need not be displayed on the cover of any out-of-state offering advertisement; however, it is the responsibility of the school to provide students with evidence that the course has been approved.

Subp. 3. **Approved course advertisements.** Advertising of

200 MINNESOTA SUPPLEMENT for Modern Real Estate Practice

approved courses must be clearly distinguishable from the advertisement of other nonapproved courses and services.

MS s 82.22 subd 13; 82.28

2800.8400 NOTICE TO STUDENTS.

At the beginning of each approved offering, the following notice shall be read to students: "This real estate educational offering is recognized by the commissioner of commerce as satisfying ____ hours of credit toward (choose one, or more, of the following: prelicensing, postlicensing, or continuing) real estate education requirements pursuant to Minnesota Statutes, section 82.22. If you have any comments about this real estate offering, please mail them to the Commissioner of Commerce, 500 Metro Square Building, Saint Paul, Minnesota 55101."

MS s 82.22 subd 13; 82.28

2800.8500 AUDITS.

The commissioner reserves the right to audit subject offerings with or without notice to the school.

MS s 82.22 subd 13; 82.28

2800.8600 DISCIPLINARY ACTION.

The commissioner may deny, censure, suspend, or revoke the approval of a coordinator, instructor, or course if it is determined that they are not in compliance with Minnesota Statutes, chapter 82 or the rules adopted thereunder.

MS s 82.22 subd 13; 82.28

2800.8700 REPORTS TO COMMISSIONER.

Continuing education credits shall be reported by the licensee on the form in part 2800.9950.

Forms will not be accepted unless they reflect the entire 45 required hours. Incomplete forms will be returned to the licensee.

Forms must be received by the commissioner no later than June 15 of the year in which the credits are due. Forms which are mailed shall be deemed timely received if addressed to: Real Estate Licensing, 500 Metro Square Building, Saint Paul, Minnesota 55101, and postmarked prior to 12:01 a.m. on June 14. Licensees are encouraged to submit the form as soon as they have completed the 45 hours of continuing education credit.

MS s 82.22 subd 13; 82.28

2800.8750 CONTINUING EDUCATION COURSE VERIFICATION.

The real estate education continuing education course verification shall be in the form in part 2800.9950.

MS s 82.22 subd 13

FORMS

2800.9905 RATING SCALE FOR INSTRUCTORS.

Ratings for applicants seeking approval as instructors of courses I, II, and III:

Points	Criteria
20	2-year degree or certificate;
40	4-year degree;
50	post graduate degree;
60	2-year real estate degree or certificate;
70	4-year real estate degree or certificate. Points may not be accumulated in the case of individuals holding more than one degree or certificate;
10	Each 45 hours of continuing real estate education attended or taught. No points will be allowed for periods of less than 45 hours;
30	First three-year period in which engaged full-time in the real estate industry as a licensed broker or salesperson or, in the case of applicants for Course III, the first three-year period in which engaged full-time in a business or profession relating to the subject being taught. No points will be allowed for an applicant who has been licensed for less than three years or who has been engaged in a related business or profession for less than three years;
10	Each full year, after the first full three years, of applicants for Course III, salesperson or, in the case each full year, after the first full three years, in which engaged full-time in a business or profession relating to the subject being taught.

MS s 82.22 subd 13; 82.28

Appendix A: Real Estate License Law and Rules and Regulations

2800.9910 FORM OF COURSE COMPLETION CERTIFICATE.

2800.9915 FORM OF APPLICATION FOR COORDINATOR APPROVAL.

MINNESOTA SUPPLEMENT for Modern Real Estate Practice

2800.9925 FORM OF APPLICATION FOR INSTRUCTOR APPROVAL.

State of Minnesota
Department of Commerce
Securities and Real Estate Division
500 Metro Square Building
St. Paul, Minnesota 55101
(612) 296-9458

APPLICATION FOR INSTRUCTOR APPROVAL FOR COURSES I, II, III

Name of Applicant

City, State, Zip | Phone (Include area code) | School/Sponsoring Entity

4 MCAR §1.41535 Instructors 2. Applicants for Course I, II, and III shall be approved if they achieve a rating of 70 points or higher based upon the scale below.

Points	
20	2 year degree or certificate
40	4 year degree
50	Post graduate degree
60	2 year real estate degree or certificate
70	4 year real estate degree or certificate
10	Each 45 hours of approved continuing real estate education attended or taught.
30	First three year period in which engaged full time in real estate industry or profession related to area of teaching.
10	Each successive year in which engaged in full time in real estate or profession relating to area of teaching.

Educational Background For Which Applicant Seeks Points

Name of School	Dates Attended	Degree

Educational Points: _____

Continuing Real Estate Education For Which Applicant Seeks Points

Total No. of Hours Attended	Total No. of Hours Taught

Continuing Education Points: _____

Professional Experience For Which Applicant Seeks Points

Place of Employment	Dates	Position Held

Experience Points: _____

TOTAL POINTS: _____

1. Do you have a real estate license in Minnesota or any other state? ☐ Yes ☐ No
   If yes, date issued: _____
   Type of License: _____
   ▶ If the answer to any of the following questions is yes, attach a detailed explanation.

2. Have you ever been the subject of any inquiry or investigation by any agency through which you have been licensed or certified?

3. Have you ever had a real estate, securities or insurance license in any state which has been suspended, revoked, cancelled or terminated?

4. Have you ever been convicted of any criminal offense (felony, gross misdemeanor or misdemeanor) in any State or Federal Court, other than traffic violations?

5. Have you ever been a defendant in any lawsuit involving claims of fraud, misrepresentation, conversion, mismanagement of funds, breach of fiduciary duty or breach of real estate contract?

6. Are you currently an officer, partner or owner of a licensed real estate company? ☐ Yes ☐ No

OVER

2800.9920 FORM OF APPLICATION FOR COURSE APPROVAL.

State of Minnesota
Department of Commerce
Securities and Real Estate Division
500 Metro Square Building
St. Paul, Minnesota 55101
(612) 296-9458

APPLICATION FOR COURSE APPROVAL FOR COURSE I, II, AND III

Instructions: 1. Attach Service of Process Form (for out-of-state applicants only).
2. Attach Instructor Approval Form if instructor has not previously been approved.

"X" applicable course: ☐ Course I ☐ Course II ☐ Course III

Course Title

Address | School/Sponsoring Entity

 | City, State, Zip | Phone (Include area code)

Course Dates: From _____ To _____ | Time _____ | Total Hours

Course Location

Name of Text | Date of Edition | Author

"X" if you certify that course material is in compliance with prescribed outlines: ☐ Yes ☐ No
If Course III is a combination of subjects, list below:

Subject	Number of Hours

Coordinator

City, State, Zip | Phone (include area code)

As coordinator of the proposed offering, I certify that the information contained in this application is correct to the best of my knowledge. I also certify that this course is not being offered by an individual, firm or business organization, the primary income of which is derived from the real estate brokerage business.

Signature of Coordinator | Date

State of _____ } ss
County of _____ }

On this _____ day of _____, 19___, appeared before me, a Notary Public, and being duly sworn, says that she/he has read the foregoing application and accompanying exhibit, and that the contents thereof are true to her/his own knowledge.

Notary Public
County

NOTARIAL SEAL

My Commission Expires

FOR OFFICE USE ONLY

Course No.	Course Title	Date Approved

Subject to Management

Signature | Title

MS s 82.28

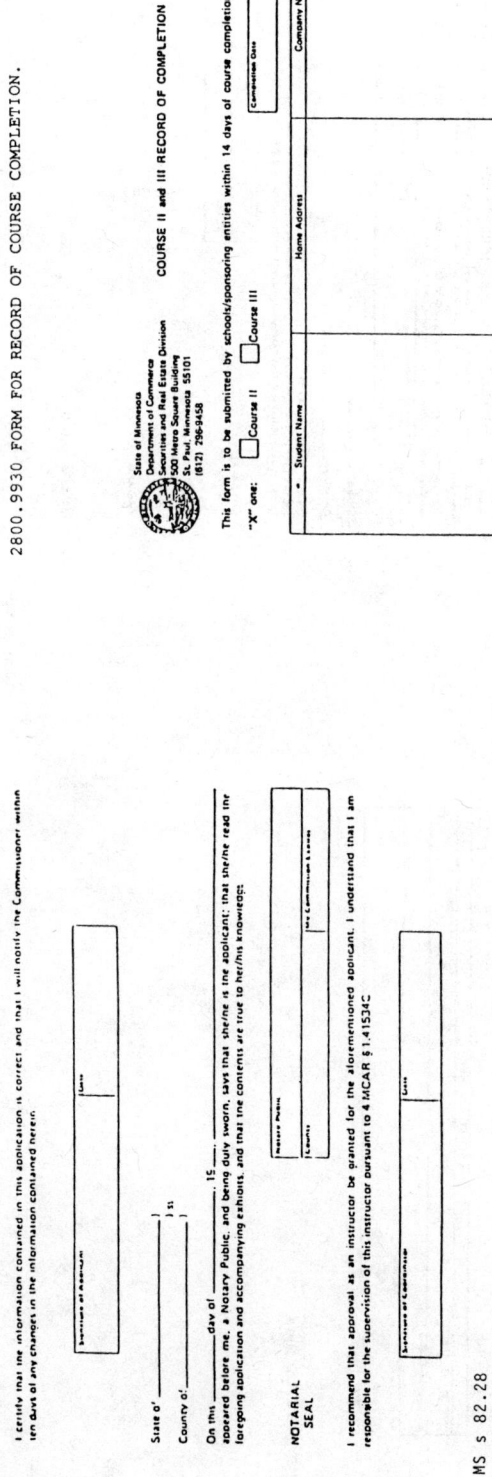

Appendix A: Real Estate License Law and Rules and Regulations   203

204 MINNESOTA SUPPLEMENT for Modern Real Estate Practice

2800.9950 FORM OF CONTINUING EDUCATION COURSE VERIFICATION.

2800.9945 FORM OF NOTICE OF SUBSEQUENT CONTINUING EDUCATION COURSE OFFERINGS.

2800.9955 FORM OF REAL ESTATE SALESPERSON AUTOMATIC TRANSFER.

MS s 82.20 subd 9

Appendix B: Subdivided Land Sales Practices Act

SUBDIVIDED LAND LAW - MINNESOTA CHAPTER 83

relating to commerce; providing various definitions applicable to the regulation of sales of subdivided lands; providing for the registration of subdivided lands; requiring the use of public offering statements; providing certain exemptions to the subdivided land statutes; providing for the rescission of subdivided land sales contracts; regulating the filing of subdivided land documents; prohibiting the publishing of false, misleading, or deceptive filing of annual reports; regulating supplemental subdivided land reports; providing for the revocation or suspension of a subdivided land registration; regulating service of process on subdivided land registration applicants; establishing prohibited practices; prescribing penalties; amending Minnesota Statutes 1982, sections 83.2, subdivisions 1, 5, 11, and by adding subdivisions; 83.21; 83.23; 83.24; 83.25, subdivision 1; 83.26; 83.27; 83.28; 83.29, by adding subdivisions; 83.30; 83.31; 83.33, subdivisions 1 and 2; 83.34, subdivision 1; 83.35; 83.36; 83.37; 83.38, subdivision 2; 83.39; 83.40; 83.41; 83.42; proposing new law coded in Minnesota Statutes, chapter 83; repealing Minnesota Statutes 1982, section 83.33, subdivision 3.

BE IT ENACTED BY THE LEGISLATURE OF THE STATE OF MINNESOTA:

Section 1. Minnesota Statues 1982, section 83.20, subdivision 1 is amended to read:

Subdivision 1. "Advertisement" means any written or printed communication or any communication by telephone or transmitted on radio, television, electronic means or similar communications media published in connection with the offer or sale of subdivided lands or any communication made to induce prospective purchasers to visit or attend and offer or sales presentation.

Section 2. Minnesota Statutes 1982, section 83.20, subdivision 5, is amended to read:

Subdivision 5. "Sale" or "sell" means every contract or agreement to convey an interest, including a leasehold interest, in subdivided land for value.

Section 3. Minnesota Statutes 1982, section 83.20, subdivision 11, is amended to read:

Subdivision 11. "Subdivision" or "subdivided land" means any real estate, wherever located, improved or unimproved, which is divided or proposed to be divided for the purpose of sale or lease, including sales or leases of any time-share interest, housing cooperative, condominium, or similar interest in real estate.

Section 4. Minnesota Statutes 1982, section 83.20, is amended by adding a subdivision to read:

Subdivision 13. "Time-share interest" means a right to occupy a unit or any of several units during intermittent time periods over a period of at least three years, including renewal options, whether or not coupled with a freehold estate or an estate for years.

Section 5. Minnesota Statutes 1982, section 83.20, is amended by adding a subdivision to read:

Subdivision 16. "Improved lots" means lots which have or will have within a two-year period from the date of purchase, a permanent residential structure thereon, and are not devoted to or used as a time share interest, cooperative apartment corporation, condominium, or similar interest in real estate.

Section 6. Minnesota Statutes 1982, section 83.21, is amended to read:

83.21 (COMMISSIONER OF SECURITIES AND REAL ESTATE TO ADMINISTER.)

Sections 83.20 to 83.42, and sections 28 and 29 shall be administered by the commissioner of securities and real estate of the Minnesota department of commerce.

Section 7. Minnesota Statutes 1982, section 83.23, is amended to read:

83.23 (REGISTRATION REQUIREMENT.)

Subdivision 1. (REGISTRATION.) It is unlawful for any person to offer or sell an interest in subdivided lands in this state unless the interest is registered under this section or the subdivided land or the transaction is exempt under section 83.26.

Subdivision 2. (NOTIFICATION.) Unless the method of offer or sale is adopted for the purpose of evasion of sections 83.20 to 83.42 and sections 28 and 29, subdivided lands may be registered by notification provided that all of the following requirements have been met:

(a) The subdivision consists of not more than 100 separate lots, units, parcels, or interests;

(b) At least 20 days prior to any offer pursuant to this subdivision, the subdivider must supply the commissioner, on forms which the commissioner may by rule prescribe, at least the following information:

(1) The name and address of the subdivider and the form and date of its organization if other than an individual;

(2) The location and legal description of the subdivision and the total number of lots, parcels, units, or interests;

(3) Either a title opinion prepared and signed by an attorney licensed to practice law in the state wherein the subdivided land is situated; or a certificate of title insurance or its equivalent acceptable to the commissioner;

(4) A copy of each instrument which will be delivered to a purchaser to evidence his interest in the subdivided lands and a copy of each contract or other agreement which a purchaser will be required to agree to or sign, together with the range of selling prices, rates, or rentals at which it is proposed to offer the lots, units, parcels, or interests in the subdivision, a list of fees the purchaser may be required to pay for amenities or membership in groups including, but not limited to, homeowners' associations, country clubs, golf courses, and other community organizations; and

(5) A copy of a signed and approved plat map or its equivalent;

(c) A filing fee of $100 has been paid;

(d) The subdivider is in compliance with the service of process provisions of section 83.39.

The commissioner may by rule or order withdraw or further condition registration by notification or increase or decrease the number of lots, units, parcels, or interests in subdivided lands permitted for registration by notification. If no stop order is in effect, no proceeding is pending, and no order has been issued under subdivision 4, a registration statement under this section automatically becomes effective at 5:00 in the afternoon on the 20th full business day after the filing of the registration statement or the last amendment, or at such earlier time as the commissioner by order determines.

The rulemaking authority in this subdivision does not include temporary rulemaking authority pursuant to chapter 14.

Subdivision 3. (QUALIFICATION.) Subdivided lands may be registered by qualification provided all of the following requirements have been met:

(a) An application for registration has been filed with the commissioner in a format which the commissioner may by rule prescribe;

(b) The commissioner has been furnished a proposed public offering statement complying with section 83.24;

(c) A filing fee of $250 plus an additional registration fee of $1 for each lot, unit, parcel, or interest included in the offering accompanies the application. The maximum combined filing and registration fees shall in no event be more than $2,500;

(d) The subdivider is in compliance with the service of process provisions of section 83.39;

(e) The commissioner has been furnished a financial statement of the subdivider's most recent fiscal year, audited by an independent certified public accountant; and, if the fiscal year of the subdivider is more than 90 days prior to the date of filing the application, a financial statement, which may be unaudited, as of a date within 90 days of the date of application.

Subdivisions in which all the improvements are complete and paid for by the developer, and for which clear title can be given the purchaser at the closing, are exempt from providing independently certified financial statements.

An application for registration under this section becomes effective when the commissioner so orders.

The rulemaking authority in this subdivision does not include temporary rulemaking authority pursuant to chapter 14.

Subdivision 4. (CONSOLIDATED REGISTRATION.) If additional subdivided lands of the same subdivider are subsequently to be offered for sale, the registration thereof may be consolidated with any earlier registration offering subdivided lands for sale if the additional subdivided lands are contiguous to those previously registered. An application for consolidation shall be accompanied by a consolidation fee of $50. If the registration is pursuant to subdivision 3, an additional registration fee of $1 shall be submitted for each lot, unit, parcel, or interest included in the consolidation if the maximum fees have not already been paid.

Section 8. Minnesota Statutes 1982, section 83.24, is amended to read:

83.24 (PUBLIC OFFERING STATEMENT.)

Subdivision 1. (DELIVERY.) A public offering statement shall be delivered to each person to whom an offer is made before or concurrently with (a) the first written offer other than offer means of a public advertisement, or (b) any payment pursuant to a sale, whichever occurs first. Each person to whom an offer is made must be afforded a reasonable opportunity to examine the public offering statement and must be permitted to retain the statement. The subdivider or his agent shall obtain a receipt, signed by the person, acknowledging that he has received a copy of the public offering statement prior to the execution of any contract or agreement to purchase any lot, unit, parcel, or interest in subdivided lands. All receipts shall be kept in files which are in the possession of the subdivider or his agent, subject to inspection by the commissioner, for a period of three years from the date of the receipt.

Subdivision 2. (FULL DISCLOSURE.) A public offering statement shall disclose fully and accurately the subdivided lands being offered and shall make known to prospective purchasers all unusual and material circumstances or features affecting the subdivided lands.

Subdivision 3. (FORM.) A public offering statement shall be in a format prescribed by rule and shall include the following:

(a) The name, principal address, and telephone number of the subdivider and of its officers and agents in this state;

(b) A general description of the subdivided lands stating the total number of lots, parcels, units, or interests to be offered;

(c) A statement which discloses whether the subdivider owns any rights or options to acquire an interest in adjacent properties, and if so, a description of the options and the locations and zoning status of the adjacent properties;

(d) A statement of the assistance, if any, that the subdivider or his agent will provide to the purchaser in the resale of the property and whether or not the subdivider or his agent will be in competition in the event of resale;

(e) The material terms of any restrictions affecting the subdivided lands and each unit or lot, including, but not limited to, any encumbrances, easements, liens, and zoning status; a statement of the subdivider's efforts to remove the restrictions; and a statement of all existing taxes and existing or proposed special taxes or assessments which affect the subdivided lands;

(f) A statement of the use for which the property is to be offered;

(g) Information concerning existing or proposed improvements and amenities and the completion dates thereof; and

(h) Additional information as may be required at the discretion of the commissioner to assure full and fair disclosure to prospective purchasers.

The rulemaking authority in this subdivision does not include temporary rulemaking authority pursuant to chapter 14.

Subdivision 4. (PERMITTED USE.) The public offering statement shall not be used for any promotional purpose before registration of the subdivided lands and after registration shall be used only in its entirety. A person may not advertise or represent that the commissioner has approved or recommended the subdivided lands or sale thereof. A portion of the public offering statement may not be underscored, italicized, or printed in larger or heavier or different color type than the remainder of the statement unless required or approved by the commissioner.

Subdivision 5. (OTHER LAW.) Any public offering statement which complies with the requirements of any federal law or the laws of any other state requiring substantially the same disclosure of information as is required by this section, may by rule or order of the commissioner be deemed to be in full or partial compliance with this section.

The rulemaking authority in this subdivision does not include temporary rulemaking authority pursuant to chapter 14.

Section 9. Minnesota Statutes 1982, section 83.25, subdivision 1, is amended to read:

Subdivision 1. No person shall offer or sell in this state any interest in subdivided lands until:

(1) He has obtained a license under chapter 82; and

(2) He has obtained an additional license to offer or dispose of subdivided lands. This license may be obtained by submitting an application in writing to the commissioner upon forms prepared and furnished by the commissioner. Each application shall be signed and sworn to by the applicant and accompanied by a license fee of $10. The commissioner may also require an additional examination for this license.

Section 10. Minnesota Statutes 1982, section 83.26, is amended to read:

83.26 (EXEMPTIONS.)

Subdivision 1. (GENERALLY; LANDS.) Unless the method of offer or sale is adopted for the purpose of evasion of sections 83.20 to 83.42, and sections 28 and 29, the following subdivided lands are exempted from sections 83.20 to 83.42:

(a) Any lands offered or sold by the United States, any state, any political subdivision of a state, or any other corporate instrumentality of one of the above;

(b) Leases of apartments, stores, offices, or similar space;

(c) Leases of rooms or space in hotels, motels, or similar space for a period of less than three years, including renewal options;

(d) Cemetery lots or interests therein;

(e) Mortgages or deeds of trust of real estate securing evidences of indebtedness;

(f) Subdivided lands which are registered as securities pursuant to the provisions of chapter 80A; and

(g) Other subdivided lands not within the intent of this chapter which the commissioner may by rule or order exempt.

The rulemaking authority in this subdivision does not include temporary rulemaking authority pursuant to chapter 14.

Subdivision 2. (GENERALLY; TRANSACTIONS.) Unless the method of offer or sale is adopted for the purpose of evasion of sections 83.20 to 83.42, and sections 28 and 29, the following transactions are exempt from sections 83.23, 83.24, 83.25, 83.28, 83.29, and 83.30:

(a) The offer or sale of an interest in subdivided land by an owner, other than the subdivider, acting as principal in a single or isolated transaction;

(b) The offer or sale of all of the subdivided lands within a subdivision in a single transaction to any person;

(c) The offer or sale of subdivided land pursuant to an order of competent jurisdiction, other than a court of bankruptcy;

(d) The offer or sale of subdivided land consisting of not more than ten separate lots, units, parcels, or interests in the aggregate;

(e) The offer or sale of subdivided lands which have been registered under section 83.23, subdivision 2, if there are no more than ten separate lots, units, parcels, or interests remaining to be sold and no material change has occurred in the information on file with the commissioner;

(f) The offer and sale of subdivided land located within the corporate limits of a municipality as defined in section 462.352, subdivision 2, which municipality has adopted subdivision regulations as defined in section 462.352, except those lands described in section 83.20, subdivisions 13, 14, and 15;

(g) The offer and sale of apartments or condominiums as defined in chapters 515 and 515A;

(h) The offer and sale of subdivided lands used primarily for agricultural purposes provided each parcel is at least ten acres in size;

(i) The offer or sale of improved lots if:

(1) the subdivider has filed with the commissiner, no later than ten business days prior to the date of the first sale, a written notice of its intention to offer or sell improved lots, which notice shall be accompanied by a fee of $50, together with a copy of the public offering statement accepted by the situs state and the standard purchase agreement

which documents are required to be supplied by the subdivider to the purchaser; and

(2) the subdivider deposits all downpayments in an escrow account until all obligations of the subdivider to the purchaser, which are pursuant to the terms of the purchase agreement to be performed prior to the closing, have been performed. The subdivider shall provide the purchaser with a purchase receipt for the downpayment paid, a copy of the escrow agreement and the name, address, and telephone number of the escrow agent. The escrow agent shall be a bank located in Minnesota. All downpayments shall be deposited in the escrow account within two business days after receipt.

The commisioner may by rule or order suspend, revoke, or further condition the exemptions contained in clauses (f), (g), (h), and (i) or may require such further information as may be necessary for the protection of purchasers.

The rulemaking authority in this subdivision does not include temporary rulemaking authority pursuant to chapter 14.

Subdivision 3. (EXEMPTION; BURDEN.) The burden of proving an exemption or an exception from a definition is upon the person claiming it.

Section 11. Minnesota Statutes 1982, section 83.27, is amended to read:

83.27 (INQUIRY AND EXAMINATION.)

The commissioner may investigate any subdivision required to be registered under sections 83.20 to 83.42, and sections 28 and 29 for the purpose of verifying statements contained in the application for registration or the public offering statement. For the purpose of such investigation, the commissioner may:

(a) Use and rely upon relevant information or data concerning a subdivision obtained by him from the federal housing administration, the United States veterans administration, or any state or federal agency having supervisory duties over real estate subdivisions which are comparable to those of the commissioner;

(b) Require the subdivider to submit reports prepared by an independent licensed or registered engineer concerning any hazard to which, in the opinion of the commissioner, any subdivision offered for disposition is subject, or concerning any other factor which affects the utility of lots, units, parcels, or interests within the subdivision and may require evidence of compliance to remove or minimize all hazards stated by competent engineering reports;

(c) Conduct an on-site inspection of each subdivision. The subdivider shall defray all actual and necessary expenses incurred by the inspector in the course of the inspection;

(d) Conduct an annual on-site reinspection of each subdivision for each of the three years after registration and thereafter make periodic on site inspections. The developer shall defray all actual and necessary expenses incurred by the inspector in the course of such inspection;

(e) Require the subdivider to deposit the expenses to be incurred in any inspection or reinspection, in advance, based upon an estimate by the commissioner of the expenses likely to be incurred. All such deposits shall be paid into the state treasury and credited to the commissioner's investigation fund, from which fund the commissioner shall have power to make disbursements to pay such expenses. Any unexpended portion shall be refunded. On field examinations made by the commissioner or his employee away from the office of the commissioner a per diem of $10 for each such person may be charged in addition to the actual expenses. Where additional technical, expert, or special services are used, the actual cost of such services may be charged in addition to actual expenses;

(f) Where an on-site inspection of any subdivision has been made under sections 83.20 to 83.42, and sections 28 and 29, an inspection of additional subdivided lands for which a subsequent application for registration is filed may be made.

Section 12. Minnesota Statutes 1982, section 83.28, is amended to read:

83.28 (SALES CONTRACT; RESCISSION.)

Subdivision 1. (CONRACT; FORM RESTRICTIONS.) Every contract for sale relating to subdivided land shall (1) state clearly the legal description of the lot, unit, parcel, or interest disposed of; (2) contain the disclosure substantially similar to that required by the federal truth in lending act, and the rules promulgated thereunder; and (3) be in recordable form.

Subdivision 2. (VOIDABLE.) Any contract or agreement for the sale of a lot, parcel, unit, or interest in a subdivision not exempt under section 83.26, is voidable at the discretion of the purchaser, for a period of three years from the date of the contract or agreement, notwithstanding the delivery of a deed to the purchaser, if the subdivision was not registered under sections 83.20 to 83.42, and sections 28 and 29 at the time of the sale, or if a current public offering statement was not given to the purchaser in accordance with section 83.24, unless subsequently thereto the subdivision is registered under this chapter and in connection therewith, the purchaser has received a written offer to repurchase the lot, parcel, unit, or interest for cash payable on closing of the repurchase, together with interest thereon from the date of purchase at the legal rate or at the rate charged on any lien paid by the purchaser, whichever is higher, less the amount of any income received from the lot, parcel, unit, or interest, and the purchaser has failed to accept the offer in writing within 30 days of its receipt. No offer of repurchase shall be effective unless a duplicate copy thereof has been filed with the commissioner at least 20 days prior to its delivery to the offeree and the commissioner has not objected to the offer within that time. The offer of repurchase shall be in the form and contain the information the commissioner by rule or order prescribes. If the purchaser no longer owns the lot, parcel, unit, or interest, the purchaser shall be entitled to maintain an action at law, and the damages shall be the consideration paid for the lot, parcel, unit, or interest together with interest thereon as specified above from the date of acquisition to the date of disposition, plus costs and reasonable attorney's fees, less the value received for the lot, parcel, unit, or interest at the date of disposition.

The rulemaking authority in this subdivision does not include temporary rulemaking authority pursuant to chapter 14.

Subdivision 3. (RESCISSION.) A purchaser has an unconditional right to rescind any contract, agreement, or other evidence of indebtedness, or revoke any offer, at any time prior to or within five days after the date the purchaser actually receives a legible copy of the binding contract, agreement, or other evidence of indebtedness or offer and the public offering statement as provided in section 83.24. Predating of a document does not affect the time in which the right to rescind may be exercised. The burden of proving that the document was not predated is upon the subdivider or lender.

Subdivision 4. (DOCUMENT LABELING.) Each contract, agreement, or other evidence of indebtedness shall be prominently labeled and captioned that it is a document taken in connection with a sale or other disposition of lands under sections 83.20 to 83.42, and sections 28 and 29.

Subdivision 5. (NOTICE TO PURCHASER.) The first contract, agreement, or other evidence of indebtedness shall prominently contain upon its face the following notice in bold type, which shall be at least 4 point type larger than the body of the document, stating, in one of the following forms:

(a) Registered by notification: "Notice to Purchaser" -- "You are entitled to rescind this agreement for any reason within five days from the date you actually received a legible copy of this document signed by all parties. The rescission must be in writing and mailed to the subdivider or his agent or the lender at the address stated in this document. Upon rescission you will receive a refund of all money paid." or;

(b) Registration by qualification: "Notice to Purchaser" -- "You are entitled to rescind this agreement for any reason within five days from the date you actually received a legible copy of this document signed by all parties and a public offering statement. The rescission must be in writing and mailed to the subdivider or his agent or the lender at the address stated in this document. Upon rescission you will receive a refund of all money paid."

The contract, agreement, or other evidence of indebtedness. Notice of rescission, if given by mail is effective when it is deposited in a mailbox properly addressed and postage prepaid. A notice of recission given by the purchaser need not take a particular form and is sufficient if it indicates by any form of written expression the intention of the purchaser not to be bound by the contract, agreement, or other evidence of indebtedness.

Subdivision 7. (WAIVER PROHIBITED.) No act of a purchaser shall be effective to waive the right to rescind as provided in this section.

Section 13. Minnesota Statutes 1982, section 83.29, is amended by adding a subdivision to read:

Subdivision 4. A document is filed when it is received by the commissioner and the proper fee is paid.

Section 14. Minnesota Statutes 1982, section 83.29, is amended by adding a subdivision to read:

Subdivision 5. No person shall publish or cause to be published in this state any advertisement offering subdivided lands subject to the registration requirements of section 83.23 which is false, misleading, or deceptive. The commissioner has 15 days in which to deny the advertising.

Section 15. Minnesota Statutes 1982, section 83.20, is amended to read:

83.30 (ANNUAL REPORT.)

Subdivision 1. (FORM; DUE DATE.) During the period a registration is effective, the subdivider shall file an annual report in a format the commissioner may by rule prescribe. Every annual report shall be due by the 120th day following the end of the subdivider's fiscal year, unless

Section 15. Minnesota Statutes 1982, section 83.30, is amemded to read:

83.30 (ANNUAL REPORT.)

Subdivision 1. (FORM; DUE DATE.) During the period a registration is effective, the subdivider shall file an annual report in a format the commissioner may by rule prescribe. Every annual report shall be due by the 120th day following the end of the subdivider's fiscal year, unless extended in writing by the commissioner for good cause.

The rulemaking authority in this subdivision does not include temporary rulemaking authority pursuant to chapter 14.

Subdivision 2. (FEE.) Every annual report filed pursuant to section 83.23, subdivision 2, shall be accompanied by a fee of $50. Every annual report filed pursuant to section 83.23, subdivision 3, shall be accompanied by a fee of $100.

Subdivision 3. (FAILURE TO FILE; EFFECT.) Failure to file the annual report shall be cause for cancellation of the registration. If canceled, the registration may be reinstated at a subsequent date following the filing of the report and payment of the appropriate fees.

Section 16. Minnesota Statutes 1982, section 83.31, is amended to read:

83.31 (CHANGES SUBSEQUENT TO REGISTRATION.)

Subdivision 1. (REPORT OF SALES.) The commissioner may by rule or order require the subdivider or his agent to submit reports of sales.

The rulemaking authority in this subdivision does not include temporary rulemaking authority pursuant to chapter 14.

Subdivision 2. (REPORT OF MATERIAL CHANGES.) A subdivider or his agent shall within 30 days report any material changes in the information contained in the application for registration or the exhibits appended thereto on file with the commissioner by submitting an application to amend accompanied by an amendment fee of $25.

Subdivision 3. (RULES; FORM OF AMENDMENT.) The commissioner may by rule define what shall be considered a material change and prescribe the format for an application to amend. The amendment shall become effective when ordered by the commissioner.

The rulemaking authority in this subdivision does not include temporary rulemaking authority pursuant to chapter 14.

Section 17. Minnesota Statutes 1982, section 83.33, subdivision 1, is amended to read:

Subdivision 1. (COMPLIANCE WITH RULES.) A person may not sell lots, units, parcels, or interests within a subdivision subject to a blanket encumbrance unless he has complied with such rules as the commissioner may promulgate concerning such sales, which rules shall be specific requirements for the protection of the purchaser.

Section 18. Minnesota Statutes 1982, section 83.33, subdivision 2, is amended to read:

Subdivision 2. (USE OF PROHIBITED PRACTICE.) The act, use, or employment by any person of any prohibited practice as set forth in section 8, with the intent that others rely thereon in connection with the offer or sale of subdivided lands not excepted from sections 83.20 to 83.42, and sections 28 and 29 is a violation of sections 83.20 to 83.42, and sections 28 and 29, whether or not any person has in fact been damaged thereby.

Section 19. Minnesota Statutes 1982, section 83.34, subdivision 1, is amended to read:

Subdivision 1. The commissioner may make necessary public or private investigations within or outside of this state to determine whether any person has violated or is about to violate sections 83.20 to 83.42, and sections 28 and 29 or any rule or order hereunder or to aid in the enforcement of sections 83.20 to 83.42, and sections 28 and 29 or in the prescribing of rules and forms hereunder.

Section 20. Minnesota Statutes 1982, section 83.35, is amended to read:

83.35 (ENFORCEMENT; POWERS OF COMMISSIONER.)

Subdivision 1. (REGISTRATION; REVOCATION OR SUSPENSION.) After notice and hearing, the commissioner may suspend or revoke a registration if he finds that the subdivider or person has:

(1) Violated any provision of sections 83.20 to 83.42, and sections 28 and 29 or any lawful order or rule of the commissioner;

(2) Directly or through an agent or employee knowingly engaged in any false, deceptive, or misleading advertising, promotional or sales methods to offer to dispose of an interest in subdivided lands;

(3) Made any material change in the advertising, plan of disposition, or development of the subdivided lands subsequent to the order of registration without obtaining prior approval from the commissioner;

(4) Offered or sold any subdivided lands which have not been registered with the commissioner unless the subdivided lands or sales thereof are exempt from registration pursuant to section 83.26;

(5) Been convicted, or if any of the subdivider's officers, directors, partners, principals, or agents has been convicted of a crime involving

fraud, deception, false pretenses, misrepresentation, false advertising, or dishonest dealing in real estate transactions, subsequent to the time of the filing of the application for registration;

(6) Disposed of, concealed, or diverted any funds or assets of any person so as to defeat the rights of subdivision purchasers;

(7) Failed faithfully to perform any stipulation or agreement made with the commissioner as an inducement to grant any registration, to reinstate any registration, or to permit any promotional plan or public offering statement;

(8) Made misrepresentations or concealed material facts in an application for registration;

(9) Permanently or temporarily been enjoined by any court of competent jurisdiction from engaging in or continuing any conduct or practice involving any aspect of land sales; or

(10) Failed to pay any filing or inspection fee required by sections 83.20 to 83.42, and sections 28 and 29.

Subdivision 2. (SERVICE OF PROCESS.) When initiating a proceeding under subdivision 1, the commissioner shall serve upon the subdivider or other person by personal service or by certified mail, a written notice of hearing setting the date, time, and place of the hearing and a statement of the allegations upon which the suspension or revocation will be based.

Subdivision 3. (CEASE AND DESIST ORDER.) The commissioner is empowered to issue and cause to be served an order requiring a person to cease and desist from violations of sections 83.20 to 83.42, and sections 28 and 29. The order shall state the reasons for its issuance and shall either order a hearing, which shall be set for no later than 20 days from the date of the order, or specify that upon the written request of the applicant, the matter will be set for hearing within 15 days after receipt of the request, provided that upon the request of the applicant a hearing may be held subsequent to the expiration of either period specified herein. All hearings shall be conducted in accordance with the provisions of chapter 14. If the person to whom a cease and desist order is issued fails to appear at the hearing after being duly notified, he shall be deemed in default, and the proceeding may be determined against him upon consideration of the cease and desist order, the allegations of which may be deemed to be true. If no hearing is requested within 30 days, the order will become final. All hearings must be conducted in accordance with chapter 14.

Subdivison 4. (AMENDMENT; REGISTRATION SUSPENSION.) Upon receipt of an application to amend or other information indicating a material change in the information on file with the commissioner, and, if the commissioner determines such action to be necessary or appropriate in the public interest or for the protection of purchasers, he may, by order, suspend the registration until such time as he is satisfied that the subdivider or his agent has made the proper changes in the public offering statement, advertising, and promotional plan to provide full and fair disclosure of the material change to the public.

Subdivision 5. (HEARING.) In the event the commissioner issues an order under subdivision 4, the order shall include in its terms a provision for a hearing within 10 days of the date of the order, specifying a date, time, and place for the hearing. Unless otherwise agreed, within 20 days of the close of the hearing record, the commissioner shall issue an order either vacating, modifying, or continuing the temporary order. If the temporary order is continued or modified he shall state his reasons therefor.

Section 21. Minnesota Statutes 1982, section 83.36, is amended to read:

83.36 (INJUNCTIONS; RECEIVERS.)

If it appears that a person has engaged or is about to engage in an act or practice constituting a violation of sections 83.20 to 83.42, and sections 28 and 29 or order hereunder, the commissioner, with or without prior administrative proceedings, may bring an action in district court to enjoin the acts or practices and to enforce compliance with sections 83.20 to 83.42, and sections 28 and 29 or any rule or order hereunder. Upon proper showing, injunctive relief or temporary restraining orders shall be granted and a receiver or conservator may be appointed. The commissioner is not required to post a bond in any court proceedings.

Section 22. Minnesota Statutes 1982, section 83.37, is amended to read:

83.37 (PENALTIES; CIVIL REMEDIES.)

Subdivison 1. (CIVIL FINE.) Any person who violates section 83.23, 83.24, 83.28, 83.29, or section 29 shall be subject to a fine of not more that $1,000 for each violation. A fine authorized by this subdivision may be imposed in a civil action brought by the attorney general on behalf of the state of Minnesota, and shall be deposited in the state treasury. Every person, agent, or employee of a person who materially aids in the act or transaction constituting the violation shall be liable jointly and severally with and to the same extent as the person.

Subdivision 2. (MISDEMEANOR PENALTY.) Any violation of sections 83.20 to 83.42 and any failure to comply with any provisions of sections 83.20 to 83.42 not enumerated in subdivision 1 shall be a misdemeanor.

Subdivision 3. (FAILURE TO PAY FEES.) Any person who fails to pay the filing or inspection fees required by sections 83.20 to 83.42, and sections 28 and 29, and continues to dispose of or offers to dispose of subdivided lands, is liable civilly in an action brought by the attorney general on behalf of the commissioner for a penalty in an amount equal to treble the unpaid fees.

Subdivision 4. (PROHIBITED PRACTICES; REMEDIES.) In the event of any prohibited practice as set forth in section 29, in addition to any other remedies, and whether or not the purchaser has in fact been damaged thereby, the purchaser may recover the consideration paid for the lot, parcel, unit, or interest in subdivided lands together with interest thereon at the legal rate from the date of payment, property taxes paid, costs, and reasonable attorneys fees, less the amount of any income received from the subdivided lands, upon tender of appropriate instruments of reconveyance. If the purchaser no longer owns the lot, parcel, unit, or interest in subdivided lands, he may recover the amount that would be recoverable upon a tender of a reconveyance, less the value of the land when disposed of and less interest at the legal rate on that amount from the date of sale.

(a) A tender of reconveyance may be made at any time before the entry of judgment.

(b) Every person who directly or indirectly controls a subdivider who may be liable under sections 83.20 to 83.42, and sections 28 and 29, every general partner, officer, or director of a subdivider, every person occupying a similar status or performing a similar function, every employee of the subdivider who materially aids in the disposition, and every agent who materially aids in the disposition is also liable jointly and severally with and to the same extent as the subdivider, unless the person otherwise liable sustains the burden of proof that he did not know and in the exercise of reasonable care could not have known of the existence of the facts by reason of which the liability is alleged to exist. There is a right to contribution as in cases of contract among persons so liable.

(c) Every person whose name or occupation gives authority to a statement which with his consent has been used in an application for registration, public offering statement, or advertising, if he is not otherwise associated with the subdivision and development plan in a material way, is liable only for false statements and omissions in his statement and only if it is proved he knew or reasonably should have known of the existence of the true facts by reason of which the liability is alleged to exist.

(d) An action shall not be commenced pursuant to this subdivision later than three years from the date the person discovers any prohibited practice set forth in section 29.

Subdivision 5. (OTHER REMEDIES.) The rights and remedies provided by this chapter shall be in addition to any and all other rights and remedies that may exist at law or in equity.

Section 23. Minnesota Statutes 1982, section 83.38, subdivision 2, is amended to read:

Subdivision 2. The commissioner may, upon request and upon the payment of the sum of $50, grant a request for a written opinion concerning the availability of any exemption in section 83.26 or interpreting any provisions of sections 83.20 to 83.42, and sections 28 and 29.

Section 24. Minnesota Statutes 1982, section 83.39, is amended to read:

83.39 (SERVICE OF PROCESS.)

Subdivision 1. (PROCEDURE.) Every applicant for registration under sections 83.20 to 83.42, and sections 28 and 29 shall file with the commissioner, in a format as by rule may be prescribed, an irrevocable consent appointing the commissioner or commissioner's successor to be the applicant's attorney to receive service of any lawful process in any noncriminal suit, action, or proceeding against the applicant or his or her successor, executor, or administrator which arises under sections 83.20 to 83.42, and sections 28 and 29 or any rule or order thereunder after the consent has been filed, with the same force and validity as if served personally on the person filing the consent. Service may be made by leaving a copy of the process in the office of the commissioner, but is not effective unless:

(a) the plaintiff, who may be commissioner in a suit, action, or proceeding instituted by him or her, forthwith sends notice of the service and a copy of the process by registered mail to the defendant or respondent at his or her last address on file with the commissioner;

(b) the plaintiff's affidavit of compliance with this subdivision is filed in the case on or before the return day of the process, if any, or within such further time as the court allows.

The rulemaking authority in this subdivision does not include temporary rulemaking authority pursuant to chapter 14.

Subdivision 2. (SERVICE ON COMMISSIONER.) When any person, including any nonresident of this state, engages in conduct prohibited or made actionable by sections 83.20 to 83.42, and sections 28 and 29, or any rule or order thereunder, and the person has not filed a consent to service of process under subdivision 1 and personal jurisdiction over this person cannot otherwise be obtained in this state, that conduct shall be considered equivalent to the person's appointment of the commissioner or the commissioner's successor to be the person's attorney to receive service of any lawful process in any noncriminal suit, action, or proceeding against the commissioner or the commissioner's successor, executor, or administrator which grows out of that conduct and which is brought under sections 83.20 to 83.42, and sections 28 and 29 or any rule or order thereunder, with the dame force and validity as if served on the person personally. Service may be made by leaving a copy of the process in the office of the commissioner, and it is not effective unless:

(a) the plaintiff, who may be the commissioner in a suit, action, or proceeding instituted by the commissioner, forthwith sends notice of the service and a copy of the process by registered mail to the defendant or respondent at his last known address or takes other steps which are reasonably calculated to give actual notice, and

(b) the plaintiff's affidavit of compliance with this subdivision is filed in the case on or before the return day of the process, if any, or within such further time as the court allows.

Subdivision 3. (CONTINUANCE.) When process is served under this section, the court, or the commissioner in a proceeding before him, shall order such continuance as may be necessary to afford the defendant or respondent reasonable opportunity to defend.

Section 25. Minnesota Statutes 1982, section 83.40, is amended to read:

83.40 (SCOPE OF SECTIONS 83.20 to 83.42, AND SECTIONS 28 AND 29.)

Subdivision 1. (IN-STATE OFFER OR SALE.) The provisions of sections 83.20 to 83.42, and sections 28 and 29 concerning offers and sales of subdivided lands apply when an offer or sale is made in this state.

Subdivision 2. (IN-STATE OFFER OR SALE DEFINED.) For the purpose of sections 83.20 to 83.42, and sections 28 and 29, an offer or sale is made in this state, whether or not either party is then present in this state, when:

(a) The offer originates from this state, or

(b) The offer is directed by the offeror to this state and received by the offeree in this state, or

(c) The subdivided lands are located in this state.

Subdivision 3. (EXCLUSIONS.) An offer or sale is not made in this state when a publisher circulates or there is circualated on his behalf in this state any bona fide newspaper or other publication of general, regular, and paid circulation which is not published in this state, or a radio or television program originating outside this state is received in this state.

Subdivision 4. (LIEN OF MORTGAGE.) Notwithstanding any provision of sections 83.20 to 83.42, and sections 28 and 29 to the contrary, sections 83.20 to 83.42, and sections 28 and 29 do not apply to or invalidate the lien of a mortgagee, nonaffiliated with the subdivider, when said lien attaches to land pledged as collateral in a transaction negotiated directly with the purchaser.

Section 26. Minnesota Statutes 1982, section 83.41, is amended to read:

83.41 (INTERSTATE RENDITION.)

In the proceedings for extradition of a person charged with a crime under sections 83.20 to 83.42, and sections 28 and 29, it need not be shown that the person whose surrender is demanded has fled from justice or at the time of the commission of the crime was in the demanding or other state.

Section 27. Minnesota Statutes 1982, section 83.42, is amended to read:

83.42 (STATUTE OF LIMITATIONS.)

The statute of limitations for actions arising under this chapter shall be three years and shall not begin to run with respect to any cause of action under this chapter, other than those set forth in section 83.37, subdivision 4, clause (d), until a conveyance describing such lot or parcel is recorded with the apprpriate recording authority. This section does not prohibit the maintenance of any action before the recording of such conveyance.

Section 28. (83.43) (CRIMINAL PENALTIES.)

Any person who willfully violates any provision of section 83.23 or section 29 or any order of the commissioner under sections 83.20 to 83.42, this section, and section 29 of which he has notice, may be fined not more than $5,000 or imprisoned not more than five years or both. Each of the acts specified shall constitute a separate offense and a prosecution or conviction for any one of the offenses shall not bar prosecution or conviction for any other offense.

Section 29. (83.44) (PROHIBITED PRACTICES.)

It is unlawful for any person, in connection with the offer or sale of any subdivided land or interest therin, directly or indirectly:

(a) to employ any device, scheme, or artifice to defraud;

(b) to make any untrue statement of a material fact or to omit to state material facts necessary in order to make the statements made, in the light of the circumstances under which they are made, not misleading; or

(c) to engage in any act, practice, or course of business which operates or would operate as a fraud or deceit upon any person.

Section 30. (REPEALER.)

Minnesota Statutes 1982, section 83.33, subdivision 3, is repealed.

Section 31. (EFFECTIVE DATE.)

Sections 1 to 30 are effective September 1, 1984.

Appendix C:

Sample Final Exam

The following 40-question sample final exam is included as a final review for the state-specific portion of the licensing exam. The questions included are similar in design to those you will encounter on the state exam.

1. Dickins and Swenson are getting married. Under the laws of Minnesota, if they do not specify otherwise, any property acquired by either after the wedding will be held under which form of ownership?

    a. tenancy in common
    b. joint tenancy
    c. tenancy by the entirety
    d. community property

2. In Minesota, upon the default of the borrower, any mortgage of real estate containing a power of sale may be:

    I. foreclosed by advertisement.
    II. sold by the mortgagee upon foreclosure.

    a. I only
    b. II only
    c. both I and II
    d. neither I nor II

3. Trust funds received by a broker may include which of the following?

    I. real estate taxes
    II. earnest money

    a. I only
    b. II only
    c. both I and II
    d. neither I nor II

4. A check received from the potential buyer shall be deposited in the listing broker's account:

    I. by the next business day.
    II. within 72 hours of offer acceptance.

    a. I only
    b. II only
    c. both I and II
    d. neither I nor II

5. What is the maximum limit on property eligible for a homestead exemption in St. Paul?

    a. 80 acres
    b. one-half acre
    c. appraised valuation of up to $30,000
    d. appraised valuation of up to $90,000

6. Minnesota law does not recognize:

    a. ownership in trust.   c. tenancy in common.
    b. joint tenancy.   d. any of the above

7. Sue Snelling lives with her 11-year-old son in a rental unit about to be converted into a condominium. How long must she be allowed to remain in the apartment following notice of conversion?

    a. 60 days   c. 180 days
    b. 120 days   d. 240 days

8. The Fifth Principal Meridian is used as a reference mark for land in:

  I. Western Minnesota.
 II. Iowa.

    a. I only   c. both I and II
    b. II only   d. neither I nor II

9. Unless a mortgage note is to be repaid without interest, a rate should be specified. If not, Minnesota statutes will impose a rate:

  I. tied to the rates of federal notes.
 II. currently of eight percent.

    a. I only   c. both I and II
    b. II only   d. neither I nor II

10. When it is agreed upon in writing by the parties, trust funds can be deposited in:

  I. the selling broker's account.
 II. an escrow agent's account.

    a. I only   c. both I and II
    b. II only   d. neither I nor II

11. Ralph Larsen's land has been forfeited for nonpayment of property taxes. He can redeem it by paying the taxes due plus:

    a. six percent annual interest.
    b. six percent annual interest plus all penalties and costs.
    c. eight and one-half percent annual interest.
    d. eight and one-half percent annual interest plus all penalties and costs.

12. The Subdivided Land Sales Practices Act requires that:

    I. all advertising must be filed with the commissioner prior to use.
    II. all property reports and annual reports must be approved by the commissioner.

    a. I only   c. both I and II
    b. II only   d. neither I nor II

13. In Minnesota, the person(s) with the authority to promulgate rules and regulations to enforce the license law is(are):

    I. the Commissioner of Commerce or his or her delegate.
    II. the Director of Real Estate.

    a. I only   c. both I and II
    b. II only   d. neither I nor II

14. When an applicant passes the broker or salesperson exam, a license is:

    I. automatically issued and sent to the broker.
    II. issued to the sales associate upon the selection of a broker.

    a. I only   c. both I and II
    b. II only   d. neither I nor II

15. If a salesperson or broker fails to complete the required real estate instruction, the individual's license will be:

    I. cancelled.
    II. suspended or revoked.

    a. I only   c. both I and II
    b. II only   d. neither I nor II

16. What information can broker Ed allow his unlicensed brother-in-law to disclose about one of his listings?

    a. its address   c. the financing options
    b. its list price   d. all of the above

17. A mechanic's lien claim arises when a general contractor has not been paid for work performed or material provided upon order of the owner for the improvement of a parcel of real estate. Such contractor has a right to:

    a. tear out the work.
    b. record a notice of lien.
    c. record a notice of lien and file a court suit within the time required by state law.
    d. have personal property of the owner sold to satisfy the lien.

18. Broker Ingrid promises a client that if he buys a certain house now, he can resell it in two years for a $9,000 profit. Ingrid's promise violates the law unless she:

    I. produces written evidence to support her claim.
    II. includes the guaranteed profit as part of the written purchase agreement.

       a. I only   c. both I and II
       b. II only   d. neither I nor II

19. Which type of listing agreement is illegal in Minnesota?

    a. net   c. exclusive right to sell
    b. multiple   d. none of the above

20. Penalties for violating Minnesota standards of licensee conduct may include:

    I. license suspension or revocation.
    II. censure of the licensee.

       a. I only   c. both I and II
       b. II only   d. neither I nor II

21. If, in connection with a sale price of $84,500, the buyer assumed the existing mortgage of $43,000 on a house, the state deed tax would be:

    a. $ 91.30.   c. $ 94.60.
    b. $185.90.   d. $132.00.

22. In Minnesota, the mortgagor is given the conveyance to the estate while the mortgagee maintains a mortgage note and the mortgage. This is known as:

    I. title theory.
    II. lien theory.

       a. I only   c. either I or II
       b. II only   d. neither I nor II

23. Where a "truth-in-housing" report is required, it must be prepared by:

   I. the city or county housing authority.
   II. a licensed private evaluator.

   a. I only   c. both I and II
   b. II only   d. neither I nor II

24. The owner of a four-unit apartment violates the law by denying accommodation because the prospective tenant is:

   I. an unmarried parent.
   II. below legal age.

   a. I only   c. both I and II
   b. II only   d. neither I nor II

25. Minnesota brokers have which of the following responsibilities regarding the records and documents of a transaction?

   I. They must give copies to all parties to the transaction.
   II. They must keep copies of all documents for five years.

   a. I only   c. both I and II
   b. II only   d. neither I nor II

26. Paula Link discovers an error in the title registration of a lot she owns. She may file a claim against:

   I. the registrar in the district court.
   II. the county recorder.

   a. I only   c. both I and II
   b. II only   d. neither I nor II

27. George Fox sells, by owner, seven houses he owns. The sales all close between February and October 1983. According to Minnesota law, Fox is acting as a:

   I. real estate salesperson.
   II. real estate broker.

   a. I only   c. both I and II
   b. II only   d. neither I nor II

28. Wilma Trim intends to move her newly purchased manufactured home from its Minneapolis mobile home court to Wisconsin as soon as the purchase papers are complete. The home is considered:

   I. a dwelling unit.
   II. not affixed to the land.

   a. I only
   b. II only
   c. both I and II
   d. neither I nor II

29. Fraudulent, deceptive, or dishonest practices by a real estate broker or salesperson include:

   I. making any material misrepresentation.
   II. paying money to an unlicensed person for assistance in the procurement of a listing.

   a. I only
   b. II only
   c. both I and II
   d. neither I nor II

30. Items that are taken as a deposit in lieu of cash and that cannot be deposited in the broker's trust account may include:

   I. Treasury bills and government certificates.
   II. a personal note.

   a. I only
   b. II only
   c. both I and II
   d. neither I nor II

31. A broker charged with misrepresentation in a lease agreement must notify:

   I. the Commissioner of Commerce within 30 days.
   II. the county real estate board within 10 days.

   a. I only
   b. II only
   c. both I and II
   d. neither I nor II

32. The decision on whether to compensate a fraud victim through the Real Estate Education, Research, and Recovery Fund is made by:

   I. any court with jurisdiction in the case.
   II. the Commissioner of Commerce.

   a. I only
   b. II only
   c. both I and II
   d. neither I nor II

33. Minnesota brokers may collect commissions upon fulfilling the terms of a(n):

   I. written listing agreement.
   II. oral listing agreement involving not more than $5,000.

   a. I only
   b. II only
   c. both I and II
   d. neither I nor II

34. A real estate broker or salesperson may have a license denied, suspended, revoked, or censured when:

   I. acting on behalf of more than one party to a transaction without consent of all parties.
   II. demanding a commission to which he or she is not entitled.

   a. I only
   b. II only
   c. both I and II
   d. neither I nor II

35. Unless otherwise stated in the purchase agreement, expenses for which the buyer is responsible include:

   a. title insurance.
   b. state deed tax.
   c. preparation of closing documents.
   d. all of the above

36. Listing agreements:

   I. must specify an expiration date.
   II. may contain an automatic extension of not more than six months.

   a. I only
   b. II only
   c. both I and II
   d. neither I nor II

37. Owners must supply buyers with an energy disclosure report:

   I. before the sale is completed.
   II. within three months after the sale is completed.

   a. I only
   b. II only
   c. both I and II
   d. neither I nor II

38. New home warranties in Minnesota guarantee:

   I. no major construction defects for 10 years.
   II. no defects from faulty plumbing installation for two years.

   a. I only
   b. II only
   c. both I and II
   d. neither I nor II

39. In Minnesota, A and B orally enter into a one-year lease. B defaults. In this situation:

    a. the parol evidence rule prohibits bringing action to enforce oral leases of one year in length.
    b. the Statute of Frauds prohibits bringing actions to enforce oral leases of one year in length.
    c. leases of only one year need not be in writing to be enforced in a court action.
    d. the Statute of Limitations does not apply to oral leases.

40. All real estate advertising must include:

    a. the price of the property.
    b. the name of the listing broker.
    c. the name of the salesperson who wrote the ad.
    d. the square footage of the lot.

Answer Key

Following the answers in this Answer Key are references to pages of this supplement where the points are discussed or explained. These references are made to help you make maximum use of the tests. If you did not answer a question correctly, <u>restudy the course material until you understand the correct answer.</u>

Chapter 5	8. c (33)	3. d (65)	11. a (93)	Chapter 21
1. b (1)	9. d (33)	4. a (66)	12. a (93)	1. b (130)
2. a (1)				2. d (131)
3. c (2)	Chapter 10	Chapter 14	Chapter 16	3. a (130)
4. d (3)	1. d (36)	1. d (72)	1. a (104)	4. d (130)
	2. c (38)	2. b (78)	2. b (103)	5. a (132)
Chapter 6	3. a (37)	3. a (69-70)	3. c (104)	6. b (132)
1. a (6)	4. c (35)	4. a (73)	4. c (103-104)	7. d (129)
2. d (5)	5. a (37)	5. c (80)	5. c (104-105)	8. d (131)
3. a (5)	6. a (38)	6. a (81-82)		9. d (131)
4. c (5)	7. b (40)	7. b (75)	Chapter 18	
	8. b (38-39)	8. b (77)	1. b (107)	Securities
Chapter 7	9. a (37)	9. c (71)	2. c (107)	1. c (147)
1. d (15)	10. d (37)	10. c (77)	3. c (108)	2. b (148)
2. c (16)		11. b (69)	4. d (108-109)	3. a (149)
3. c (16-17)	Chapter 11	12. b (78)	5. a (108-109)	4. c (147)
4. d (16)	1. d (43)	13. b (78)		
5. a (16)	2. c (45)	14. c (79)	Chapter 19	License Exam
	3. c (44-45)	15. a (75)	1. b (111)	1. c (156)
Chapter 8	4. c (44)	16. a (71)	2. b (113)	2. d (156)
1. b (21)	5. b (45)	17. a (73)	3. a (111)	3. a (156)
2. c (19)	6. c (45)	18. a (80)	4. c (114)	4. b (156)
3. a (19)			5. d (111)	5. d (156)
4. c (21)	Chapter 12	Chapter 15	6. c (112)	6. a (156)
5. a (21)	1. d (59)	1. b (87, 88)		7. a (157)
6. c (21)	2. a (58)	2. a (91)	Chapter 20	8. a (156, 157)
	3. c (60)	3. c (89)	1. c (126)	
Chapter 9	4. c (60)	4. a (92)	2. a (122)	9. b (157)
1. b (30)	5. c (58)	5. d (87)	3. a (121)	10. c (157)
2. c (30)	6. b (58)	6. c (88)	4. d (123)	11. b (158)
3. c (29)		7. d (89)	5. b (123)	12. b (158)
4. b (29)	Chapter 13	8. b (90)	6. b (126)	13. c (158)
5. d (30)	1. d (66)	9. a (90)	7. d (118)	14. d (158)
6. d (33)	2. a (66)	10. a (91)	8. b (119)	15. a (158)
7. c (33)				

License Exam (cont.)

16. a (158)
17. a (158)

Sample Final Exam

1.	a	21.	a
2.	c	22.	b
3.	c	23.	b
4.	a	24.	a
5.	b	25.	a
6.	a	26.	a
7.	c	27.	b
8.	c	28.	c
9.	d	29.	c
10.	c	30.	c
11.	b	31.	d
12.	a	32.	a
13.	a	33.	a
14.	d	34.	c
15.	a	35.	a
16.	a	36.	c
17.	c	37.	d
18.	b	38.	c
19.	d	39.	c
20.	c	40.	b

Index

A
Ad valorem tax, 35-38
Adverse possession, 58
Air rights, 17
Alien real estate ownership, 19-20
Antitrust
    allocation of customers or markets, 3
    penalties, 3
    price fixing, 3

B
Blockbusting, 131
Blue sky law, 147
Brokerage
    agency and commission, 1-2
    broker-salesperson relationship, 2
    dual agency, 2
    ethical considerations, 2-3

C
Certificate of compliance, 6
Closing the transaction
    closing problem, 138-144
    closing statement, 137
    documents needed, 135-36
    procedures, 136
    prorations, 138
    title evidence, 135
Conditional use, 112
Condominium Act
    consumer disclosure, 21-22
    creation of condominium, 20
    flexible condominium, 22
    operation and administration, 21
    ownership, 20-21
    termination, 22
Contract alterations, 45
Contract, capacity to, 43
Contract for deed, 93-94
Co-ownership, 19

D
Deeds
    involuntary alienation, 58
    voluntary alienation, 57-58
Defeasible fee estate, 15
Descent and distribution, 58-59

E
Earnest money, receipt of, 45
Earnest money contract, 44
Easement by prescription, 16
Environmental legislation, Minnesota, 114
Escrow agreement, 46
Estates in land, 15

F
Fair Housing Act, federal, 129-31
Foreclosure
    attorney's fees, 91
    deficiency, 91
    judicial, 89
    nonjudicial, 89
    redemption, 90
    sale, 89-90
    surplus, 91
Foreign language documents, 65
Frauds, statute of, 43

H
Homestead exemption, 15-16
Homestead tax
    benefits, 16
Human Rights Act
    blockbusting, 131
    discriminatory practices, 129-31
    enforcement, 132

exemptions, 131
financial discrimination/redlining, 131

I

Installment contract, 46
Investment contract, 141-42

J

Judgments, 40

L

Landlord-Tenant Act
    automatic renewals, 103
    destruction of premises, 104
    landlord information disclosure, 103-104
    landlord's remedies, 104-105
    notice of absence, 104
    rent, 103
    security deposits, 104
    tenant's rights, 105
    termination of tenancy, 104
Leasehold estates, 103-105
License Law
    advertising, 80
    broker's responsibilities, 78
    broker-salesperson relationship, 76
    Commissioner of Commerce, 72
    commissions, 80
    continuing education, 76-77
    contracts and documents, 77-78
    denial, suspension, and revocation, 81-82
    disclosure, 79
    Education, Research, and Recovery Fund, 74
    ethical considerations, 80
    exemptions, 71
    funds, care and handling of, 78-80
    legal actions, 82
    licensing procedure, 72-74
    licensing requirements, 72
    records, 79
    standards of conduct, 81-82
    who must be licensed, 69-71
Lien theory, 87
Life estates, legal, 15
Limitations, statute of, 44
Limited broker's license, 73
Lis pendens, 40
Listing agreements
    exclusive-agency, 5
    exclusive-right-to-sell, 5
    multiple, 5
    net, 5
    open, 5

M

Mechanics' liens, 38-39
Minor's contracts, 43
Misrepresenting by silence, 2
Mobile homes, 70
Mortgage loans
    assumption, 88
    commitments, 87
    deed, 93, 94
    discount points, 88
    due-on-sale clauses, 88
    graduated payments, 92
    junior, 87
    recording, 87-88
    registration tax, 88
    renegotiable rate, 92
    reverse, 93
Municipal Housing and Redevelopment Act, 111

N

New-home warranty legislation, 7
Notice of default, 93

O

Out-of-town seller, 46

P

Partition suits, 19
Plain Language Contract Act, 44
Power of sale, 87
Principal meridians, 29
Property distribution
    homestead, 59
    nonhomestead, 59
Purchase agreement, 44-46

R

Recording documents, 65
Rectangular survey system, 29
Residential market value
    comparison, 108-109
    value estimates, 107

S

Securities
    antifraud provision, 148-49

    broker/dealer, 148
    definition, 147
    penalties, 149
    registration, 148
Sheriff's certificate of sale, 90
Shoreland criteria, 112-13
State deed tax, 58
Statutory interest rate, 92
Subcontractors' liens, 39-40
Subdivided Land Sales Practices Act
    advertising, 122-23
    annual report, 124
    blanket encumbrances, 123-24
    changes subsequent to registration, 124
    exemptions, 118
    inspection of records, 124
    investigation and proceedings, 125
    land registration, 119-20
    licensing, 118-19
    other operating procedures, 125
    penalties, 126
    prohibited acts, 125
    public offering statement, 121-22
    sales contracts, 123
    scope of the act, 117
Subdivision plat, 29-30

T

Tax assessment
    agricultural classification, 35-36
    appeals, 36
    exemptions and credits, 36
    homestead benefits, 35
    limited market value, 36
Tax delinquency, 37
Tax payment, 37
Tax rate, 36-37
Tax sale, 37
Termination of homestead, 16
Title evidence, 66
Title insurance, 66
Torrens system, 66
Trust accounting, 46
Trust deed, 88
Truth-in-housing report, 6

U

Uniform Commercial Code, 67
Uniform Condominium Act, 20-23
Urea formaldehyde disclosure, 6-7
Usury, 91-92

V

Variance, 112

W

Wills, 60

Z

Zoning
    county, 112
    municipality, 111-12
    region, 112
Zoning amendment, 112

Introducing
The Competitive Edge Book Program
from Real Estate Education Company

SPECIAL FREE BOOKLET

Call or write for your no-obligation free copy

As a new member of the real estate profession, you are eligible to become a charter member of our Competitive Edge Book Program and receive all these special benefits:

- free booklet entitled "How About a Career in Real Estate?"
- free subscription for all Real Estate Education Company catalogs
- save up to 25% on the real estate professional "Library League" special monthly book offer
- increase your sales and commissions through our continuing education programs

You are under no obligation to ever purchase a book.

FILL IN THE COUPON OR CALL – TOLL-FREE (800)621-9621. In Illinois, (800)572-9510.

Name _____
Company _____
Address _____
City/State/Zip _____

15-DAY FREE EXAMINATION ORDER CARD

REAL ESTATE EDUCATION COMPANY
a Longman Group USA company

Please send me the books I have indicated. I'll return any books I don't want for a full refund within the 15-day period without further obligation.

Detach, Sign, and Mail in Postage-Paid envelope today!

NAME _____
ADDRESS _____
CITY _____
STATE _____ ZIP _____
TELEPHONE # _____

New And Best-Selling Real Estate Books

	Order #		Price	Total Amount
☐ 1.	1926-01	Classified Secrets	$29.95	_____
☐ 2.	1970-02	Guide to Passing the Real Estate Exam (ACT)	$14.95	_____
☐ 3.	1556-10	Fundamentals of Real Estate Appraisal, 3rd ed.	$31.95	_____
☐ 4.	1557-10	Essentials of Real Estate Finance, 3rd ed.	$31.95	_____
☐ 5.	1961-01	The Language of Real Estate, 2nd ed.	$21.95	_____
☐ 6.	1512-10	Mastering Real Estate Mathematics, 4th ed.	$21.95	_____
☐ 7.	1970-04	Questions & Answers to Help You Pass the Real Estate Exam (ETS), 2nd ed.	$14.95	_____
☐ 8.	1559-01	Essentials of Real Estate Investment, 2nd ed.	$31.95	_____
☐ 9.	1970-03	How To Prepare for the Texas Real Estate Exam, 3rd ed.	$14.95	_____
☐ 10.	1510-01	Modern Real Estate Practice, 10th ed.	$31.50	_____
☐ 11.	1510-	License law supplements for Modern Real Estate Practice available for many states. Indicate the state you're interested in _____	$ 9.95	_____
☐ 12.	1510-02	Modern Real Estate Practice Study Guide, 10th ed.	$ 9.95	_____
☐ 13.	1909-01	New Home Sales	$19.95	_____
☐ 14.	1907-01	Power Real Estate Listing	$14.95	_____
☐ 15.	1907-02	Power Real Estate Selling	$14.95	_____
☐ 16.	1512-15	Practical Real Estate Financial Analysis: Using the HP-12C Calculator	$19.95	_____
☐ 17.	1551-10	Property Management, 2nd ed.	$31.95	_____
☐ 18.	1974-01	Protecting Your Sales Commission: Professional Liability in Real Estate	$24.95	_____
☐ 19.	1929-01	Real Estate Advertising	$24.95	_____
☐ 20.	1965-01	Real Estate Brokerage: A Success Guide	$29.95	_____
☐ 21.	1560-01	Real Estate Law	$32.95	_____
☐ 22.	1970-01	The Real Estate Education Company Real Estate Exam Manual, 3rd ed. (ETS)	$14.95	_____
☐ 23.	1513-01	Real Estate Fundamentals	$22.50	_____

Book Total

PAYMENT MUST ACCOMPANY ALL ORDERS: (check one)
☐ check or money order (payable to Real Estate Education Company)
☐ charge to my credit card (circle one) VISA or MASTERCARD or AMEX
Account No. _____ Exp. date _____
Signature _____

OR CALL OUR TOLL-FREE ORDERING HOTLINE (800) 621-9621 WITH YOUR CHARGE CARD (Illinois residents please call (800) 572-9510)

IL Res. add 8% Sales Tax
Postage/Handling $2.00 + .50 postage for each book
TOTAL

REAL ESTATE EDUCATION COMPANY

GUIDE TO PASSING THE REAL ESTATE EXAM
By Lawrence Sager

Guide to Passing the Real Estate Exam is the only manual designed specifically for the ACT salesperson and broker exams. Provides additional test-taking drills . . . helps you review important topics . . . and gives the additional confidence you need to pass the ACT real estate exam.

This ACT-style exam manual features . . .
- point-by-point outlines in sections corresponding to the four topic areas of the exam—real estate law, valuation, finance, and special fields
- alphabetical glossary
- diagnostic tests that aid you when identifying areas that require additional study
- hundreds of ACT-style practice questions
- one sample sales and one sample broker exam—both with the answers fully explained
- math review
- section on exam strategies—how to prepare mentally and physically—how to follow directions . . . how to develop a strategy for studying . . . and how to guess.

Check box #2 on the order card $14.95   order number 1970-02

FUNDAMENTALS OF REAL ESTATE APPRAISAL, 3rd edition
By William L. Ventolo, Jr. and Martha R. Williams. James Boykin, Consulting Editor

Thorough and concise explanation of real estate appraisal. Covers—in detail—the cost approach . . . market comparison approach . . . and income approach to appraising. NEW TO THIS EDITION . . .
- information on the ways financing techniques affect appraised value—provides numerous examples to give a hands-on feel for this critical element in current appraisals
- section on solar heating added to aid understanding of this form of developing technology as it relates to an appraiser's everyday work
- complete, up-to-date discussion of zoning and depreciation and the way each affects a parcel's value

Numbers and figures have been updated throughout the text to reflect current costs and values of real estate. Features end-of-chapter exams plus glossaries of appraisal and construction terms.

Check box #3 on the order card $31.95   order number 1556-10

ESSENTIALS OF REAL ESTATE FINANCE, 3rd edition
By David Sirota

Popular real estate finance book includes current, up-to-date information—text has been completely revised to include complete coverage of financing methods and instruments in use today. Includes comprehensive discussion of the sources and techniques of financing. Book is clearly written and well organized, while workbook format encourages note-taking.

Special features of the third edition of *Essentials of Real Estate Finance* include . . .
- text revised to reflect changes in laws —you won't have to search for up-to-date information to use . . . Everything you need is included!
- over 50 graphs, charts and tables have been completely updated—emphasize basic principles and apply them to current market conditions
- sample forms and contracts have been incorporated into the appropriate sections for easy reference
- glossary of real estate terms included for quick review

Check box #4 on the order card $31.95   order number 1557-10